Actionable Intelligence
in Healthcare

Data Analytics Applications

Series Editor: Jay Liebowitz

PUBLISHED

Actionable Intelligence for Healthcare
by Jay Liebowitz, Amanda Dawson
ISBN: 978-1-4987-6665-4

Sport Business Analytics: Using Data to Increase Revenue and Improve Operational Efficiency
by C. Keith Harrison, Scott Bukstein
ISBN: 978-1-4987-6126-0

FORTHCOMING

Data Analytics Applications in Law
by Edward J. Walters
ISBN: 978-1-4987-6665-4

Data Analytics for Marketing and CRM
by Jie Cheng
ISBN: 978-1-4987-6424-7

Data Analytics in Institutional Trading
by Henri Waelbroeck
ISBN: 978-1-4987-7138-2

Actionable Intelligence in Healthcare

Edited by
Jay Liebowitz
Amanda Dawson

CRC Press
Taylor & Francis Group
Boca Raton London New York

CRC Press is an imprint of the
Taylor & Francis Group, an **informa** business

AN AUERBACH BOOK

CRC Press
Taylor & Francis Group
6000 Broken Sound Parkway NW, Suite 300
Boca Raton, FL 33487-2742

First issued in paperback 2022

© 2017 by Taylor & Francis Group, LLC
CRC Press is an imprint of Taylor & Francis Group, an Informa business

ISBN 13: 978-1-03-247686-5 (pbk)
ISBN 13: 978-1-4987-7993-7 (hbk)

DOI: 10.1201/9781315208442

Publisher's Note
The publisher has gone to great lengths to ensure the quality of this reprint but points out that some imperfections in the original copies may be apparent.

Library of Congress Cataloging-in-Publication Data

Names: Liebowitz, Jay, 1957- editor. | Dawson, Amanda, PhD, editor.
Title: Actionable intelligence in healthcare / Jay Liebowitz and Amanda Dawson.
Other titles: Actionable intelligence in health care
Description: Boca Raton : Taylor & Francis, a CRC title, part of the Taylor & Francis imprint, a member of the Taylor & Francis Group, the academic division of T&F Informa PLC, 2017.
Identifiers: LCCN 2016046829| ISBN 9781498779937 (hardback : alk. paper) | ISBN 9781315208442 (ebook)
Subjects: LCSH: Medical informatics--Data processing. | Medical records--Data processing. | Computational biology--Methods. | Big data. | Data mining.
Classification: LCC R858 .A364 2017 | DDC 610.285--dc23
LC record available at https://lccn.loc.gov/2016046829

**Visit the Taylor & Francis Web site at
http://www.taylorandfrancis.com**

**and the CRC Press Web site at
http://www.crcpress.com**

From Jay: To Dr. Jason Liebowitz and Dr. Anat Chemerinski
and their patients, where analytics, intuition, humanism,
and evidence-based research are always welcomed.

From Amanda: We thank each of the authors for devoting their time
and effort toward this book. I'd like to thank my physician mentors,
Buddy Hammerman and Lisa Snyder, for always providing their clinical
feedback and granting me the time to pursue more sophisticated
analytic approaches and special projects like this book. Special thanks
to David Dundas for providing excellent support and editing.

Contents

Foreword

Actionable Intelligence in Healthcare can take many forms, from informing health policymakers on effective strategies for the population to providing direct and predictive insights on patients to healthcare providers so that positive outcomes can be achieved. Additionally, it can assist those performing clinical research where relevant statistical methods are applied to both identify the efficacy of treatments and improve clinical trial design, along with healthcare data standards groups through which pertinent data governance policies are implemented to ensure quality data are obtained, measured, and evaluated for the benefit of all involved. Although the obvious constant thread among all of these important healthcare use cases of actionable intelligence is the data at hand, such data in and of itself merely represents one element of the full healthcare data analytics structure.

Data collection and data governance policies and procedures must be established before any analysis. Doing so allows for the relevant questions to be answered in actionable ways and proper evaluation methods to be performed through repeatable and statistically valid practices. Such attempts at data collection and data governance must not precede the formulation of the hypothesis to be tested, the ascertainment of the strategic question to be appraised, or the identification of the population outcome of consequence to the community under evaluation. Once the point-at-issue has been agreed upon by all parties involved, then and only then can the concept of "Big Data" and its characteristics of volume, velocity, variety, and even veracity be tackled. Reversal of this order, where data are located first and questions are framed second, only leads to evaluations where data often lack the intended veracity and where needless assumptions are made because of the absence of variety; thus, frequency of data falls short of the requirements for appropriate statistical assessment, while data volumes become unmanageable as the scope of the data continually expands in an attempt to meet the needs of the questions being asked of them.

The subsequent steps to *healthcare data analytics* may be familiar to some, perhaps even most of you, but within each of these steps resides a fine detail that, if overlooked, results in the ultimate failure of *Actionable Intelligence in Healthcare*. With the central question in mind, and data in place, which supports the proper review, the transformation of data into information can proceed unequivocally. Information is derived through transformations based on known relations within data, along with a general understanding of business or clinical constructs. While data represent facts, information translates these facts into associations with causes and effects. Within this transformation, principle-centered data analytics must be performed to ensure that the associations derived can and will support the underlying queries and must be framed with respect to the business, clinical, or community audience.

Through the appropriate compilation of information—with an overarching intent of identifying key causes and effects from associations within data—knowledge can be imparted to interested parties and audiences. This knowledge provides a basis for action and integration of new experiences and information, though in and of itself it does *not* allow for actionable intelligence to be achieved. It is often here where data analytics in healthcare falls vastly short. Knowledge is only relative and can quickly become obsolete or outdated. As knowledge is simply information contextualized, it is within this contextual framework where analytic methods must be robust to the variety of confounding and mitigating factors, as well as adaptive to the clinical, business, or public demands. In order to achieve true actionable intelligence, focus must be not only on the "how" of the assessed associations within the data but also on the "why" of the findings encapsulated in the interest and empowerment of those who need to act upon such knowledge.

With an accurate evaluation of "why" the classified causes and effects arose, then and only then can understanding evolve within clinical, business, and community settings. These understandings must rely on a carefully constructed narrative of findings and conclusions, which should be coupled with both static and interactive data visualizations to engage audiences, meeting them at their current level of perception along with the direction to answer their questions: "What is the point?" and "Why is this important to us?" It should also tell them how these new understandings can be put into motion to achieve constructive changes desired, to improve current undertakings, or to provide the underpinning for further and more positive knowledge and understanding to be formed. Such narratives and data visualizations need to build upon currently vetted knowledge and understanding, even if they refute a specific previous insight, in order to establish trust and rapport with those who will act based on these understandings.

Given understandings presented within the frameworks outlined in the preceding paragraphs, the definitive goal of the true "wisdom of crowds" can be realized. Wisdom is the application of understandings toward a common or greater good, and *Actionable Intelligence in Healthcare* presents significant details on how proper healthcare-related questions should be formulated, how relevant data must be transformed to associated information, and the processing of information into relative knowledge. It also indicates to clinicians, researchers, and the public why this new knowledge is meaningful and how best to apply such a newfound understanding for the betterment of all involved.

David Napoli

Editors

Dr. Jay Liebowitz is the distinguished chair of applied business and finance at Harrisburg University of Science and Technology. He previously was the Orkand Endowed Chair of management and technology in the Graduate School at the University of Maryland University College (UMUC). He served as a professor in the Carey Business School at Johns Hopkins University. He was ranked one of the top 10 knowledge management researchers/practitioners out of 11,000 worldwide, and was ranked #2 in KM Strategy worldwide according to the January 2010 *Journal of Knowledge Management*. At Johns Hopkins University, he was the founding program director for the Graduate Certificate in Competitive Intelligence and the Capstone Director of the MS-Information and Telecommunications Systems for Business Program, where he engaged over 30 organizations in industry, government, and not-for-profits in capstone projects. Prior to joining Hopkins, Dr. Liebowitz was the first knowledge management officer at NASA Goddard Space Flight Center. Before NASA, Dr. Liebowitz was the Robert W. Deutsch Distinguished Professor of information systems at the University of Maryland-Baltimore County, professor of management science at George Washington University, and chair of artificial Intelligence at the U.S. Army War College. Dr. Liebowitz has been selected as the Fulbright Visiting Research Chair in business at Queen's University in Canada for Summer 2017. He has lectured and consulted worldwide.

Dr. Amanda Dawson is the corporate director of research at Select Medical, where she oversees clinical research and quality improvement initiatives for a health care network with nearly 150 nationwide long-term acute care and inpatient rehabilitation hospitals and over 1000 outpatient provider clinics. Prior to joining Select Medical, Dr. Dawson was a research fellow in biomedicine at Albert Einstein Hospital's Moss Rehabilitation Research Institute. She earned a PhD in experimental psychology from Penn State University and completed her postdoctoral training in physical medicine and rehabilitation from the University of Pennsylvania Medical School. Dr. Dawson's research has been supported by DHHS funding through contracts and grants from the NIH, CDC, and state Departments of Health. Over the last decade, she has published numerous articles on hospitalized patient outcomes and stroke rehabilitation. Her research involves characterizing clinical practice patterns, measuring the impact of clinical interventions, and predicting patient outcomes over time.

Contributors

Sergei Ananyan
Megaputer Intelligence, Inc.
Bloomington, Indiana

Shivaram Poigai Arunachalam
Mayo College of Medicine
Rochester, Minnesota

Diane Berry
OutsideView
Califon, New Jersey

Michael Brimacombe
Kansas University Medical Center
Kansas City, Kansas

Mark A. Caron
Geneia LLC
Harrisburg, Pennsylvania

Jieshi Chen
Carnegie Mellon University
Pittsburgh, Pennsylvania

Matthew M. Churpek
The University of Chicago
Chicago, Illinois

Amanda Dawson
Select Medical
Mechanicsburg, Pennsylvania

Artur Dubrawski
Carnegie Mellon University
Pittsburgh, Pennsylvania

Mary B. Engler
NIH/National Institute of Nursing
   Research
Bethesda, Maryland

Aryya Gangopadhyay
University of Maryland Baltimore
   County
Catonsville, Maryland

Arif Khan
University of Sydney
Sydney, New South Wales, Australia

Minjae Kim
Columbia University Medical Center
New York, New York

Kyun Hee (Ken) Lee
Johns Hopkins University
Baltimore, Maryland

Jay Liebowitz
Harrisburg University of Science and
   Technology
Harrisburg, Pennsylvania

David Napoli
Colorado HealthOP
Greenwood Village, Colorado

Lavi Oud
Texas Tech University Health Sciences
  Center
Odessa, Texas

Kalyan S. Pasupathy
Mayo College of Medicine
Rochester, Minnesota

L. Nelson Sanchez-Pinto
The University of Chicago
Chicago, Illinois

Mustafa Sir
Mayo College of Medicine
Rochester, Minnesota

Uma Srinivasan
Capital Markets Cooperative Research
  Centre
Sydney, New South Wales, Australia

Pamela A. Tamez
NIH/National Institute of Nursing
  Research
Bethesda, Maryland

Shahadat Uddin
University of Sydney
Sydney, New South Wales, Australia

Rose Yesha
University of Maryland Baltimore
  County
Catonsville, Maryland
and
Rutgers University, Newark
Newark, New Jersey

Chapter 1

Empowering Clinician-Scientists in the Information Age of Omics and Data Science

Pamela A. Tamez and Mary B. Engler

Contents

1.1 Introduction

A new era of individualized care, driven by new diagnostics and therapeutic strategies, is rapidly emerging. This era will provide unprecedented opportunities in research focused on targeted prevention and treatment strategies. Research strategies using individual variability in each person's genes, environment, and lifestyle are needed to take advantage of these opportunities. Clinician-scientists will need training to learn about these approaches to precision health, expand their skills, and develop new approaches. Several research and training opportunities include the following: the National Institutes of Health (NIH) Precision Medicine Initiative, the National Institute of Nursing Research (NINR) 1-week intensive boot camps, massive open online courses, workshops provided by professional societies, and resources provided by NIH initiatives and funded programs (such as Big Data to Knowledge [BD2K] and Clinical and Translational Science Awards [CTSA]). Within this chapter, we will discuss how advances in the omics sciences, biotechnology, and data science will enable clinician-scientists to engage with patients and implement timely and effective interventions to improve patient outcomes.

Because of 21st-century advances in science and technology and changing patient demographics, healthcare providers need to be ready to incorporate this new information and new actionable knowledge toward precision health and improved patient's lives. One scientific advance affecting practice is the sequencing of the human genome (Lander et al. 2001; Venter et al. 2001). Information from the Human Genome Sequencing Project has significantly accelerated medical advances and clinical practice. The development of innovative high-throughput capturing technologies, such as DNA sequencing and analysis methods, have since provided access to multiple types of data, from genetic and expression data to metabolic and protein profile data. As a result, the omics science era has evolved with focused areas in genomics, transcriptomics, epigenomics, proteomics, and metabolomics. The term *omics* originally stemmed from systems-level studies involving all genes or gene products and has rapidly expanded to include many other systems and interactions, such as all microbes (microbiomics), the interaction of nutrition and genes (nutrigenomics), and genetics in drug responses (pharmacogenomics).

In addition to the omics sciences, big data or data science provides varied sources of data, such as from personal biosensors, environmental inputs, electronic health records (EHR), clinical data, claims, and public health (Brennan and Bakken 2015; Tenenbaum 2016). Big data in healthcare and the life sciences is complex, voluminous, and diverse in the data types and speed at which it is generated. These data sets are considered too large and complicated for typical data processing methods, and thus, the term *big data* was coined. However, when these data are able to be synthesized and analyzed with sophisticated methodology, patterns, trends, and associations can be understood and used to help inform healthcare decisions that may potentially improve patient care, lower costs, and save lives (Belle et al. 2015; Gligorijevic et al. 2016; Knowledgent White Paper 2015). Integrating big data analytics into clinical practice may also have an important impact on prevention, diagnosis, and treatment of disease. There is the potential to complement traditional clinical practices by adding contextual information so that the clinical professional can make better informed decisions on clinical care.

The availability of these high dimensional data coalesces with the drive to deliver precision medicine (Collins and Varmus 2015) and to create a Learning Healthcare System (LHS) (Olsen et al. 2007) (Figure 1.1). One goal of precision medicine is to

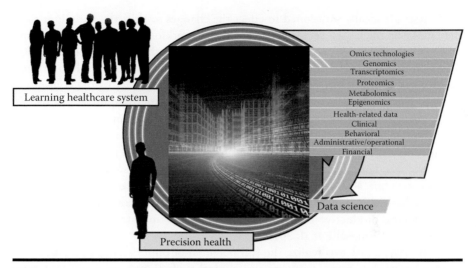

Figure 1.1   Precision Health Model and the Learning Healthcare System (LHS). Biological samples obtained from large diverse populations in biobanks and repositories are analyzed and processed through omics technologies (from genes to all gene products) and linked to an individual's health-related data or other varied sources of data into large complex data sets. Data science translates the omics and health-related data into knowledge. Big data analytics is helpful in determining patterns, trends, and associations to develop actionable healthcare information and precision health, such as personalized diet or nutrients (nutrigenomics), drug prescriptions based on the right drug and the right dose at the right time (pharmacogenomics), or individualized targeted cancer therapies (cancer genomics). Data from the individual will feed back into the circle. With enough individual data points, medicine and care can move toward an LHS. The move will be from evidence-based practice toward practice-based evidence.

deliver actionable healthcare information to patients based on their lifestyle, genes, and environment (Collins and Varmus 2015). Clinicians will use these data to tailor treatment and prevention therapies for an individual patient. Evidence generated from that individual's therapy can serve as data to feed into the LHS. One aim of the LHS is to create an evidence cycle where evidence is generated, applied, and refined. The paradigm will shift from evidence-based practice, where clinical care decisions are based on the use of current best evidence, to practice-based evidence or the generation of evidence through collection of real-world data (Embi and Payne 2013; Tenenbaum 2016). The evidence cycle will create a healthcare system that evolves, providing tailored therapies to individual patients, incorporating knowledge gained from each experience, and ultimately improving the health of persons and populations. Translation becomes bidirectional in LHS (Tenenbaum 2016).

Nurses are ideally positioned to effect the changes to shift the paradigm since they make up the largest sector in the healthcare workforce and are poised to have an essential role in redesigning healthcare that is responsive to patient needs (IOM [Institute of Medicine] 2011). Nurses advocate for the individual, family, and community and have a scientific understanding of care delivery across the continuum of care. Nurse scientists have experience working in interdisciplinary teams and employing data science techniques, both of which are important to transform data into knowledge (Brennan and Bakken 2015). Such large and complex data sets are being generated and used by nurse scientists to promote and improve the health of individuals, families, and communities. Nursing science is uniquely primed to contribute to new advances that make use of the omics and data sciences. Nursing expertise has made significant contributions within large multidisciplinary teams by developing productive community collaborations and strengthening translational science (Sampselle et al. 2013).

However, in order to realize the full potential of omics technologies and data science knowledge, nurse scientists and clinical professionals need to build competencies in omics and informatics (Conley et al. 2015; Genomic Nursing State of the Science Advisory Panel et al. 2013). The challenges are to keep well informed and up to date on a field that is continuously evolving, to understand how these technologies affect patient care, to interpret data into knowledge, and to deliver actionable information to patients. Learning how advances in the omics sciences, genomic medicine, and data science are incorporated into healthcare will empower clinicians to engage with patients and implement timely and effective interventions to improve patient outcomes.

We provide a framework for delivering actionable healthcare information. We define different omics technologies, provide opportunities for training, and describe efforts to form large, multidisciplinary, productive, and collaborative teams. We conclude by discussing how advances in the omics sciences, biotechnology, and data science have enabled clinician-scientists to engage with patients and implement timely and effective interventions to improve patient outcomes.

1.2 Building Genomic Competency: Defining Omics Sciences

The sequencing of the human genome was a technological breakthrough. It provided scientists with a comprehensive view of genetic structure and function and moved candidate gene studies toward comprehensive approaches for studying the genetic underpinnings of disease (Green et al. 2011). In cataloging genomic information, the Human Genome Project shed new light on the roles of noncoding RNAs and regulatory regions, allowed for comparative analyses of protein-coding regions across organisms, and accelerated the discovery of the genetic bases for common diseases through technologies, such as genome-wide association studies

(Lander 2011). Sequencing can now be performed on the whole exome to study protein-coding regions (~1.5% of the total genome) or on the whole genome to study both protein-coding and noncoding regions, which provides additional information on regulatory regions. A framework for cataloging other molecular entities, such as RNA, protein, metabolites, and others, has been developed as a result of the advances in sequencing technologies (Table 1.1).

While genomics offers a comprehensive view of an organism's genetic material, it is a static view (Topol 2014). To understand cellular dynamics, other molecules, such as RNA, proteins, and metabolites, can be investigated and measured. Transcriptomics, which measures RNA and gene expression, details the cellular transcriptional response to a perturbation. One technique to measure gene expression is microarray analysis, which quantifies the relative abundance of mRNA transcripts and elucidates the cellular response under different conditions or stages of development. RNA-Seq is another more precise technique as it not only captures mRNA but also measures microRNA, small RNA, lincRNA, ribosomal RNA, and transfer RNA. Information on gene fusions, alternatively spliced transcripts, and posttranscriptional changes is also gained with RNA-Seq methodology (Topol 2014; Wang et al. 2009). Comprehensive analysis of proteins, which are the functional entities of a cell, can be accomplished through proteomics. A primary goal of proteomics is to understand how proteins and protein complexes readjust over time and space under different conditions (Altelaar et al. 2013). This technology can be used to confirm genomic studies, compare protein profiles under different cellular conditions, reveal subcellular spatial organization of proteins and protein complexes, identify posttranslational modifications that regulate protein activity, and identify biomarkers for prognostic or diagnostic purposes. The aim of metabolomics is to identify and measure small molecules that are chemically, physically, structurally, and functionally diverse (Cacciatore and Loda 2015). Metabolites are a third class of molecule to study cellular dynamics. They are heterogeneous and include products and intermediates from biochemical reactions, ions, sugars, and lipids, and their range of concentrations can span nine orders of magnitude. Metabolomics has been employed to cross-validate other omics studies, to identify biomarkers for disease and drug effects, and to measure small molecules from nutrient intake, and pharmaceuticals, and the host microbiome (Cacciatore and Loda 2015; Kaddurah-Daouk et al. 2015).

Sequencing and omics technologies are being employed to increase our understanding of factors that determine an individual's response, and examples include cancer genomics, pharmacogenomics, and nutrigenomics. Cancer genomics, which uses sequencing technology to identify mutations that drive cancer growth, has allowed diagnosis to move from histology-based to genomic-based; it also reveals the mutations underlying drug resistance and hence treatment failure (Mardis 2015). Whole-genome sequencing has been employed to identify mutations that cause acute myeloid leukemia, hereditary pancreatic cancer, colon cancer, and other types of cancer (Kilpivaara and Aaltonen 2013). Sequencing cancer genomes has

Table 1.1   Building Genomic Competency: Technologies and Definitions

Term	Definition	Reference
Genomics	Systematic sequencing and characterization of an organism's genetic material; has contributed toward a greater understanding of cancer etiology, rare disease diagnosis, and pharmacogenomics.	Green et al. 2011
Trancriptomics	The science of documenting the various types of transcripts (messenger, long non-coding, and small RNAs); of delineating the transcriptional unit (start and stop sites, splicing junctions, and posttranscriptional modifications); and of quantifying gene expression.	Wang et al. 2009
Proteomics	The science that identifies and quantifies all proteins in a sample.	Altelaar et al. 2013; Cox and Mann 2007
Metabolomics	The science that quantifies and characterizes small molecules, or metabolites; can generate biochemical profiles and provide insight into the physiology of an organism or pathology in a disease state.	Cacciatore and Loda 2015
Epigenomics	The study of modifications by chemical compounds that are added to the entirety of an individual's DNA (genome) as a way to regulate the activity (expression) of all genes within the genome.	www.ghr.nlm.nih.gov; Friedman and Rando 2015
Cancer genomics	Sequencing of tumor samples for comparisons between cancer genomes and normal tissue DNA.	Kilpivaara and Aaltonen 2013; Mardis 2015; Rafii et al. 2014; Vogelstein et al. 2013

(Continued)

Table 1.1 (Continued)   Building Genomic Competency: Technologies and Definitions

Term	Definition	Reference
Pharmacogenomics	The study of how genes and genetic variation influence drug response. The goal is to determine which genetic variants will influence drug metabolism— pharmacokinetics or pharmacodynamics.	Relling and Evans 2015
Nutrigenomics	The study to identify and characterize genetic variants that influence response to nutrients.	Engler 2009; Fenech et al. 2011; Ordovas and Corella 2004
Microbiomics	The microbiome is defined as the collection and genetic information of all bacteria, viruses, archaea, and other microbial organisms as well as their environment and biological niche.	Cho and Blaser 2012
Big data	A complex or large data set that cannot be processed using conventional systems or fit into current database architectures; characterized by large volume, velocity (fast pace at which it is generated), and variety (heterogeneous types of data).	Beyer and Laney 2012

provided information on the typical number of mutations, the types of changes (mutational, epigenetic) that occur over time to drive cancer growth, and the signaling and biochemical pathways that different tumors share (Vogelstein et al. 2013). Clinical applications include the development of small-molecule inhibitors that target signaling pathways (Vogelstein et al. 2013), the development of personalized immunotherapy (Partners Healthcare 2016), and the generation of patient-specific data to improve drug development (Partners Healthcare 2016). The latter two have been cited as "disruptive" technologies that will have the greatest impact on cancer care in the next 10 years (Partners Healthcare 2016).

Pharmacogenomics and nutrigenomics use sequencing to provide information on how an individual's genetic makeup influences the metabolism of drugs and nutrients, respectively. The goal of the former is to tailor the correct dose and correct drug to the right individual (Relling and Evans 2015). If a variant in a drug-metabolizing gene is found to increase drug clearance of a specific drug, then either a different drug or a different dose can be prescribed. One goal of nutrigenomics is to be able to recommend a personalized diet and to personalize nutrition (Engler 2009; Ordovas and Corella 2004).

Several groups are working to integrate these technologies for a multi-omics approach to care. Microbiome research is one emerging area that is using multiple omics technologies to determine how the microbiome affects human health and disease (Cho and Blaser 2012; Integrative H. M. P. Research Network Consortium 2014). Sequencing and metagenome analysis has provided insight into the numbers and types of organisms that make up the host microbiome. Many microbial organisms cannot be cultured; thus, metagenome analysis is a method to determine taxonomy and composition. Transcriptomics provides a dynamic view of how host and microbes respond to each other, to different conditions, or to disease states. Metabolomics reveal how microbes and host communicate biochemically with one another.

Integrating multi-omics approaches moves care and medicine toward a tailored, or personalized, approach. Topol suggests building a geographic information system view of the person and presents the idea that the individual will be the conduit of information flow of these technologies and will serve as the principal driver of medicine (Topol 2014). He depicts how omics tools will affect an individual over the lifespan and how information from that individual can be used to inform care decisions for other family members and subsequent generations. Chen and colleagues have undertaken a massive effort to integrate these technologies and created an integrated personalized omics profile for an individual over a 14-month period (Chen et al. 2012). The analysis revealed that several molecular components changed over time and across healthy and diseased states. Importantly, it provided actionable healthcare information and showed a risk for type 2 diabetes. Notably, the individual made significant lifestyle changes to mitigate his risk.

Moreover, a systems biology approach is rapidly being used in the context of precision health to understand the many complex molecular levels and interactions in biological systems from a holistic view. This approach combines and integrates data, that is, genomic, transcriptomic, proteomic, and metabolomic, from the different high-throughput omics platforms and technologies. The systems biology approach will be helpful to identify the molecular events and mechanisms in the onset and progression of disease and can lead to biomarker discovery and identification of novel nutritional or drug targets. Personalized interventions would be tailored to the individual's omics profile to promote wellness and to prevent or treat disease (Pathak and Dave 2014). Some institutions, such as Stanford Medicine in California, are currently using this "precision health" approach to provide targeted, predictive, and personalized care to help individuals thrive based on their unique factors, including genetics and environmental factors (http://med.stanford.edu/news).

Translational bioinformatics is another new discipline important in the transformation of data into actionable knowledge in this era of precision health (Tenenbaum 2016). Specifically, it is defined by the American Medical Informatics Association (http://www.amia.org) as "the development of storage, analytic, and interpretive methods to optimize the transformation of increasingly voluminous biomedical data, and genomic data, into proactive, predictive, preventive, and participatory health." Notably, translational bioinformatics bridges the gap between bench research and the bedside clinical care application by focusing on clinical "big data" or the use of EHR data for discovery, genomics, and pharmacogenomics in routine clinical care; omics for drug discovery and repurposing; and personal genetic testing and associated ethical, legal, and social issues (Tenenbaum 2016).

1.3 Building Genomic Competency: Working in Interdisciplinary Teams

Because integrating omics and data science into practice is complex and multifaceted, no one profession can work in isolation. We provide examples of training opportunities and initiatives that build large, multidisciplinary teams and share best practices.

The NINR at the NIH, Bethesda, Maryland, stimulates innovation in nursing science and contributes toward the scientific development of nurse scientists (Grady and Gough 2015). Two intensive, tuition-free training courses offered by the NINR are the Boot Camp and Summer Genetics Institute (Cimino 2014; NINR 2016). The purpose of each program is to increase the research capability of graduate students, faculty, and clinicians. The boot camp is a week-long program designed around a theme, such as Big Data (2014–2015) or Precision Health: From Omics to Data Science (2016–2017), to explore methods and strategies that can be incorporated into research or clinical practice or research proposals. Every other year, a new theme highlights an emerging area of science. The Summer Genetics Institute is an annual month-long training program that provides participants with a foundation in molecular genetics appropriate for use in research and clinical practice. There are also no-cost, online courses, such as the NINR "Developing Nurse Scientists," the NINR Grantsmanship workshop (seven modules), a series of NINR YouTube videos, and courses in clinical research and clinical pharmacology that the NIH Clinical Center offers (NIH/CC 2016). NINR has several funding opportunities and grant mechanisms to advance the training of nurse scientists, such as fellowships, career development awards, and the NIH Loan Repayment Program.

Many initiatives that require large, interdisciplinary teams have been launched. One example is the Precision Medicine Initiative Cohort Program (now called the *All of Us Research Program*) that NIH launched to translate genome information into better and more effective therapies (NIH/PMI/AoU 2016). One goal is to recruit 1 million participants who will share their genome, biological specimens, and data from clinical records and personal health trackers. The aim is to create new ways for patients to become active participants in their care and treatment, to share and protect health information, and to build an infrastructure that turns data into knowledge (Terry 2015). It is a large-scale effort that brings together several government agencies with more than 40 private-sector organizations (The White House Office of the President 2016).

A second example is the NIH Big Data to Knowledge (BD2K) initiative, which provides resources and grant money for training and acts as a hub for the data science community. One training goal is to allow a larger community of researchers to access and analyze big data. Toward this aim, 12 BD2K centers (NIH/BD2K 2016) have been funded, and several have disseminated training workshops, symposia, courses, and research software. The NIH BD2K initiative is creating a Commons to share technological solutions and digital products that are FAIR (Findable, Accessible, Interoperable, and Re-usable) and shared in a virtual space (Bourne et al. 2015). The aim is to add tools to this space and monitor usage to learn the value these provide to the research community.

The Clinical and Translational Science Award (CTSA) Consortium is an exemplar framework for developing multidisciplinary translational teams (Calhoun et al. 2013). One important aspect of the CTSA Consortium is to train the next generation of clinical and translational researchers. Its central hub provides information on best practices (NIH/CTSA 2016a) and resources for education and training (NIH/CTSA 2016b). The best practices section contains white papers and links to information on comparative effectiveness research, metrics for biostatistical and epidemiological collaborations, principles of community engagement, among many other areas. The education and training section provides information on mentor development, core competencies in clinical and translational research, a learning center, and other tools. The consortium has cataloged data from across multiple sites to provide a searchable, open access database that will facilitate and accelerate clinical and translational science (Shirey-Rice et al. 2014).

The National Patient-Centered Clinical Research Network (PCORnet) is another resource, and its mission is to create teams of health researchers, patients, and health systems that work together to improve medical treatment and advance medical knowledge. It is an initiative of the Patient-Centered Outcomes Research Institute and is creating a network of networks to share data across systems so that teams may query big data sets and conduct studies more efficiently. The PCORnet is being built over several stages, and once fully operational, teams of researchers, health systems, and patients will access the network, perform queries, and use data to improve healthcare (Selby et al. 2015).

1.4 Knowledge Discovery—How Data Can Be Translated to the Clinical Setting

When teams and technologies are integrated, then basic science data and big data can inform clinical practice. We provide several examples of how data can be translated to the clinical setting and into knowledge that will improve patients' lives.

One of the first examples is provided by Worthey and colleagues who reported on a case study of a male child of 15 months who presented with poor weight gain and a lower gastrointestinal abscess (Worthey et al. 2011). Despite multiple rounds of treatment and multiple diagnoses, including Crohn disease, remission was never long-lasting, and symptomatology worsened. In order to ensure that a subsequent aggressive treatment would work, the team decided to perform whole-exome sequencing to discover the underlying disease-causing mutation. They identified a mutation in the gene X-linked inhibitor of apoptosis (*XIAP*) and proceeded with progenitor cell transplant, a known intervention for this mutation. This treatment allowed for a significant recovery with no recurrence of gastrointestinal disease, and the authors suggest that success was unlikely without whole-exome sequencing to identify the causative mutation and to subsequently implement a known intervention. Further, their findings on the biology of mutated *XIAP* contribute to a better understanding of the pathogenesis of inflammatory bowel disease. The authors conclude that building multidisciplinary teams, clinical data sets, and infrastructure will be essential to realize the benefits of whole-exome sequencing.

Genomic information is also being used to understand and guide drug treatment options. Tang and colleagues reported on a clinical trial that tested whether insulin secretion would improve in patients with type 2 diabetes when the adrenergic receptor is pharmacologically blocked (Tang et al. 2014). A genetic variant in the alpha(2A)-adrenergic receptor (*ADRA2A*) gene is associated with defective insulin release and increased risk of type 2 diabetes patients. The team tested whether yohimbine, which blocks the receptor, would improve insulin secretion in patients with the risk variant. They found that 30 min after yohimbine administration, insulin secretion improved in patients with the risk variant and was similar to patients without this variant. The authors conclude that it is feasible to tailor treatment of type 2 diabetes according to genotype.

Genomics has been the lead technology in clinical and translational science. However, other omics technologies are also being utilized to provide information in the clinical setting. Guo and coauthors detail their methodology and results incorporating metabolomics to complement genomic sequencing (Guo et al. 2015). Their aim was to enhance medical interpretation of disease risk of a small cohort of volunteers, who were of normal health, who provided medical records and a three-generation family pedigree, and whose exomes were sequenced (Gonzalez-Garay et al. 2013). Plasma samples were collected from these 80 volunteers, and nearly 600 metabolites were profiled and cross-referenced with clinical data and whole-exome sequences. In one volunteer, an altered fructose metabolic profile correlated with a variant aldolase gene, which had previously been associated with fructose intolerance. This volunteer was identified as a potential asymptomatic carrier for autosomal recessive fructose intolerance, and diet planning was recommended to avoid liver and kidney damage, which can result from persistent fructose intolerance. The authors profile 10 cases as part of an effort to link pathogenic alleles to biochemical function and clinical condition and conclude that metabolomics can aid in interpreting genomic data, in improving diagnosis, and in evaluating risk assessment.

Nutrigenomics also provides insight into actionable healthcare information, and the study outlined here is a large-scale example of personalizing diets. Zeevi and colleagues tested whether personalized diets could modify postmeal glucose responses and hence potentially mitigate metabolic consequences (Zeevi et al. 2015). Having high postmeal glucose levels is a major risk factor for prediabetes and type 2 diabetes; hence, the authors undertook a study to measure interperson variability of after-meal glycemic responses. They collected data from daily food logs, blood measurements, microbiome samples, anthropometrics, and continuous glucose monitoring in an 800-person cohort and measured postmeal glycemic responses. The authors found high interperson variability to identical meals. They devised an algorithm to predict the postprandial glycemic response and successfully validated it using a separate 100-person cohort. Then, they tested how the algorithm performed in a dietary intervention study when compared to the gold standard. A diet was designed as "good" or "bad," depending on whether it was predicted to decrease or increase postmeal glucose responses, respectively. Interestingly, foods that were part of the "good" diet for some participants constituted the "bad" diet for others. The authors show that the algorithm was comparable to experts in designing diets and the "good" diet lowered postmeal glycemic responses. Participants on this diet showed fewer glucose spikes and fluctuations when compared with those on the "bad" diet, and their gut microbiota shifted toward taxa reported to have beneficial effects. The authors show that high-dimensional data can be translated into actionable information in the form of a personalized diet. The authors suggest that a one-size-fits-all diet will be of limited use with high interpersonal variability.

These examples offer a view of what molecular data can provide, and the impetus is growing to incorporate these types of data into the EHR. Several biobanks have been ramping up patient recruitment to link biological specimens with clinical data from the EHR (Carey et al. 2016; Karlson et al. 2016; Olson et al. 2013; Roden and Denny 2016). The aim is to accelerate translational research by aggregating clinical, molecular, and demographic information. Roden and Denny discuss examples that use EHRs to discover gene variants associated with thyroid conditions, resistance to malaria infection, susceptibility to herpes zoster, and characteristics of platelet counts and erythrocyte traits (Roden and Denny 2016). They also detail studies using BioVU, the Vanderbilt DNA biobank, to predict drug responses based on genomic information. In comparing how differently data are gathered between a prospective study and EHR, they present the idea of phenome-based discovery. Because EHR data are not gathered in a prospective manner with control and cases, the team developed the Phe-WAS software that generates control and case populations to identify disease-causing genetic variants (Denny et al. 2010). They argue that approaches to scanning and interrogating the phenome will be valuable in generating actionable healthcare information.

Healthcare big data, available from EHR and clinical data repositories, can accelerate translational science to create actionable healthcare information. However, data and nursing data, which represent a significant amount of information included in the EHR, need to be structured and normalized (Westra et al. 2015b). Such data can then be analyzed many times to ask different questions. An example is provided by data used to study home care of elderly adults. The data were used to model interventions (Monsen et al. 2009; Westra et al. 2010), predict hospitalizations (Monsen et al. 2011), evaluate high-risk medication regimens and hospital readmission (Dierich et al. 2011; Olson et al. 2014), improve oral medication management (Westra et al. 2011b), and discover which interventions improved urinary and bowel incontinence (Westra et al. 2011a). The authors argue for standardizing nursing terminology so that nursing data are interoperable and available when and where it is needed. Collaboration across agencies and systems will make nursing data actionable and has the potential to improve interventions, improve consistency of care and compliance, and support research in interventions (Westra et al. 2010).

1.5 Conclusions

As direct providers of care, patient advocates, researchers, scientists, and educators, nurses play an important role in improving patient outcomes and implementing timely and effective interventions. With strong expertise in clinical care, risk assessment, health promotion, and translation science, nurse scientists also have a critical role in multidisciplinary teams. They add context so that bench scientists can apply their research to the clinic (Sampselle et al. 2013). They bring patient, family, and community perspectives to the application of these technologies, interpret science findings, and create interventions that patients can comprehend and act on (Brennan and Bakken 2015). Nursing is uniquely prepared to adapt and respond to the requirements of highly advanced data processing, computing, and analysis by applying knowledge from many scientific disciplines to professional practice (Brennan and Bakken 2015, Westra et al. 2015a).

Omics and data science technologies will continue to affect the way healthcare is delivered. This chapter provides many opportunities and examples to decrease knowledge gaps. Ultimately, trained and knowledgeable nurses and nurse scientists will be key drivers to improved patient care and better outcomes in the current complex and diverse healthcare environments.

References

Altelaar, A. F., J. Munoz, and A. J. Heck. 2013. Next-generation proteomics: Towards an integrative view of proteome dynamics. *Nat Rev Genet* 14 (1):35–48. doi: 10.1038/nrg3356.

Belle, A., R. Thiagarajan, S. M. Soroushmehr, F. Navidi, D. A. Beard, and K. Najarian. 2015. Big data analytics in healthcare. *Biomed Res Int* 2015:370194. doi: 10.1155/2015/370194.

Beyer, Mark A. and Douglas Laney. 2012. *The Importance of 'BigData': A Definition.* Stamford, CT: Gartner.

Bourne, P. E., V. Bonazzi, M. Dunn et al. 2015. The NIH Big Data to Knowledge (BD2K) initiative. *J Am Med Inform Assoc* 22 (6):1114. doi: 10.1093/jamia/ocv136.

Brennan, P. F. and S. Bakken. 2015. Nursing needs big data and big data needs nursing. *J Nurs Scholarsh.* doi: 10.1111/jnu.12159.

Cacciatore, S. and M. Loda. 2015. Innovation in metabolomics to improve personalized healthcare. *Ann N Y Acad Sci* 1346 (1):57–62. doi: 10.1111/nyas.12775.

Calhoun, W. J., K. Wooten, S. Bhavnani, K. E. Anderson, J. Freeman, and A. R. Brasier. 2013. The CTSA as an exemplar framework for developing multidisciplinary translational teams. *Clin Transl Sci* 6 (1):60–71. doi: 10.1111/cts.12004.

Carey, D. J., S. N. Fetterolf, F. D. Davis et al. 2016. The Geisinger MyCode community health initiative: An electronic health record-linked biobank for precision medicine research. *Genet Med.* doi: 10.1038/gim.2015.187.

Chen, R., G. I. Mias, J. Li-Pook-Than et al. 2012. Personal omics profiling reveals dynamic molecular and medical phenotypes. *Cell* 148 (6):1293–307. doi: 10.1016/j.cell.2012.02.009.

Cho, I. and M. J. Blaser. 2012. The human microbiome: At the interface of health and disease. *Nat Rev Genet* 13 (4):260–70. doi: 10.1038/nrg3182.

Cimino, A. 2014. From HeLa cells to nanotechnology. *NIH Catalyst.*

Collins, F. S. and H. Varmus. 2015. A new initiative on precision medicine. *N Engl J Med* 372 (9):793–5. doi: 10.1056/NEJMp1500523.

Conley, Y. P., M. Heitkemper, D. McCarthy et al. 2015. Educating future nursing scientists: Recommendations for integrating omics content in PhD programs. *Nurs Outlook* 63 (4):417–27. doi: 10.1016/j.outlook.2015.06.006.

Cox, J. and M. Mann. 2007. Is proteomics the new genomics? *Cell* 130 (3):395–8. doi: 10.1016/j.cell.2007.07.032.

Denny, J. C., M. D. Ritchie, M. A. Basford et al. 2010. PheWAS: Demonstrating the feasibility of a phenome-wide scan to discover gene-disease associations. *Bioinformatics* 26 (9):1205–10. doi: 10.1093/bioinformatics/btq126.

Dierich, M. T., C. Mueller, and B. L. Westra. 2011. Medication regimens in older home care patients. *J Gerontol Nurs* 37 (12):45–55. doi: 10.3928/00989134-20111103-02.

Embi, P. J. and P. R. Payne. 2013. Evidence generating medicine: Redefining the research-practice relationship to complete the evidence cycle. *Med Care* 51 (8 Suppl 3):S87–91. doi: 10.1097/MLR.0b013e31829b1d66.

Engler, M. B. 2009. Nutrigenomics in cardiovascular disease: Implications for the future. *Prog Cardiovasc Nurs* 24 (4):190–5. doi: 10.1111/j.1751-7117.2009.00058.x.

Fenech, M., A. El-Sohemy, L. Cahill et al. 2011. Nutrigenetics and nutrigenomics: Viewpoints on the current status and applications in nutrition research and practice. *J Nutrigenet Nutrigenomics* 4 (2):69–89. doi: 10.1159/000327772.

Friedman, N. and O. J. Rando. 2015. Epigenomics and the structure of the living genome. *Genome Res* 25 (10):1482–90. doi: 10.1101/gr.190165.115.

Genomic Nursing State of the Science Advisory Panel, K. A. Calzone, J. Jenkins et al. 2013. A blueprint for genomic nursing science. *J Nurs Scholarsh* 45 (1):96–104. doi: 10.1111 /jnu.12007.

Gligorijevic, V., N. Malod-Dognin, and N. Przulj. 2016. Integrative methods for analyzing big data in precision medicine. *Proteomics* 16 (5):741–58. doi: 10.1002/pmic.201500396.

Gonzalez-Garay, M. L., A. L. McGuire, S. Pereira, and C. T. Caskey. 2013. Personalized genomic disease risk of volunteers. *Proc Natl Acad Sci U S A* 110 (42):16957–62. doi: 10.1073/pnas.1315934110.

Grady, P. A. and L. L. Gough. 2015. Nursing science: Claiming the future. *J Nurs Scholarsh* 47 (6):512–21. doi: 10.1111/jnu.12170.

Green, E. D., M. S. Guyer, and National Human Genome Research Institute. 2011. Charting a course for genomic medicine from base pairs to bedside. *Nature* 470 (7333):204–13. doi: 10.1038/nature09764.

Guo, L., M. V. Milburn, J. A. Ryals et al. 2015. Plasma metabolomic profiles enhance precision medicine for volunteers of normal health. *Proc Natl Acad Sci U S A* 112 (35):E4901–10. doi: 10.1073/pnas.1508425112.

Integrative H. M. P. Research Network Consortium. 2014. The Integrative Human Microbiome Project: Dynamic analysis of microbiome-host omics profiles during periods of human health and disease. *Cell Host Microbe* 16 (3):276–89. doi: 10.1016 /j.chom.2014.08.014.

IOM (Institute of Medicine). 2011. *The Future of Nursing: Leading Change, Advancing Health.* Washington, DC: National Academies Press.

Kaddurah-Daouk, R., R. Weinshilboum, and Pharmacometabolomics Research Network. 2015. Metabolomic signatures for drug response phenotypes: Pharmacometabolomics enables precision medicine. *Clin Pharmacol Ther* 98 (1):71–5. doi: 10.1002/cpt.134.

Karlson, E. W., N. T. Boutin, A. G. Hoffnagle, and N. L. Allen. 2016. Building the Partners HealthCare Biobank at Partners Personalized Medicine: Informed consent, return of research results, recruitment lessons and operational considerations. *J Pers Med* 6 (1). doi: 10.3390/jpm6010002.

Kilpivaara, O. and L. A. Aaltonen. 2013. Diagnostic cancer genome sequencing and the contribution of germline variants. *Science* 339 (6127):1559–62. doi: 10.1126 /science.1233899.

Knowledgent White Paper. 2015. Big Data Analytics in Life Sciences and Healthcare: An Overview. Last modified May 3, 2016. https://knowledgent.com.

Lander, E. S. 2011. Initial impact of the sequencing of the human genome. *Nature* 470 (7333):187–97. doi: 10.1038/nature09792.

Lander, E. S., L. M. Linton, B. Birren et al. 2001. Initial sequencing and analysis of the human genome. *Nature* 409 (6822):860–921. doi: 10.1038/35057062.

Mardis, E. 2015. Cancer genomics. *F1000Res* 4. doi: 10.12688/f1000research.6645.1.

Monsen, K. A., B. L. Westra, S. C. Oancea, F. Yu, and M. J. Kerr. 2011. Linking home care interventions and hospitalization outcomes for frail and non-frail elderly patients. *Res Nurs Health* 34 (2):160–8. doi: 10.1002/nur.20426.

Monsen, K. A., B. L. Westra, F. Yu, V. K. Ramadoss, and M. J. Kerr. 2009. Data management for intervention effectiveness research: Comparing deductive and inductive approaches. *Res Nurs Health* 32 (6):647–56. doi: 10.1002/nur.20354.

NIH/BD2K. 2016. BD2K Centers. Accessed May 2, 2016. https://datascience.nih.gov.

NIH/CC. 2016. Clinical Research Courses. Accessed May 2, 2016. http://clinicalcenter .nih.gov/training/training1.html.

NIH/CTSA. 2016a. CTSA best practices. Accessed May 2, 2016. https://ctsacentral.org /consortium/best-practices/.

NIH/CTSA. 2016b. CTSA education and training. Accessed May 2, 2016. https://ctsa central.org/consortium/education-and-training/.

NIH/PMI/AoU. 2016. Accessed December 21, 2016. https://www.nih.gov/AllofUs -Research-Program.

NINR. 2016. NINR homepage. Accessed May 20, 2016. http://www.ninr.nih.gov/.

Olsen, L. A., D. Aisner, J. M. McGinnis, and Institute of Medicine (US) Roundtable on Evidence-Based Medicine. 2007. *The Learning Healthcare System: Workshop Summary.* Washington, DC: National Academies Press.

Olson, C. H., M. Dierich, and B. L. Westra. 2014. Automation of a high risk medication regime algorithm in a home health care population. *J Biomed Inform* 51:60–71. doi: 10.1016/j.jbi.2014.04.004.

Olson, J. E., E. Ryu, K. J. Johnson et al. 2013. The Mayo Clinic Biobank: A building block for individualized medicine. *Mayo Clin Proc* 88 (9):952–62. doi: 10.1016 /j.mayocp.2013.06.006.

Ordovas, J. M. and D. Corella. 2004. Nutritional genomics. *Annu Rev Genomics Hum Genet* 5:71–118. doi: 10.1146/annurev.genom.5.061903.180008.

Partners Healthcare. 2016. Disruptive Dozen: The 12 technologies That Will Drive Cancer Care in the Next Decade. World Medical Innovation Forum, Boston, MA.

Pathak, R. R. and V. Dave. 2014. Integrating omics technologies to study pulmonary physiology and pathology at the systems level. *Cell Physiol Biochem* 33 (5):1239–60. doi: 10.1159/000358693.

Rafii, A., C. Touboul, H. Al Thani, K. Suhre, and J. A. Malek. 2014. Where cancer genomics should go next: A clinician's perspective. *Hum Mol Genet* 23 (R1):R69–75. doi: 10.1093/hmg/ddu234.

Relling, M. V. and W. E. Evans. 2015. Pharmacogenomics in the clinic. *Nature* 526 (7573):343–50. doi: 10.1038/nature15817.

Roden, D. M. and J. C. Denny. 2016. Integrating electronic health record genotype and phenotype datasets to transform patient care. *Clin Pharmacol Ther* 99 (3):298–305. doi: 10.1002/cpt.321.

Sampselle, C. M., K. A. Knafl, J. D. Jacob, and D. J. McCloskey. 2013. Nurse engagement and contributions to the clinical and translational science awards initiative. *Clin Transl Sci* 6 (3):191–5. doi: 10.1111/cts.12020.

Selby, J. V., L. Forsythe, and H. C. Sox. 2015. Stakeholder-driven comparative effectiveness research: An update from PCORI. *JAMA* 314 (21):2235–6. doi: 10.1001/jama .2015.15139.

Shirey-Rice, J., B. Mapes, M. Basford et al. 2014. The CTSA Consortium's Catalog of Assets for Translational and Clinical Health Research (CATCHR). *Clin Transl Sci* 7 (2):100–7. doi: 10.1111/cts.12144.

Tang, Y., A. S. Axelsson, P. Spegel et al. 2014. Genotype-based treatment of type 2 diabetes with an alpha2A-adrenergic receptor antagonist. *Sci Transl Med* 6 (257):257ra139. doi: 10.1126/scitranslmed.3009934.

Tenenbaum, J. D. 2016. Translational bioinformatics: Past, present, and future. *Genomics Proteomics Bioinformatics* 14 (1):31–41. doi: 10.1016/j.gpb.2016.01.003.

Terry, S. F. 2015. Obama's precision medicine initiative. *Genet Test Mol Biomarkers* 19 (3):113–4. doi: 10.1089/gtmb.2015.1563.

The White House Office of the President. 2016. FACT SHEET: Obama Administration Announces Key Actions to Accelerate Precision Medicine Initiative. Accessed May 3, 2016. https://www.whitehouse.gov/the-press-office/2016/02/25/fact-sheet-obama -administration-announces-key-actions-accelerate.

Topol, E. J. 2014. Individualized medicine from prewomb to tomb. *Cell* 157 (1):241–53. doi: 10.1016/j.cell.2014.02.012.

Venter, J. C., M. D. Adams, E. W. Myers et al. 2001. The sequence of the human genome. *Science* 291 (5507):1304–51. doi: 10.1126/science.1058040.

Vogelstein, B., N. Papadopoulos, V. E. Velculescu, S. Zhou, L. A. Diaz, Jr., and K. W. Kinzler. 2013. Cancer genome landscapes. *Science* 339 (6127):1546–58. doi: 10.1126 /science.1235122.

Wang, Z., M. Gerstein, and M. Snyder. 2009. RNA-Seq: A revolutionary tool for transcriptomics. *Nat Rev Genet* 10 (1):57–63. doi: 10.1038/nrg2484.

Westra, B. L., T. R. Clancy, J. Sensmeier, J. J. Warren, C. Weaver, and C. W. Delaney. 2015a. Nursing knowledge: Big data science—Implications for nurse leaders. *Nurs Adm Q* 39 (4):304–10. doi: 10.1097/NAQ.0000000000000130.

Westra, B. L., G. E. Latimer, S. A. Matney et al. 2015b. A national action plan for sharable and comparable nursing data to support practice and translational research for transforming health care. *J Am Med Inform Assoc* 22 (3):600–7. doi: 10.1093/jamia/ocu011.

Westra, B. L., C. Oancea, K. Savik, and K. D. Marek. 2010. The feasibility of integrating the Omaha system data across home care agencies and vendors. *Comput Inform Nurs* 28 (3):162–71. doi: 10.1097/NCN.0b013e3181d7812c.

Westra, B. L., K. Savik, C. Oancea, L. Choromanski, J. H. Holmes, and D. Bliss. 2011a. Predicting improvement in urinary and bowel incontinence for home health patients using electronic health record data. *J Wound Ostomy Continence Nurs* 38 (1):77–87.

Westra, Bonnie, Sanjoy Dey, Gang Fang et al. 2011b. Interpretable predictive models for knowledge discovery from home-care electronic health records. *Journal of Healthcare Engineering* 2 (1):55–74. doi: doi:10.1260/2040-2295.2.1.55.

Worthey, E. A., A. N. Mayer, G. D. Syverson et al. 2011. Making a definitive diagnosis: Successful clinical application of whole exome sequencing in a child with intractable inflammatory bowel disease. *Genet Med* 13 (3):255–62. doi: 10.1097/GIM .0b013e3182088158.

Zeevi, D., T. Korem, N. Zmora et al. 2015. Personalized nutrition by prediction of glycemic responses. *Cell* 163 (5):1079–94. doi: 10.1016/j.cell.2015.11.001.

Chapter 2

Making Data Matter: Identifying Care Opportunities for US Healthcare Transformation

Mark A. Caron

Contents

The US healthcare system has been undergoing a foundational and fundamental transformation driven largely by two key federal laws:

1. The Health Information Technology for Economic and Clinical Health (HITECH) Act, which was part of the American Recovery and Reinvestment Act (ARRA) and was passed on February 17, 2009
2. The Patient Protection and Affordable Care Act (PPACA) also called the Affordable Care Act (ACA) and Obamacare, which was enacted on March 23, 2010

The HITECH Act focused on driving and enabling adoption and implementation of electronic health records (EHRs) and the digitization of the healthcare system. This was done by connecting three Meaningful Use stages with key criteria and regulations such as the use of computerized physician order entry or CPOE. Each of the three stages required an attestation that organizations had met progressively more challenging requirements and therefore were eligible for reimbursements as structured under the law. The Centers for Medicare and Medicaid Services (CMS) and the Office of the National Coordinator for Health IT (ONC), created by the HITECH Act, defined the criteria and regulations for each stage. Both HITECH and ACA also leverage and enhance the Health Insurance Portability and Accountability Act of 1996 (HIPAA).* The ACA required the US Department of Health and Human Services (HHS) to define operating rules for HIPAA's transactions and how they are communicated between different systems. There are many other provisions contained in both laws, and additional information can be found online.

While the Affordable Care Act may be best known for its focus on expanding access to health insurance for America's uninsured population, other key provisions within the law were intended to drive substantial delivery system reforms in terms of how care is delivered as well as complementary payment reforms. For decades, the US healthcare system has been paid through fee-for-service (FFS) payment models and schedules. Expensive and inefficient, this system is responsible for substantial differences in cost for services rendered by hospitals and physicians as well as significant differences in the quality of those services and their outcomes.

ACA provisions allow for the creation and piloting of new care delivery models, such as Accountable Care Organizations (ACOs), while shifting from an FFS or "volume"-based payment models to "value"-based care models that focus on the quality of care delivered with fixed and incentive-based reimbursement tied to outcomes. ACOs can be defined in the simplest way as a network of physicians, hospitals, and other providers that share in the responsibility for providing care and care coordination of medical services while taking financial risk of the patient who is assigned to a member primary care physician (PCP). With more than 825 ACOs

---

* HIPAA (http://www.hhs.gov/hipaa/for-professionals/).

serving 28 million Americans, a fundamental shift to value-based care delivery is underway.

This chapter in not intended to cover the HITECH Act or ACA law in their entirety as there is significant information available online at HealthIT.gov,* which details all of the components and provisions of each law. Nor is it intended to be a deep detailed technical and analytic body of work but to introduce and inform the reader on why these laws are significant in enabling the change necessary to provide physicians, clinicians, and constituents, including the patient, the data and information needed to deliver quality value-based care.

These laws are undoubtedly the fundamental drivers of the transformation in the US healthcare system. By integrating the disparate stakeholders with the data utilized to manage their patients and workflows, data modeling, and advanced technologies, advanced analytics platforms can provide a 360° view of the patient to all stakeholders. This 360° view is critical to managing the health of patients and populations in this new quality value-based care world.

2.1 Digitizing Healthcare—Connecting the Islands of Data

Before the HITECH Act and the era of EHR implementation and Meaningful Use, many hospitals, physicians, clinicians, and care facilities provided limited data electronically. Much of these data were still in paper format. As of April 2015, the ONC reported an increase from 27.6% to 75.5% of hospitals using a basic EHR from 2011 to 2014 (see Figure 2.1).†

2.1.1 Within 3 Years, Three Quarters of Hospitals Had a Basic EHR System

While industry standard bodies strive for transmission and format standards to pass information between constituents providing connectivity, the ONC developed a vision in 2013 for a Nationwide Health Information Network made up of several components including authentication, messaging standards, and a security and trust framework for exchanging health information across disparate and diverse constituents. These efforts are intended to address the shortcomings of EHRs in terms of interoperability and are important for long-term interoperability and

---

* HealthIT.gov (https://www.healthit.gov/).
† ONC Data Brief No. 23 April 2015. Adoption of Electronic Health Record Systems among US Non-Federal Acute Care Hospitals: 2008–2014 (https://www.healthit.gov/sites/default /files/data-brief/2014HospitalAdoptionDataBrief.pdf).

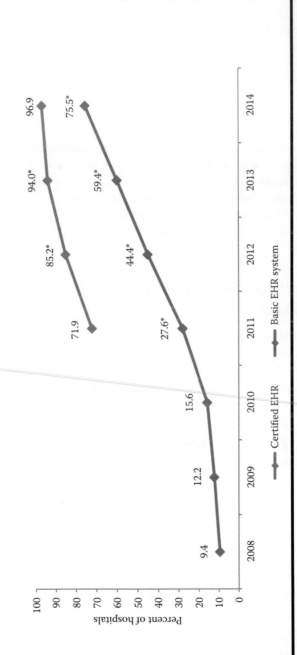

Figure 2.1 Percentage of non-federal acute care hospitals with adoption of at least a basic EHR with notes system and possession of a certified EHR: 2008–2014. Basic EHR adoption requires the EHR system to have a set of EHR functions. A certified EHR is EHR technology that meets the technological capability, functionality, and security requirements adopted by the U.S. Department of Health and Human Services. *Significantly different from previous year ($p < 0.05$). In 2014, three out of four (76%) hospitals had adopted at least a basic EHR system. This represents an increase of 27% from 2013 and an eightfold increase since 2008. Nearly all reported hospitals (97%) possessed a certified EHR technology in 2014, increasing by 35% since 2011. Possession means that the hospital has a legal agreement with the EHR vendor, but is not equivalent to adoption. (From ONC/American Hospital Association [AHA], AHA Annual Survey Information Technology Supplement.)

exchange of healthcare information to improve the quality of care and support value-based care models (see Figure 2.2).*

Interoperability, as defined by the Health Information and Management Systems Society, describes the extent to which systems and devices can exchange data and interpret those shared data. For two systems to be interoperable, they must be able to exchange and subsequently present data such that they can be understood by a user.

The topic of interoperability is a huge one; for this discussion, the focus is on the higher level of data categories that are needed to build a complete picture of a patient later in this chapter. A recent article in *Modern Healthcare*† states that Health Information Exchange (HIE) use is definitely rising, citing a December 2015 report completed by AHRQ‡ in which HIE adoption has increased over time with 76% of US hospitals exchanging information in 2014. The effectiveness has been difficult to quantify and the impact is less clear. From the perspective of interoperability, notwithstanding that core Meaningful Use measures have been met as required by HITECH, the industry has a ways to go to exchange complete sets of information and data integrated into clinical workflows in a longitudinal fashion to realize the goals of Triple Aim§ and fulfill the ONC's 10-year vision of an interoperable healthcare IT ecosystem.

The assumption is that interoperability challenges will diminish over the next decade, and while various levels of maturity exist across the country today, significant interoperability hurdles remain. These include ones that need to be addressed to enable the capture and integration of longitudinal data sources required by the Triple Aim.

2.2 Achieving the Triple Aim in Healthcare

The Institute of Healthcare Improvement (IHI), an independent, not-for-profit organization driving innovation and results for healthcare improvement worldwide, developed a three-pronged framework to optimize health system performance. The aptly named Triple Aim focuses on the following:

- Improving patient experience of care (quality and satisfaction)
- Improving the health of populations
- Reducing the per capita cost of healthcare

---

* Connecting Health and Care for the Nation: A 10-Year Vision to Achieve an Interoperable Health IT Infrastructure (https://www.healthit.gov/sites/default/files/ONC10yearInteroperabilityConceptPaper.pdf).
† Modern Healthcare—HIE use definitely rising; impact less clear (http://www.modernhealthcare.com/article/20151218/NEWS/151219860).
‡ AHRQ—Agency for Healthcare Research and Quality (http://www.ahrq.gov/).
§ The IHI Triple Aim (http://www.ihi.org/engage/initiatives/tripleaim/pages/default.aspx#.V26qcUZhLak.mailto).

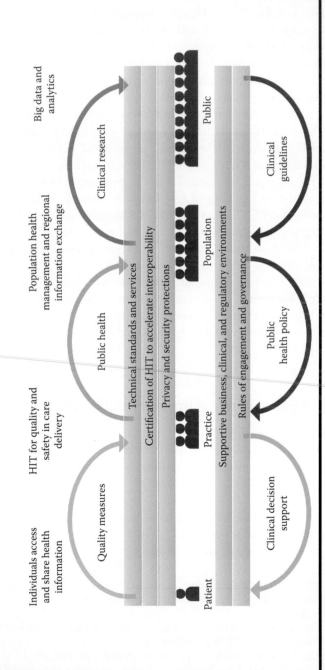

Figure 2.2 Health IT ecosystem—ONC 10-year vision.

These three dimensions are foundational to achieving cost and quality goals of ACOs and population health initiatives. The Triple Aim also defines key areas of measurement and outcomes to achieve the goals mentioned above:

1. Key measures for *improving patient experience* of care include the following:
   a. Global experience questions from patient, member, or populations surveys
   b. Care of experience measures based on key dimensions such as the Institute of Medicine, Joint Commission Quality Check, HHS Hospital Compare—Medicare data, Healthcare Effectiveness Data and Information Set (HEDIS),* and internal clinical practice management measures
2. Key health outcomes measures for improving the *health of the population* such as the following:
   a. Mortality and health/functional status measured by HHS Community Health Status Indicators, mortality rates, and years of potential life lost
   b. Disease burden as it pertains to incidence and prevalence and also predictive modeling scores forecasting future health and resource needs
   c. Behavioral and physiological factors such as the following:
      i. Smoking, alcohol use, physical activity, and diet that can be captured via health risk assessments
      ii. Blood pressure, body mass index, cholesterol, and blood glucose as measured through examination
3. The key measures to monitor *reducing the per capita cost of healthcare* include the following:
   a. Total cost per member of the population per month or PMPM as measured via payer claims, EHR data, and Medicare information. These look at utilization, primary care, and other areas of healthcare cost and utilization.
   b. Hospital and emergency department utilization and costs. In addition to the above sources, HEDIS contains utilization measures and focuses on procedures, inpatient stays, surgery, and prescription drugs.

For a better understanding of Triple Aim measures, please refer to *A Guide to Measuring Triple Aim: Population Health, Experience of Care, and Per Capita Cost.*[†] These three key areas of focus are paramount to achieving the overall goals of the Triple Aim.

Equally important are building the organization with the people, processes, information, and technology and successfully implementing them. (Figure 2.3

---

* What is HEDIS (http://www.ncqa.org/hedis-quality-measurement/what-is-hedis).
† Guide to Measuring Triple Aim (http://www.jvei.nl/wp-content/uploads/A-Guide-to-Measuring-the-Triple-Aim.pdf).

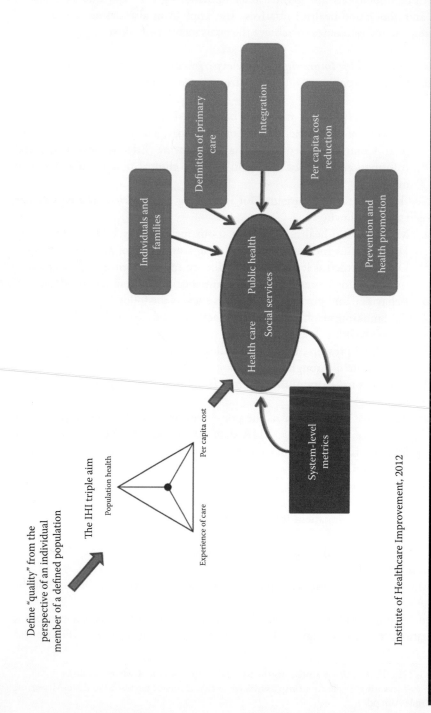

Institute of Healthcare Improvement, 2012

Figure 2.3 Design of a Triple Aim enterprise.

describes these functions at a high level.) Another consideration is the fact that the continuum of care is longitudinal in nature. Rarely does one stakeholder—whether a delivery system, physician group, or hospital—have all the needed medical, clinical, pharmaceutical, and behavioral health resources at their disposal to ensure a fully integrated approach to population health management (PHM) or individual care.

Adding to this challenge is the ability of patients to travel for work or vacation or perhaps spend time living in different geographic locations and having healthcare needs met by nonaffiliated providers. Simply missing a laboratory test that was completed but not captured in the patient's record will affect a provider's quality scores and show up as a gap in care. Similarly, if a patient were to receive medical or clinical services, which may include indicators of a new diagnosis without their PCP's knowledge, this could also create a change in their acuity or risk adjustment and is described as a coding gap.

Looking at the varied constituents of the healthcare ecosystem and the Triple Aim framework, the data for providing a comprehensive and accurate picture of a patient's health are a complex and complicated array of sources, types, frequency, and importance. More importantly, incorporating all the data sources and using them to understand the current and future healthcare needs from chronic care to rising risk issues to prevention are essential for driving to value-based care and overall PHM. Information from health payer claims, laboratories, patient-provided information, pharmaceutical, wellness/fitness, demographic/psychographic, and EHR data such as Continuity of Care Document (CCD) and Admission Discharge Transfer (ADT) messages are all critical information sources.

In the new world of value-based care, transitional care, care coordination, and care management, all utilize and leverage these key sources of information to understand where patients are in the care of their illness or disease in the post-acute settings and to ensure that any gaps in their care plans and care needs are met to achieve quality measures. There is a financial component associated with this as well, but for this, discussion is focused on identifying the gaps tied to delivering quality care. The evolution to value-based care also creates the need for a longitudinal view that follows the patient through every care setting.

2.3 A Closer Look at Data Sources

For the purpose of this chapter, the Workgroup for Electronic Data Interchange (WEDI) definition of gaps in care is used, which is the discrepancy between evidence-based best practices and the care that is actually delivered to the patient.*

---

* http://www.wedi.org/knowledge-center/white-papers-articles/white-papers/resources/2016
/03/31/closing-gaps-in-care-through-health-data-exchange

As mentioned, two types of gaps exist: (1) how a patient's diagnosis is coded, which describes the patient's acuity (how ill a patient is) and (2) a gap in care. Both gaps require a set of data to evaluate and determine if they exist. Coding gaps are important as they tie to the patient acuity, risk score, and the level of resources needed for care. These resources are tied to reimbursement models from CMS and commercial payers to cover providers' efforts to care for the patient. Risk adjustment is covered later in the chapter.

To get a better understanding of how to ensure care needs are met and that gaps in care are identified and brought to the care team's attention, it is important to look deeper at the data sets that figure into this shift to value-based care and where the data may reside. Enrollment data, medical (professional and facility, e.g., hospitals), pharmacy, vision, and mental health claims data are key data sets that help enable and determine if a gap in care may exist.

Enrollment data provide the necessary information regarding the payer, member information, benefits, coverage, demographics, and so on. It is the data that a physician or hospital checks when a patient shows up for services. These data use the 834 Benefit Enrollment and Maintenance standard HIPAA transaction, which enables electronic transmission to stakeholders.

Medical claims data include diagnosis; the date, place, and type of service; the procedure performed; who performed the service; and also financial information like charges and paid amounts. These claims include specific ICD-10 (International Statistical Classification of Diseases and Related Health Problems) diagnosis codes and also CPT (Current Procedural Terminology) procedures codes or HCPCS (Healthcare Common Procedure) codes, which identify the services performed by the provider. Medical claims use the 837P (Professional) electronic HIPAA transaction standard to send these claims, which is the same as the CMS 1500 paper claim form.

Facility claims utilize similar coding standards such as ICD procedure codes and are found on facility or hospital claims. Facility claims use the 837I (Institutional) electronic HIPAA transaction standard to transmit, which is the same as UB 04 and CMS1450 facility claims. Facility claims include diagnosis, procedure(s), revenue codes, discharge information, and other data elements. Many payers, including CMS, utilize DRGs (Diagnosis-Related Groups) as a way of categorizing medical procedures and associated services to support that procedure to standardize reimbursement. CMS and payers use a DRG grouper to map these ICD-10 codes within the claim to the associated DRG. Groupers scan the claim at the line level and perform the mapping. Claims can have multiple lines to them representing additional ICD-10 codes as well.

Pharmacy claims provide a limited set of data that are still critical in helping to identify gaps. Typically, a pharmacy claim includes patient identifiers, prescription drug information such as the NDC identifier code (National Drug Code assigned by the Food and Drug Administration), when it was filled, the number of refills, and paid amounts. The diagnosis is not included but can be found on medical and hospital claims. From an analytics perspective, there is work that needs to be completed to map the prescribed drug to the appropriate patient diagnosis.

Clinical data can come in the form of a CCD, which contains a patient summary and core administrative and clinical information. The CCD is electronically transferred to the next care provider or can be requested by the previous one. The transmission standard is based on the HL7 (Health Level Seven) Clinical Document Architecture. CCDs support SNOMED (Systematized Nomenclature of Medicine) medical terms and LOINC (Logical Observation Identifiers Names and Code), which applies universal code names to medical laboratory observations. ADT transactions also play an important role in providing a trigger event that a patient has been admitted, discharged or transferred to another facility. These messages alert care managers, care team members, and other key stakeholders that an event has occurred with this patient and communicate pertinent information regarding the event.

Vision claims data are also electronically transmitted using HIPAA Compliant 837 standard formats as described above. ICD-10, CPT, and HCPCS are used.

Behavioral health claims are electronically transmitted using HIPAA Compliant 837 as well as *DSM-5 (Diagnostic and Statistical Manual of Mental Disorders, Fifth Edition)*, which is now mapped to ICD-10-CM codes for diagnosis and also CPT codes for the provided procedure or service. *A note on behavioral health and EHR implementation:* A March 2016 *Health Affairs* study found that only 2% of the surveyed psychiatric hospitals had an EHR system implemented by 2012.* In contrast to hospitals and physician practices, there were no federal incentives to encourage behavioral health organizations to deploy EHRs. The lack of EHRs poses significant challenges to the healthcare industry's ability to manage population health effectively because of the lack of data, clinical notes, and records that are important to understanding a patient's overall health, and the absence of integration and interoperability.

Other data sources are also becoming available, which will enhance the richness of predictive models, including health risk assessments, psychographic data (data about a person's values, attitudes, interests, traits, etc.), consumer information patient-supplied data, and fitness and clinical wearables, to name a few.

2.4 Turning Data into Insights

Now that the key data sources needed to be brought together to create meaningful insights for the various stakeholders in the transition to value-based care have been identified, the next step is to review the steps necessary to build those insights. Because a detailed deep dive would go far beyond the scope of this or any single chapter, the review is high level.

---

* Hospitals Ineligible for Federal Meaningful-Use Incentives Have Dismally Low Rates of Adoption of Electronic Health Records (http://content.healthaffairs.org/content/31/3/505 .abstract).

At the outset, it is important to understand how value-based care (VBC) and value-based reimbursement (VBR) relationships work. The move to PHM and VBR requires that providers are reimbursed in a risk-based model. Providers bear financial risk, and the quality of their patient is measured to ensure that they meet metrics such as HEDIS and satisfy evidence-based guidelines for improved outcomes. These contractual relationships are often tied to some form of ACO model with commercial payers or with CMS for Medicare and Medicaid enrollees.

2.5 Understanding Risk

Risk as it relates to PHM and healthcare in this chapter is defined as one or more entities assuming the financial risk for caring for patients and meeting quality measures. Risk factors are key in understanding the current medical and lifestyle condition of members and predicting their current and future needs and potential costs, and ultimately the financial risk. There is a large body of existing work in the industry regarding healthcare risk and the addition of new data sources to improve the accuracy of predictive models and lead to prescriptive models, all of which are outside the scope of this chapter. A more definitive and descriptive source of information on this subject can be found in *Healthcare Risk Adjustment and Predictive Modeling* by Ian Duncan.*

In an ACO or PHM relationship, patients are identified and attributed to a PCP and then stratified by their risk groupings such that a provider understands which patients are the most ill (high risk), patients that may be pre-disease state or pre-chronic (rising risk), and those who are well and require the least intervention (healthy).

Utilizing the models described below enables the appropriate risk adjustment and scoring for each patient. Leveraging commercial grouper technologies provides known and proven algorithms that help build consistency across providers and payers. The CMS Hierarchical Condition Category (HCC) Risk Adjustment model was developed in the 1990s for Medicare and continues to evolve today. At a conceptual level, what HCCs do are to categorize diseases into 79 categories that map to ICD-10 codes (see www.cms.gov) and use the HHS HCC Risk Adjustment model for individual and small group market products under the Affordable Care Act. HHS HCC categorizes diseases into 127 categories that map to ICD-10 codes. It is important that physicians and staff properly code patients annually to reflect their health conditions. Missed or improper documentation or coding (coding gap) can reduce the patient acuity and hence risk score. These missed codes can also occur if a patient seeks services outside of the PCP's knowledge, which again reinforces the need for a longitudinal view of all patient medical, clinical, pharmacy, or laboratory services. These risk scores tie to resource needs and reflect patient acuity, which corresponds to the appropriate financial reimbursement.

---

* Healthcare Risk Adjustment and Predictive Modeling Paperback—2011 by FIA, FCIA, MAAA Ian Duncan FSA (Author).

Quality of care is a significant component of this shift to value-based care. Gaps in care can occur when the standard of care that is appropriate and necessary to care for a patient who is diagnosed with a condition or chronic illness is not being fulfilled. An example would be if a patient has been diagnosed as a diabetic and the standard of care requires a hemoglobin A1c test every 3 or 6 months. If a laboratory test is not received by the PCP, nor a claim for that service appears, a gap in care exists. For each of the chronic diseases, standards of care exist for physicians and the care team to manage that patient's condition(s). Some patients have multiple comorbidities, and with each diagnosis comes standards of care to manage those patients and the population to meet quality outcomes and measures.

Quite the challenge isn't it? Physicians, clinicians, hospitals, and other providers need to meet Triple Aim and HEDIS measures going forward to satisfy the requirements of value-based care and the goals of VBRs. So it is a significant tracking and management challenge requiring the ability to consume data from multiple payers, sources, and constituents in the healthcare continuum to meet the care demands of their patients and achieve the quality outcomes. In many ways, this is a classic big data challenge.

2.6 Bringing It All Together

As previously mentioned, the challenge the healthcare industry faces is that it is a longitudinal process that requires a solution or platform that can integrate into an existing HIE, if one exists, or more importantly where one does not exist, capture the data necessary from those various sources to create a complete picture of all of a patient's services. Claims data can give us a longitudinal picture of the patient and where they received services, but it may be insufficient to close a gap in care; supplemental or other source data may be required. The solution or platform also needs capabilities to ingest all of the sources of data; to utilize risk models to determine patient identification, attribution, and stratification to mention a few; and to translate all of these structured and unstructured data (such as clinical notes, etc.) into actionable insights driving clinical workflows for a care team to manage their patients.

Figure 2.4 shows a market-leading PHM solution, the Theon platform,* which solves for these complex problems and enables physicians, hospitals, delivery systems, payer organizations, and even employers to realize the Triple Aim goals and manage their VBR and VBC relationships. The Theon platform creates a 360° patient-centric view within the care continuum and healthcare stakeholders.

Figure 2.5 depicts the Theon platform's architecture, which is a cloud-based, HIPAA-compliant, secured, real-time platform as a service.

---

* Theon, Care Modeler, Care Collaborator, Care Engager, and Care Optimizer are registered trademarks of Geneia LLC. Theon diagrams and architecture are owned and provided as a courtesy by Geneia LLC and are used only with permission; all other rights are reserved.

Theon
CARE OPTIMIZER

Understanding **savings
or cost-avoidance**
opportunities

Care administrators
and providers in ACOs,
PCMHs, P4P, MSSP

Theon
CARE COLLABORATOR

Identifying **care pattern
variation** and opportunities
to **coordinate care**

Physicians, hospitals, care
managers

Theon
CARE ENGAGER

Employer-focused
analytics and **consumer**
tools

Employers, brokers,
payers, consumers

Theon
CARE MODELER

**Care and risk
arrangement modeling
tool** for healthcare
business users

Care providers, payers,
care data teams

Figure 2.4 The Theon platform provides a 360°, patient-centered view that enables organizations to successfully manage and improve population health and performance of value-based contracts. The Theon platform provides each stakeholder specific views of the patient, member, or employee, filtered and driven by role-specific business, clinical, and HIPAA-compliant rules.

The Theon platform shown is composed of key enabling technologies that include the following:

- *Clinical Integration Engine*—An interoperability hub for integrating standards-based, real-time, right-time clinical, administrative, and consumer data feeds from various constituents. Whether they are participating in an HIE, EHR, skilled nursing or long-term care facility, payer, or an independent organization, integration and interoperability are achieved through an HIE-compatible integration layer. This layer also includes a Master Patient Index capability to match the right patients with their health information.
- *Big Data Engine*—A HADOOP engine that provides the ability to consume unstructured data, clinical health pathways, healthcare consumer segmentation data, pricing information, and a myriad of other potential sources that can be used to meet clinical measures, expanded analytical model development, and clinical workflow needs.
- *Care Modeler Module*—Care and risk arrangement modeling tool for healthcare business users in which key algorithms for identifying and creating insights and action are defined. Models include the following:
  - Identification and attribution of a population to a physician.
  - Care and coding opportunities are identified, condition identification and stratification; base cohorts such as coronary artery disease, heart failure, diabetes, and other customized cohorts are determined.

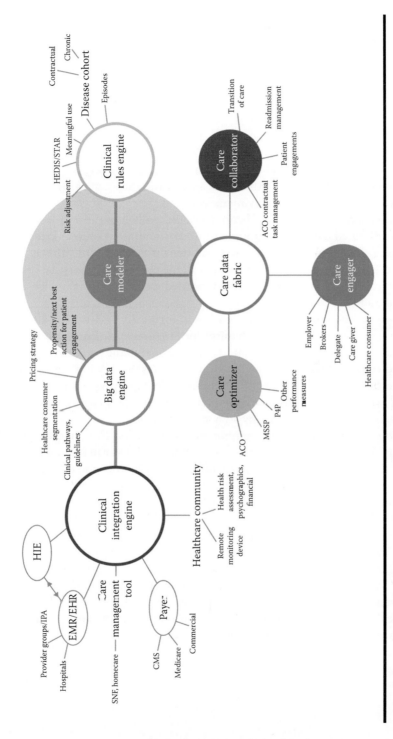

Figure 2.5 Unified platform ingests and analyzes consumer, clinical, biometric, and claims data.

- Risk stratification such as condition and demographic risk and Medicare Risk Adjustment Factor/HHS Commercial Risk Adjustment are calculated and customized, as well as evolving models using additional consumer sources.
- Predictive statistical analysis and enrichment for data.
- Big data analysis to understand patient engagement models, disease prevalence, and care patterns.

■ ***Clinical Rules Engine***—Calculates rule sets and measures such as HEDIS/STAR, Meaningful Use, Medicare Access & CHIP Reauthorization Act (MACRA), episodic and disease cohort measures whether payer-specific, contractual, or chronic. Other rules and measure sets can easily be added to accommodate new and evolving measures.

■ ***Care Data Fabric***—The Theon platform pulls together structured and unstructured data sets in atomic, summary, and nonrelational areas to present a single source of truth in a multitenant environment. This is known as the Care Data Fabric. These data include claims, pharmacy, laboratories, clinical data from EHRs, patient-generated data clinical wearables, Fitbits, and more.

■ ***Care Collaborator module*** (screenshot in Figure 2.6)—The Care Collaborator module provides the mechanism for physicians, patients, and their care teams to act on gap-in-care opportunities related to the patient's plan of care, and collaborate and manage toward the success of each individual member and their goal of better health. It also provides reporting capabilities including watch lists, activity manager, population explorer, patient explorer, and action reports as well as many ad hoc capabilities.

■ ***Care Engager module*** (screenshot in Figure 2.7)—This module provides employers, brokers, and payers with analytics and performance measurement of those members/employees regarding care utilized, cost of care, quality measures associated with providers delivering care as well as services in and out of network, to name a few key features.

■ ***Care Optimizer module*** (screenshot in Figure 2.8)—Intended for care administrators, including shared risk partners and quality-based programs such as ACOs, CMS Patient Centered Medical Homes, or any pay-for-performance organization (e.g., P4P, P4Q, MSPP, DSRIP); this module provides the ability to create refined views of the population at the level of the payer, health system, a customer-created program, a site/office, a specific product such as Medicare Advantage, or a physician, and shows cost of care, quality performance, and physician referral patterns.

Figure 2.6 The Theon platform's Care Collaborator module delivers insights at the point of care, integrating seamlessly into provider workflows and helping care teams identify care pattern variations, gaps in care, and opportunities for better care coordination.

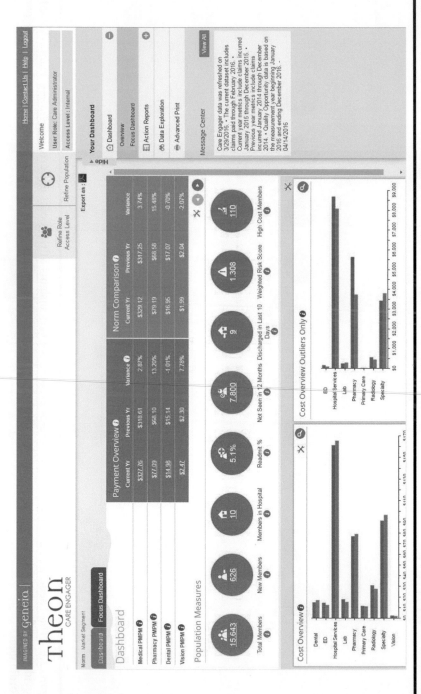

Figure 2.7 The Theon platform's Care Engager module delivers employer-focused insights and healthcare engagement tools that help employers better understand and control healthcare spend.

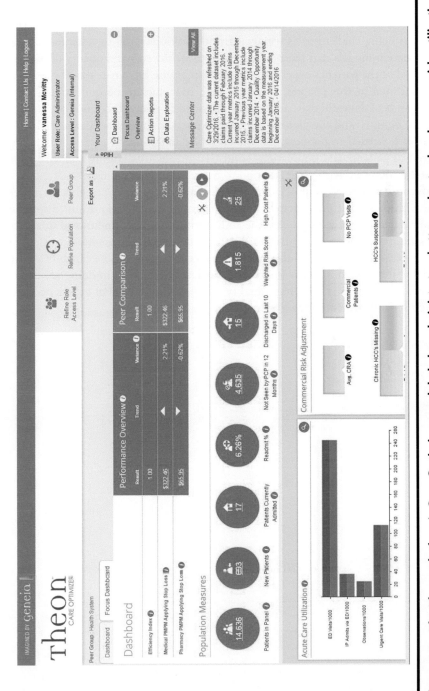

Figure 2.8 The Theon platform's Care Optimizer module helps administrators better understand and manage risk, utilization, and cost, and improve performance in value-based contract arrangements.

2.7 Summary

The US healthcare system and industry are in a period of great transformation. The industry is being challenged as it moves from traditional FFS to value-based risk reimbursement models that put providers at risk for the cost and quality of patient care as well as the patient's experience of care, otherwise known as the Triple Aim.

As outlined in this chapter, this challenge continues to be quite significant. Many islands of data still exist and care is provided in many disconnected settings across the country and the globe. To meet the goals of the Triple Aim and PHM, a solution is needed to connect and integrate the longitudinal care that is being delivered to patients and population—and that means that coding and care gaps need to be addressed within the solution to meet quality outcomes.

Advanced analytics can provide more robust and more timely insights than ever before with expanded data models now consuming many various and disparate data sources. Big data tools provide the ability to take in vast amounts of unstructured data and convert these disparate data into actionable insights provided to the appropriate care team member as well as to the patient. These capabilities are essential if the United States is to achieve the Triple Aim and, in doing so, meets the needs of its citizenry with high-quality outcomes, high level of experience and satisfaction, and cost efficiency.

Chapter 3

Turning Data into Enhanced Value for Patients

Kyun Hee (Ken) Lee

Contents

3.1 Introduction

In the past decade, billions of dollars were invested in revamping the information technology (IT) infrastructure for hospitals and healthcare providers. Software companies such as EPIC and Cerner are increasing their market presence and providing strategic direction on how electronic medical record (EMR) systems are designed, implemented, and utilized. These systems reduce redundancies in workflows and provide a single platform for data collection and querying. Yet, as countless bits of data get accumulated in every organization's servers, a clear strategy around leveraging the data assets to achieve goals such as Institute for Healthcare Improvement's three aims has not been clearly defined. The three aims are as follows: (1) improving patient experience of care including quality and satisfaction, (2) improving the health of populations, and (3) reducing the per capital cost of healthcare.

While there are many challenges to develop an effective and scalable business intelligence and data analytics capability within any healthcare organization, this chapter gives an overview of how two groups within a large health system successfully leveraged data to deliver tangible benefits to patients and the organization. The objective of the two case studies Patient Blood Management (PBM) and Enhanced Recovery After Surgery (ERAS) is to provide real-life examples of how data can be converted into action and improved results.

Hospitals are under immense pressure to reduce their operating costs. Traditional payment models that rely on additional volume for increased profit margins are phasing out and new payment models such as population health-based Accountable Care Organizations are forcing hospitals to take more financial risk on the services that they provide. A prime example of this trend can be found in the State of Maryland where the Center for Medicaid and Medicare Services approved a pilot program for all the hospitals in Maryland to have limits on annual revenues, essentially putting the entire state under a capitated payment model for hospital services.[1] Although cost-saving initiatives have always been part of the annual budget cycle at every hospital, the changing landscape in reimbursement is forcing hospitals to take unprecedented measures in improving quality and reducing costs.

3.2 Blood Management

3.2.1 Background

PBM programs are becoming popular among hospitals because the program is designed to educate clinicians on transfusion guidelines that would lead to safer care and lower cost. Blood transfusion is an ideal target area because it is the most commonly performed procedure and one of the top five most overused procedures.[2] In the United States, at least $3 billion is spent every year on red blood cells (RBCs) alone.[3]

A PBM program involves multiple stakeholders including anesthesiologists, intensivists, hospitalists, and blood bankers. Existing studies summarizing PBM programs indicate that multidisciplinary interventions are necessary to be successful. The program is based on landmark randomized controlled trials that prove the appropriateness of using threshold laboratory values before administering transfusions. For example, when patients have hemoglobin levels above 7 g/dL, then RBC transfusion is not recommended for non–cardiovascular-related diagnosis and non-bleeding patients.[4] The thresholds exist for all four types of blood: RBC, plasma, platelet, and cryoprecipitate. Educational materials, best practice alerts (BPAs) on the ordering form, and data are also critical elements to the program that enhance the enforcement of the thresholds. Collecting accurate and timely data, reporting results, and sharing the results with the appropriate providers are important factors to drive improvements. Furthermore, clinician engagement and leadership are key ingredients to fully execute the plan and sustain the success.

3.2.2 Business Imperative

Before the PBM program officially started, the Johns Hopkins Health System hired external consultants to assess potential areas of cost savings throughout the organization. Based on the assessment, supply chain was an area where most of nonlabor cost could be reduced. Like many organizations, the executive leadership team was committed to avoiding reductions in workforce, and supplies became a primary target area for cost reduction.

More than 150 potential initiatives were identified by the supply chain team, and the PBM program was one of the top five areas where the most savings could be realized. The opportunity analysis was conducted by using national benchmarks on utilization of blood units. When the first report on the blood-related opportunity was published, internal stakeholders, such as the administrator of the blood bank and clinical leaders, challenged the consultants by requesting details on the assumptions and sources of benchmark data. After multiple iterations of refining the opportunity analysis, which led to excluding certain patient populations because of high complexity and selecting comparable institutions for benchmarking purposes, the analysis still showed significant cost savings potential.

After confirming the opportunity, the next step was to define what was needed to realize the opportunity. Teams from finance, supply chain, quality, and the blood bank formed a workgroup to develop a business plan based on the potential opportunity and the resources needed to achieve the savings. The business planning process also required input from each of the five hospitals within the health system because while the system level leaders determined the opportunity and were responsible for providing support to the hospital level leaders, the local hospitals were ultimately accountable for the results.

In any business plan, these elements are always included: revenue, expense, and program-related costs. Since the PBM program did not require a complex financial arrangement, the projected financials were developed on a simple operating statement. In terms of revenue, PBM did not have any impact because revenue was governed under a capitation arrangement with the state. On the other hand, the program had a direct impact on expenses to the hospital, and some upfront cost was needed to hire staff for the PBM program.

The impact on the hospital's expense was modeled by comparing the actual utilization of the four types of blood products—RBC, plasma, platelet, and cryoprecipitate—with the benchmarks. Differences in units per patient between the actual result and benchmarks for the four blood products were used to project the maximum cost savings potential by multiplying the differences by the annual utilization of those products and then multiplying the result by the acquisition cost per unit of each blood product. During this exercise, the business planning group debated about the use of acquisition cost versus overall cost, which includes overhead and any other cost other than the price (i.e., acquisition cost). The overall cost could be three to five times the acquisition cost.[5] After much debate, the group concluded that using the acquisition cost to project potential savings was a more accurate and concrete approach that would eliminate any doubt on the program's effectiveness. If the overall costs were used, developing an accurate way of accounting for the overhead costs and how they are allocated would have been detrimental to measuring the program's success because it is dependent on subjective assumptions that could be easily challenged.

Once the potential cost savings were calculated, the program-related costs needed to be developed. The program was going to be led by a physician who was an expert in blood transfusions, and additional help from IT staff, analysts, and improvement coordinators was needed. The total program-related costs offset the potential cost savings, yet the net savings were still significant. The business plan was compiled with all these factors in consideration, and it was presented and approved by the executive leadership.

The business planning process took 6 months to complete. After the plan was approved, each respective team members had to execute their part of the plan. The physician champion reprioritized efforts from other obligations such as clinical time and research to the PBM program, the quality improvement department recruited a transfusion specialist to serve as the clinical project coordinator supporting the physician, the supply chain department positioned itself to challenge the blood vendor on the prices, the health system blood bank leadership team worked with the hospital level blood banks to elicit their participation, the analytics teams worked together to harmonize data and reports throughout the system, and the IT teams worked together to implement BPAs in the computerized physician order entry. The BPAs were used to standardize guidelines across the health system.

3.2.3 PBM Data and Analytics

The PBM program at the Johns Hopkins Health System involved five hospitals in Maryland and Washington, DC. Three hospitals were using Epic, one was using Meditech, and one was using Eclipsys Sunrise as their EMR at the time the program started, although all of them were using Epic after 2 years, which enabled a more efficient data extraction process. The EMRs were used to identify patients and their attributes such as location of transfusions and ordering provider. In addition, laboratory results such as hemoglobin levels were acquired from the laboratory information system and the dispensed number of units was acquired from the blood bank information system.

Before starting the program, a significant amount of time was spent on planning the data and analytics requirements. This was the first time in the history of the organization that an effort was made to create a harmonized health system level data and reporting infrastructure related to blood utilization; hence, careful planning and execution were important to ensure that all the relevant stakeholders were included and that decisions on data uses and report designs were reviewed and approved as a group. During the first 6 months, eight IT and business analyst personnel worked together, led by the Analytics Project Management Office (APMO) that served in an integrating function for the group. The team members represented all the five hospitals, and they were experts in information systems and data related to PBM in their own hospital. As a baseline assessment, each member was asked to share how each hospital was extracting, transforming, and loading (ETL) the data related to PBM. An inventory of all the existing reports and analyses was also compiled. To the team's surprise, every hospital had a unique strength, yet no hospital had the best comprehensive approach. For example, one hospital had a robust data infrastructure but the analytics capabilities were immature while another hospital had well-designed reports and analytics tools but the data were not as comprehensive or accurate. The project quickly turned from a simple data integration task to a transformational project that required a redesign of how the health system should approach PBM analytics.

Before the eight members were engaged, every hospital had systems architects and analysts who worked in their siloes. In general, a systems architect's role is to extract, transform, and load (ETL) data into a database that business analysts or business intelligence developers could access and develop dashboards and analyses. When the team members shared what they were doing in the ETL process and what the analysts were producing for frontline providers and managers, common themes emerged and the APMO saw an opportunity to realize economy of scale with key processes.

The APMO's role was critical in bringing the group together and finding areas of optimization in the existing processes. The APMO team consisted of two out of the eight members in the analytics team and their background was in finance, analytics, quality, and project management. During weekly meetings with the eight members, the APMO recorded notes and specification from each hospital while sharing all the information transparently with the team. At the same time, determining the strategy, assigning tasks, and tracking progress were APMO's responsibilities.

The leader of the APMO was also trained in change management and transformational leadership that were useful when getting every member on board to achieve the goal. Initially, a few members of the team were reluctant to collaborate, and this reaction is common when engaging data stewards who have a strong sense of ownership. Knowing how to get the right data and calculate accurate metrics gives power to the person who holds the knowledge, and it becomes a part of the person's proprietary identity within the organization. The effort to breakdown siloes and openly share everyone's processes could have been seen as a threat to that perceived authority. After a few meetings of explaining the purpose of the team's collaboration and the ultimate goal, everyone was on board.

The most intriguing observation was that when anyone developed ways to extract data or to calculate metrics using sophisticated formulas, many became highly protective of the methodologies and lacked the impetus to be transparent. This phenomenon, which is more appropriate for a psychological study, will be a key issue to overcome as health systems develop a more consolidated approach to data and analytics especially in decentralized organizations.

Despite the psychological challenges, the APMO was able to remove the barriers and started to focus everyone's energy on developing a strategy and specific milestones. There were several components of the project that needed clear direction: data model, metric calculation, validation process, visualization, report designs, and customer needs.

There were two data models developed for PBM. One was at the patient encounter level and the other was at the individual blood order level. The patient-level data model included any attribute and measure related to the patient's encounter such as outcomes on quality, length of stay, and complications. These measures were only useful at the patient level because they were not attributable to a specific order. The order-level data model contained data on every blood order and the corresponding laboratory results: hemoglobin levels for RBC orders, international normalized ratio (INR) for plasma orders, and platelet count for platelet orders. Since cryoprecipitate was not frequently used and the financial impact was minimal, the PBM program did not invest much time in it. Along with the laboratory results, the order-level data model contained the number of units ordered each time.

The primary outcomes to measure the success of the PBM program were as follows: total units ordered, transfused units per patient, cost reduction, complications, and length of stay. Each of these measures was available for the four blood products and for each hospital. The results were also available at the department and provider level. Process measures that were identified as the key drivers of the outcomes were blood orders in compliance with guidelines and number of units ordered each time. The process measures were also available at the department and provider level. An important distinction in the use of these two types of measures—outcome measures and process measures—is worth highlighting. The outcome measures were more important for the PBM program, hospital, and health system leadership because they were directly related to the patients and the organization. However, the process measures were more important for the frontline providers who were being asked to comply with the guidelines. Without the ability to track their ordering patterns, the frontline providers would not have been convinced that improvements could be made.

After the ETL and metric calculation steps, the importance of validating the process and accuracy of the data could not be overemphasized. In most instances, especially around quality- and clinical-related data, the rigor that is found in financial audits is nonexistent. The issue stems from inadequate data infrastructure for quality and clinical reporting and lack of standards to define ETL steps including clear formulas with explicit inclusion and explicit criteria. There are national efforts led by prominent institutions such as the Agency for Healthcare Research and Quality and the National Quality Foundation to tackle this issue, yet the journey has just begun. To validate the PBM-specific ETL process and metric calculations, the APMO worked with other parties such as blood vendors, blood banks in the hospitals, and other data sources within the health system. At the end of the exercise, every stakeholder was in agreement that the EMR-based ETL process and the results were accurate enough to proceed. During the validation process, no two sources of data had the same results. For example, the total number of RBC units at one hospital was different when the result from the EMR-based ETL, blood vendor, and blood bank reports were compared to each other. The discrepancies could have been attributed to timing of reports, missing data, and other noncontrollable issues, yet the results were similar. Since the EMR-based ETL provided the most granular level of detail related to the PBM program, it was determined to be the sole source of data for dashboards, reports, and analyses.

The visualization of the outcome and process measures was critical in converting data into information that could be metabolized by the frontline providers. For the measures that were listed previously, interactive dashboards were developed to enable dynamic filtering by provider, service, and type of blood product. For the process measures, best practice guidelines related to triggers were incorporated in the visualizations as conditional statements. For simplicity, green and red colors were used to track compliance. For example, the monthly graphs for RBC compliance had green for orders that were associated with hemoglobin values <7 g/dL and red for orders associated with hemoglobin values ≥8 g/dL. For RBC, values between 7 and 8 were considered to be yellow because the guidelines were flexible for patients with cardiovascular conditions. For plasma, green was used if the INR value was ≥1.5 and red was used if the value was <1.5 before ordering. Last, for platelets, green was used if the platelet count was <50,000 and red was used if the value was ≥50,000. In essence, green indicated that the blood order was appropriate (i.e., followed the guideline) and red indicated that the order was unnecessary. Both outcome and process measures were tracked on a monthly basis and the physician leader of the health system's PBM program sent reports to each hospital's Chief Medical Officers.

The distribution of monthly results required more strategic thinking than anticipated because the executives, hospital leaders, and frontline providers had different needs at their respective levels. Furthermore, the use of online interactive dashboards was not as popular as the team expected for the broader audience beyond the analytics teams. Hence, to provide what each stakeholder needed, the physician leader of the PBM program sent out monthly e-mails to each stakeholder groups with the relevant reports in static portable document format (PDF). Many recipients preferred the PDF to the online dashboard because they had busy schedules and wanted immediate and easy access to the reports as e-mail attachments rather than logging into a server and clicking through different buttons to get the information they needed. Until there is broad adoption of business intelligence tools among nontechnical users, the need for static reports will likely not disappear.

While the interactive dashboards and static reports are helpful in evaluating retrospective performance, they are limited in their ability to answer questions that might arise from the information provided. For example, an orthopedic surgeon reached out to the APMO and inquired about the impact of using tranexamic acid for his patients. The surgeon hypothesized that his need to order blood decreased because tranexamic acid can reduce blood loss. The APMO promptly developed a process to answer ad hoc inquiries and completed the analysis. The results showed that the timing of tranexamic acid usage matched well with a dramatic reduction in transfusion. Furthermore, the APMO developed capabilities to conduct advanced statistical analyses for physicians who were engaged in research by engaging a biostatistician.

3.2.4 Results

The PBM program's first year met the business plan targets and continued to generate value for patients and the organization. More than $1 million was saved and complication rates decreased. The educational materials and cultural transformation around blood transfusions worked well and the analytics teams were successful in delivering solutions to the program. Based on the initial success, the health system leadership decided to continue funding the program and supporting the expansion of the program to reach more frontline providers. Similar to any intervention, sustainability and scalability will continue to be a challenge. From the analytics perspective, all the data feeds were automated and the production of measures, dashboards, and reports were almost completely automated. Hence, the scalability and sustainability were not critical concerns. However, for the physician leader and the operational teams, sustainability and scalability were not as easy because of constant turnover in staff, which meant that the PBM program needed to continue the education on guidelines and constantly push providers to comply.

3.3 Enhanced Recovery after Surgery

3.3.1 Background

Enhanced Recovery After Surgery (ERAS) is based on protocols that surgeons use to streamline pre- and postoperative care for surgical patients admitted to the hospital.[6,7] Its goal is to reduce infections and improve other outcomes while complying with recommended tasks. Ultimately, it would enhance the value of patient care, which is similar to the PBM program, yet the ERAS program incorporates a broader set of process and outcome measures. The ERAS program had more in-depth data and analytics requirements, and it was only implemented at one hospital instead of the entire health system. Hence, it was a relatively narrower yet deeper approach to data analytics compared to the PBM program, which only had a handful of measures applied throughout the health system.

The ERAS program was focused on colorectal surgery because of several reasons: (1) the infection rates were high, (2) surgeon leadership was available, and (3) the ERAS protocol for colorectal surgery was successful in other institutions. Senior leaders in the Department of Surgery and the hospital demanded improvements in the infection rates and reduction of length of stay as a result of the ERAS program.

An advantage of using existing improvement tools such as the ERAS program is that there are other institutions trying to achieve the same goals. During the implementation phase, the team visited other institutions to observe how others were implementing the program.

3.3.2 Enhancing Overall Value

Colorectal surgery has high infection rates owing to the site of surgery, and length of stay in the hospital could be easily prolonged as a result of infections. At the Johns Hopkins Hospital, the colorectal surgery team was asked to reduce the infection rates, and the team went beyond expectations by looking at the problem from a total value perspective. Value is defined as quality and service over cost.[8] It is measured with outcomes while processes drive the outcomes. The outcomes of interest in the ERAS program were infection rates, patient satisfaction, length of stay, and cost. Some examples of process measures were preoperative education, early mobilization, and chlorhexidine bathing. In total, there were more than 30 process measures that were initially developed. The hypothesis was that the chosen process improvements would drive the outcomes.

Implementing the ERAS program came at a cost. Although shifting resources and reprioritizing work are always on top of hospital executives' minds, translating the concept to operations has proven to be difficult in most cases. Hence, the ERAS program leaders had to develop a business plan that showed its potential impact on the financial and quality outcomes. The business case was supported by reduction of cost through lower length of stay and fewer infections. Similar to the PBM business plan, the ERAS program was approved and investments in surgeon time, analysts, IT staff, and nurses were made.

3.3.3 ERAS Data and Analytics

The data and analytics requirements for the ERAS program included more outcome and process measures than the PBM program, thus enabling a richer environment for advanced analytics. Since the program was only implemented at one hospital, IT and analytics resources who were dedicated to that specific hospital were engaged unlike the PBM program.

The following detailed measures were collected. The list was compiled after multiple iterations working with the clinicians because there was an initial gap between what the clinicians expected and what could be achieved based on the EMR data. Most of the limitations were based on the lack of granular attributes that could be tied to an intervention.[6]

Outcome Measures—length of stay, National Surgical Quality Improvement Program surgical site infection rates, patient experience, and cost.
Process Measures—preoperative education, mechanical bowel preparation with oral antibiotics, chlorhexidine bathing, multimodal analgesia with thoracic epidurals or transversus abdominis plane blocks, restricted intravenous fluids protocol, early mobilization, and resumption of oral intake.

Both outcome and process measures were collected from various sources for each patient who underwent surgery. The process of collecting the data, similar to how the PBM data were collected, required multiple ETL jobs and validation. While the steps were critical in achieving success, they are similar to rudimentary data collection processes. However, the story behind how the process measures listed above were selected deserves more elaboration.

When the ERAS program started, more than 30 different processes were deemed to play a critical role in the outcomes. The clinical analytics team spent many hours defining the specifications and collecting data on the process measures. However, after collecting enough data over time, statisticians were engaged to apply advanced analysis methods that would combine the outcome and process measures and determine the most valuable processes that were contributing to the improvements in outcomes. Unlike averages or totals that require little or no statistical knowledge, conducting regression analyses and applying other statistical techniques is what is sometimes referred to as data science. Through the exercise, the statistician was able to identify the process measures that had the most meaningful impact, and the ERAS operational team was able to eliminate efforts that were determined to be ineffective and, hence, are able to focus more efforts on processes that had real impact. Taking the power of data science to another level, the analytics team and the statistician worked with application developers to design a predictive tool that surgeons could use for identifying patients who were at risk of leading to an unfavorable outcome. Although the ability to predict the patients who might have unfavorable outcomes was a good concept, the analytics team quickly learned that the sample size based on one hospital's colorectal surgery volume was insufficient to have any impact on the surgeons' decision making.

3.4 Summary

The two case studies covered in this chapter—PBM and ERAS—demonstrated how raw data from the source systems were translated into a useful enabler for clinicians to improve quality and reduce unnecessary costs. Gathering requirements, accessing the data, and developing appropriate tools are important ingredients. However, building trust with other team members and maintaining relationships are also critical, especially in a large organization where resources are decentralized. To get buy-in from multiple stakeholders for enterprise-level projects, transparently sharing the purpose and maintaining constant communication are good first steps in building a collaborative network.

3.5 Future Direction

Many hospitals are struggling with how to develop an efficient and effective data analytics infrastructure governed with mature policies and procedures. While small-scale solutions could be delivered by working around these hurdles, maximizing the return on data assets will be possible when resources are coordinated and focused on extracting data, creating metrics, and sharing common goals. At the same time, building a culture of managing with data will accelerate the metabolism of information generated by analysts and data scientists so that the nontechnical audience would ultimately change behavior and make decisions that contribute to higher value. Technical skills are essential but not impactful if the end users are not able to absorb the information generated by the technical teams. To succeed in delivering value, any analytics professional will need to consider both technical requirements and business priorities while being cognizant about simple yet practical solutions.

References

1. Sharfstein, Joshua; Kinzer, Donna; Colmers, John. An update on Maryland's all-payer approach to reforming the delivery of health care. *JAMA Internal Medicine.* 175 (7) (2015): 1083–1084.

2. Pfuntner, Anne; Wier, Lauren; Stocks, Carol. Most Frequent Procedures Performed in U.S. Hospitals, 2010. HCUP Statistical Brief no. 149 (2013). Agency for Healthcare Research and Quality, Rockville, MD. Available at http://www.hcup-us.ahrq .gov/reports/statbriefs/sb149.pdf.

3. Toner, Richard; Pizzi, Laura; Leads, Brian et al. Costs to hospitals of acquiring and processing blood in the US. *Appl Health Econ Health Policy.* 9 (1) (2011): 29–37.

4. Hebert, Pail; Carson, Jeffrey. Transfusion threshold of 7 g per deciliter—The new normal. *NEJM.* 371 (15) (2014): 1459–1461.

5. Shander, Aryeh; Hofmann, Axel; Ozawa, Sherri et al. Activity-based costs of blood transfusions in surgical patients at four hospitals. *Transfusion.* 50 (4) (2010): 753–765.

6. Wick, Elizabeth; Galante, Daniel; Hocson, Deborah et al. Organizational culture changes results in improvement in patient-centered outcomes: Implementation of an integrated recovery pathway for surgical patients. *J Am Coll Surg.* 221 (2015): 669–677.

7. McLeod, Robin; Aarts, Mary-Anne; Chung, Frances et al. Development of an enhanced recovery after surgery guideline and implementation strategy based on the knowledge-to-action cycle. *Ann Surg.* 262 (2015): 1016–1025.

8. Porter, Michael. What is value in health care? *NEJM.* 363 (26) (2010): 2477–2481.

Chapter 4

Data Analytics for the Clinical Researcher

Minjae Kim

Contents

4.1 Introduction

The amount of healthcare data collected continues to grow at unprecedented rates, with total US data in 2011 containing 150 exabytes (10^{18} bytes) and soon reaching the zettabyte (10^{21} bytes) and yottabyte (10^{24} bytes) levels (Raghupathi and Raghupathi 2014). Large healthcare organizations, often in conjunction with commercial enterprises with specialization in Big Data, are using Big Data analytics to improve the efficiency of healthcare delivery and to reduce costs while improving health outcomes.* The sheer size of the available data is staggering and meaningful uses to improve clinical care and patient outcomes and to reduce costs are constantly being pursued. For the clinical researcher, the increasing availability of data of all different types presents new opportunities to conduct research to identify important areas where patient care may be improved.

The goal of the chapter is to present a broad introduction to the opportunities available through the use of large data sets to conduct observational clinical research. Analytics using these data sets will be explored, which allow the clinical researcher to formulate and to test important hypotheses related to clinical care and outcomes. Their advantages and limitations will be discussed as well as the overall spectrum of evidence in clinical medicine and how studies using these data sets fit into this paradigm. Examples of available data sets and analytical methods that will guide clinical researchers in identifying the best sources of data and the optimal methodological approaches for their research question will be reviewed.

4.2 Posing the Research Question

Many clinical research questions center around the effects of an intervention or exposure on specific outcomes. *Does daily aspirin use reduce the risk of a heart attack? Does exposure to secondhand smoke increase the risk of lung cancer?* Hypotheses are often generated from direct clinical observations, and at this stage, it is unclear whether these observations represent true associations with an outcome or if they are confounded by subconscious biases that may not be recognized. For example, a novel intervention that has not been formally tested may seem to improve outcomes in a small sample of patients, but the provider may be subconsciously applying this intervention only to patients that are likely to have a good outcome. Once an observation has been noted, there are many necessary steps that must be undertaken in order to determine if the intervention or exposure has a significant clinical effect, and in which population of patients the effects are seen.

To illustrate the utility of research studies using large data sets, an example from the field of anesthesiology will be used, specifically: *Does the use of neuraxial (spinal or epidural) anesthesia, compared to general anesthesia, improve outcomes in patients undergoing orthopedic surgery of the lower extremity?* Neuraxial anesthesia, initially developed in the late 19th century, is increasingly being used for many different types of surgical procedures. There are potential benefits to the use of neuraxial anesthesia but its overall use in lower-extremity orthopedic procedures remains relatively low in the United States today, with a recent study showing that 75% of primary hip and knee arthroplasties were performed solely with general anesthesia (Memtsoudis et al. 2013). There may be a myriad of reasons for this, including

---

* http://www-03.ibm.com/industries/ca/en/healthcare/documents/Data_driven_healthcare
  _organizations_use_big_data_analytics_for_big_gains.pdf; accessed August 8, 2016.

surgeon and anesthesiologist preferences, patient comorbidities and preferences, and a lack of knowledge or belief in the purported benefits of neuraxial anesthesia.

In the early 1990s, Buckley (1993) observed that many anesthesiologists thought neuraxial anesthetic techniques to be superior over general anesthesia for orthopedic surgery, mainly on theoretical grounds that were not supported by evidence available at that time. Since then, there has been a considerable amount of research trying to compare the anesthetic techniques and their relative effects on outcomes, but to date, the evidence has been mixed. If the true benefits of neuraxial anesthesia and the patients most likely to benefit from it could be identified, there could be significant implications for many stakeholders, including patients, providers, and payors.

4.3 Hierarchies of Evidence

In order to understand the potential value of any research project, the clinical researcher must understand different types of research studies and how they fit into the spectrum of clinical evidence. In an ideal setting, both the outcome and the *counterfactual outcome* (Rothman et al. 2008), that is, the resulting outcome had the individual received the alternative intervention or exposure instead of the one they actually received, would be identified, allowing one to determine the effect of the intervention or exposure in the individual and, when aggregated across many individuals, the average effect in the sample. Obviously, this is a philosophical concept that is not possible to assess in reality, but methodologies can be used to approximate this scenario.

To that end, the randomized controlled trial is the "gold standard" for measuring the effects of interventions in clinical studies. If the randomization process is done properly, in aggregate, the treatment group and control group will be similar with respect to unmeasured confounders and the outcomes will not be biased by these confounders. However, there are limitations to randomized controlled trials, including cost and time constraints, difficulties in enrolling sufficient numbers of patients, and imperfect randomization, with biases potentially introduced by personnel involved in the trial (Greenhalgh 1997). Randomized controlled trials typically have specific inclusion criteria, raising the issue of generalizability to broader populations of patients. There may be ethical considerations preventing certain types of studies, such as the exposure of subjects to potential harm. Randomized controlled trials, and meta-analyses of randomized controlled trials, are at the top of the "hierarchy of evidence" with respect to clinical investigations (Greenhalgh 1997; Guyatt et al. 1995):

1. Systematic reviews and meta-analyses
2. Randomized controlled trials with definitive results (confidence intervals do not overlap threshold clinically significant effect)

3. Randomized controlled trials with nondefinitive results (point estimate suggests clinically significant effect but confidence intervals overlap threshold)
4. Cohort studies
5. Case–control studies
6. Cross-sectional surveys
7. Case reports

As described in Section 4.2, many research questions begin with clinical observations and progress from the bottom of the hierarchy to the top, with initial observations reported through case reports and case series (7) and then through observational studies (4–6), followed by randomized controlled trials (2–3) and systematic reviews and meta-analyses (1).

In the neuraxial versus general anesthesia example, an early published report of the potential benefits of neuraxial anesthesia over general anesthesia was the retrospective review at a specialty orthopedic hospital that made significant changes to their anesthetic practice for elective total hip and knee arthroplasty at a specific time point, including the preferential use of neuraxial anesthesia over general anesthesia (Sharrock et al. 1995). Comparing outcomes before and after the change, they observed a threefold reduction in mortality, suggesting that neuraxial anesthesia may be beneficial. However, these results were far from conclusive, as there were many other factors potentially contributing to this effect, including changes to other aspects of perioperative management, improvements in surgical technique, and changes in the underlying patient population.

Many randomized controlled trials that evaluate differences in clinical outcomes with neuraxial and general anesthesia have been performed, but to date, the results are inconclusive. Meta-analyses of randomizsed controlled trials have not been able to identify significant differences in most major outcomes, including mortality, but there are many methodological problems with the trials, such as inadequate sample sizes and problems with randomization and blinding (Barbosa et al. 2013; Guay et al. 2016; Macfarlane et al. 2009; Parker et al. 2004); thus, there are still many unanswered questions. The remainder of the chapter will focus on observational research conducted with large data sets and the ways in which the proliferation of data has contributed to the understanding of this clinical issue.

4.4 Data Sources

While many researchers collect primary data by enrolling patients into studies, the focus here will be on secondary sources of data. There are a wide variety of data sources, both public and proprietary, available to clinical researchers. Some data sets are freely available, but many require membership in a specific organization or a fee to access the data. Government agencies, such as the Agency for

Healthcare Research and Quality (AHRQ), Centers for Medicare & Medicaid Services (CMS), and the Centers for Disease Control and Prevention (CDC), are common sources of data used in observational clinical studies. Online resources, such as the compendium organized by the Society of General Internal Medicine,* may facilitate the search for an appropriate data set.

Once the research question has been defined, the characteristics of the study will need to be determined in order to identify the most suitable data set, such as the underlying patient population, the intervention or exposure of interest, the outcome, and other variables that might be associated with both the exposure and the outcome (confounders). An advantage to using large data sets is that they tend to reflect "real-world practice" without being limited to the strict inclusion criteria of clinical trials; hence, they may have better generalizability. Not all research questions are well suited for analysis using large data sets and a primary limitation is the availability of relevant variables required for proper analysis.

4.4.1 Administrative Data

Administrative data sets are extensively used in healthcare research and offer many advantages (Mazzali and Duca 2015). The data are collected as part of routine hospital processes and can be representative of large segments of the population, including region, state, and the nation as a whole. Table 4.1 lists some widely used administrative data sets available from AHRQ and CMS. Other proprietary sources of administrative data exist, such as large healthcare networks and insurance claims data, but access to these data sets may be more limited. As the data sets are relatively easy to assemble, large cohorts are available and can be analyzed more rapidly than when collecting primary data. It is important to understand the purpose of the data set and the method of data collection so that the limitations of the data set can be understood. Administrative data sets are typically used for billing purposes, and this must be kept in mind when assessing the validity and quality of the variables contained in the data set. If, for example, reimbursement depends on the presence of certain elements, the validity and quality of those elements may be different from those that do not affect reimbursement. The discharge abstract is generated by a medical coder reviewing the medical record; thus, the presence of codes depends on accurate documentation of procedures and diagnoses by the clinical provider. A user new to a particular data set should spend a considerable amount of time becoming familiar with the structure and coding procedures of the data set so that it may be used appropriately.

Administrative data sets typically contain basic demographic information, such as age, race, and sex, with protected health information often omitted because of privacy regulations, though identifying data may be used to link different data sources or to follow individual patients over time. Data on socioeconomic status,

* http://www.sgim.org/communities/research/dataset-compendium; accessed August 11, 2016.

Table 4.1   Examples of Large Data Sets Used in Clinical Research

Administrative Data Sets		
Source	Data Set	Notes
AHRQ	Healthcare Cost and Utilization Project (HCUP)[a]	
	National Inpatient Sample (NIS)	20% stratified sample of inpatient discharges from US community hospitals, excluding rehabilitation and long-term acute care hospitals.
	Kids' Inpatient Database (KID)	National sample of hospital inpatient stays for patients younger than 21 years of age.
	Nationwide Emergency Department Sample (NEDS)	National sample of emergency department visits, including patients who are admitted as well as not admitted.
	Nationwide Readmissions Database	National sample of discharge data and readmissions after discharge.
	State Inpatient Databases (SID)	Universe of inpatient discharge abstracts in participating states.
	State Emergency Department Databases (SEDD)	Discharge data on all emergency department visits not resulting in an admission, in participating states.
CMS	Medicare Provider Analysis and Review (MEDPAR)[b]	Claims from Medicare beneficiaries at inpatient hospitals and skilled nursing facilities.
	Medicaid Analytic eXtract (MAX)[c]	Enrollment and claims data for enrollees of Medicaid and the Children's Health Insurance Program (CHIP) (state level).
Surveys		
Source	Data Set	Notes
AHRQ	Medical Expenditure Panel Survey (MEPS)[d]	Large-scale survey of families and individuals, medical providers, and employers regarding use, cost, and payment for health services.

(Continued)

Table 4.1 (Continued)   Examples of Large Data Sets Used in Clinical Research

Surveys		
Source	*Data Set*	*Notes*
CDC	National Center for Health Statistics[e]	
	National Health Interview Survey	Started in 1957, collecting data on a broad range of healthcare topics.
	National Health and Nutrition Examination Survey	Assesses health and nutritional status of children and adults. Data are collected from interviews and physical examinations.
	National Survey of Family Growth	Collects data on family life, marriage and divorce, and reproductive health.
Other Data Sets		
ACS	National Surgical Quality Improvement Program (NSQIP)[f]	Patient-level, aggregate data with risk factor and clinical outcome data on general, vascular, and other specialty surgery patients.
PCORI	Patient-Centered Clinical Research Network (PCORnet)[g]	Network of clinical data research networks and patient-powered research networks with focus on sharing health information for research.

Note: ACS, American College of Surgeons; AHRQ, Agency for Healthcare Research and Quality; CDC, Centers for Disease Control and Prevention; CMS, Centers for Medicare & Medicaid Services; PCORI, Patient-Centered Outcomes Research Institute.

[a] http://www.ahrq.gov/research/data/hcup/index.html
[b] https://www.cms.gov/Research-Statistics-Data-and-Systems/Files-for-Order/IdentifiableDataFiles/MedicareProviderAnalysisandReviewFile.html
[c] https://www.cms.gov/Research-Statistics-Data-and-Systems/Files-for-Order/IdentifiableDataFiles/MedicaidAnalyticExtractMAX.html
[d] https://meps.ahrq.gov/mepsweb/
[e] http://www.cdc.gov/nchs/surveys.htm
[f] https://www.facs.org/quality-programs/acs-nsqip/program-specifics/participant-use
[g] http://www.pcori.org/research-results/pcornet-national-patient-centered-clinical-research-network/clinical-data-and-0
URL data are current as of August 11, 2016.

geography, and cost are often available as well. Clinical information is represented by diagnosis and procedure codes, such as the International Classification of Diseases, Ninth Revision, Clinical Modification (ICD-9-CM) and Current Procedural Terminology codes. (As of October 1, 2015, the United States has transitioned to ICD-10-CM coding.) For clinical studies, these codes are used to extract the cohort to be used in the study. For instance, if the population of interest were diabetic patients, the selection criteria might be patients with a primary diagnosis of 250.*xx*, representing the ICD-9-CM code range for primary diabetes mellitus. The fourth and fifth digits of this particular ICD-9-CM code represent complications and the type of diabetes (type 1, type 2, or juvenile type), respectively, allowing for further categorization of patients, if necessary.

The primary purpose of administrative data is not for clinical research; hence, there may be biases attributed to errors in coding that must be assessed. Patients with a diagnosis code may not actually have the disease and patients with the disease may be missing the diagnosis code, and coding practices may vary between different hospitals contained in the data set. Validation studies should be performed to determine whether the strategy for extracting a particular cohort is reliable and valid; whether the data set contains adequate information on variables necessary for proper adjustment for confounders, such as comorbidities and risk factors; and whether the outcomes are also valid and reliable. Many important clinical outcomes, especially for surgery, procedures, and childbirth, can be coded using AHRQ's Patient Safety Indicators,* and many of them have been rigorously validated in the literature.

4.4.2 Surveys

Longitudinal surveys are conducted by government agencies, such as the CDC and US Census Bureau, to collect data on specific topics over time. They include random samples of subjects that are designed to be representative of healthcare in the United States. Examples include the National Health and Nutrition Examination Survey, assessing the health and nutritional status of adults and children, and the National Survey of Family Growth, assessing family life and reproductive health issues. Patients are not the only subjects of longitudinal studies. For example, the National Ambulatory Medical Care Survey is conducted using a sample of physicians that provide outpatient and emergency department care. Table 4.1 provides examples of longitudinal surveys conducted by AHRQ and the CDC.

---

* http://www.qualityindicators.ahrq.gov/Modules/PSI_TechSpec_ICD10_v60.aspx; accessed August 11, 2016.

4.4.3 Other Data Sets

Other types of data sets are available, and the clinical researcher should investigate whether suitable ones exist in their area of interest. Data may be collected from the electronic health records of the researcher's own institution, and internal procedures should be followed for obtaining this type of data. Clinical trials collect a large amount of data, and they may be suitable for secondary analysis to answer research questions that may not have been part of the original aims of the study. In the fields of surgery and anesthesiology, there are several initiatives aimed at improving the quality of perioperative care, including the National Surgical Quality Improvement Program (NSQIP) of the American College of Surgeons* and the Anesthesia Quality Institute of the American Society of Anesthesiologists.† Both programs provide secondary data sets to researchers at member institutions that are suitable for observational clinical studies in perioperative outcomes. Another example is the United States Renal Data System,‡ focusing on patients with chronic kidney disease and end-stage renal disease.

In recognition of the potential for the large amount of data being collected by healthcare institutions for clinical research, in 2014, the Patient-Centered Outcomes Research Institute (PCORI) funded PCORnet, an initiative designed to aggregate clinical data for comparative effectiveness research through a network of Clinical Data Research Networks (CDRNs) and Patient-Powered Research Networks (PPRNs).§ As the CDRNs and PPRNs develop, they may be an important source of data for future clinical research.

Observational studies using large data sets have played an important role in the study of the comparative effectiveness of general anesthesia versus neuraxial anesthesia on patient outcomes in orthopedic surgery, with different types of data sets used in the analyses. For example, Memtsoudis et al. (2013) used an administrative data set from a commercial source and Neuman et al. (2012, 2014) took advantage of the availability of anesthetic management data in administrative data sets from New York State, while O'Hara et al. (2000) used data from a clinical trial on perioperative blood management to conduct a secondary analysis of anesthetic technique in hip fracture surgery.

4.5 Data Analysis

Once a data set has been identified and the analysis cohort has been assembled, the clinical researcher must prepare the data set for analysis. This includes examining

---

* https://www.facs.org/quality-programs/acs-nsqip; accessed August 11, 2016.
† https://www.aqihq.org; accessed August 11, 2016.
‡ https://www.usrds.org; accessed August 11, 2016.
§ http://www.pcori.org/research-results/pcornet-national-patient-centered-clinical-research-network; accessed August 15, 2016.

the variables for completeness and consistency as well as translating the raw data into the variables that will be used in the analysis. The data sets can become very large and spreadsheet software is inadequate for use in maintaining and analyzing the data; hence, the researcher must become familiar with software packages that will facilitate the use of the data sets. Commonly used packages include SAS (SAS Institute Inc., Cary, North Carolina), Stata (StataCorp LP, College Station, Texas), IBM SPSS Statistics (International Business Machines Corp., Armonk, New York), and R (R Foundation for Statistical Computing, Vienna, Austria).

The clinical researcher must become familiar with statistical methodology to analyze the data, such as logistic regression, linear regression, and Cox proportional hazards regression, with the nature of the data determining the specific methodology that is used. Detailed descriptions and comparisons of various statistical methodologies are outside the scope of this chapter, but a few issues related to the analysis of observational data will be highlighted.

Data sets used in observational research can contain very large sample sizes and may be especially useful in establishing differences in outcomes when the outcomes are relatively rare. However, the large sample sizes can lead to a plethora of statistically significant p values (Lin et al. 2013) and the researcher must be careful in the interpretation of results and must always determine the clinical relevance of any statistically significant findings (Armijo-Olivo et al. 2011). In addition, there are many types of bias and potential errors that must be considered when interpreting the results of analyses using large data sets (Kaplan et al. 2014). There are many assumptions inherent in the design of any study and statistical model, and sensitivity analyses should be conducted to verify the robustness of the primary findings (Delaney and Seeger 2013). A sensitivity analysis is a separate analysis conducted after changing a specific aspect of the data or analysis in order to determine if and how the results change with a particular modification. For instance, sensitivity analyses can be conducted to determine the effects of a change in the underlying statistical model, the presence of unmeasured confounders, or the use of specific subpopulations of the sample. Missing data are frequently encountered in large data sets used in observational studies and rigorous methods to account for missing data should be applied (Groenwold et al. 2012).

Another common problem with observational studies is related to the fact that there may be significant differences in the underlying characteristics of the comparison groups that affect the outcome, or selection bias. Randomization avoids this issue, theoretically leading to equivalent groups of patients with respect to unmeasured confounders. There are statistical techniques aimed at accounting for the nonrandom nature of the samples in observational studies, such as propensity score and instrumental variable methods. A propensity score is the probability that an individual receives a particular treatment based on known characteristics and can be used to account for selection bias (Austin 2011). An instrumental variable is a variable that is correlated with the exposure or treatment but not with the outcome and can be used to account for measurement error and omitted variables (Newhouse and McClellan 1998). Both propensity score (Neuman et al. 2012) and instrumental variable (Neuman et al. 2014) methods have been used in the analysis of neuraxial versus general anesthesia in orthopedic surgery patients.

4.6 Translating the Evidence

While research studies using large data sets may be performed efficiently, they still must be conducted rigorously to ensure that the results have merit. There are frameworks for assessing the quality of observational studies, such as the GRACE principles, which ask whether (1) the study plans were prespecified before the study was conducted; (2) the study was conducted in a manner consistent with good practice and described in sufficient detail for replication; and (3) the interpretation of the study is valid (Dreyer et al. 2010). The findings of a single study, no matter how novel, should not be evaluated in isolation but must be examined in the context of the available evidence. Are the results consistent with prior findings, including other observational studies and randomized controlled trials? It is increasingly being acknowledged in the medical community that many studies, including both observational and randomized trials, suffer from limitations and biases that are likely to minimize the veracity of significant findings, such as small sample sizes, small effect sizes, flexible study designs, and conflicts of interest (Ioannidis 2005). Publication bias remains an issue, with "negative" observational and laboratory-based studies more likely to be affected than randomized controlled trials (Easterbrook et al. 1991). Therefore, a lack of published studies with no significant effects should not be taken as proof that studies with these results do not exist.

In the evaluation of neuraxial versus regional anesthesia techniques, observational studies have been important in understanding their comparative effectiveness in patients undergoing orthopedic surgery. There are observational studies demonstrating a mortality benefit with neuraxial anesthesia (Hunt et al. 2013; Memtsoudis et al. 2013; Neuman et al. 2012), and reviews of observational studies suggest that neuraxial anesthesia is associated with reduced mortality and morbidity, including thromboembolic events, blood loss, and transfusion (Luger et al. 2010; Opperer et al. 2014). However, several observational studies have failed to demonstrate a mortality benefit with neuraxial anesthesia (Neuman et al. 2014; O'Hara et al. 2000; Patorno et al. 2014). These conflicting results do not imply that the studies were invalid or conducted improperly, but they reveal the complexity of the issue and the limitations of the available evidence. Taken together, when accounting for all of the available evidence, including those from randomized controlled trials and observational research using large data sets, it is clear that the topic is of great importance to those affected and that large randomized clinical trials are required to address this issue, such as the multicenter pragmatic clinical trial recently funded by PCORI with a budget of $12 million.* Thus, while studies using large data sets cannot definitely answer this research question, they contributed to the available evidence that was necessary to justify the commitment of significant resources for further evaluation.

4.7 Conclusions

The proliferation of healthcare data presents new opportunities for clinical researchers to conduct studies on topics that may not have been feasible or practical with a randomized controlled trial as well as to provide the evidence base that can serve as the justification for conducting new randomized trials. While administrative data sets have tended to be the main source of data for clinical research using large data sets, the increasing availability of electronic health record data and efforts by organizations such as PCORI to aggregate it for clinical research should make electronic health data an important source for future studies and allow for more clinical data to be incorporated into research studies.

While randomized controlled trials remain the "gold standard" for evidence in clinical research, there is a role for observational studies using large data sets, and with careful application, they can make significant contributions to the clinical evidence base. The researcher undertaking a study using a large data set must take into consideration all of the inherent limitations and potential biases of these studies when interpreting the results of their analyses. Observational studies using large data sets can have a significant role in the spectrum of evidence of clinical research and should be embraced by the medical community as a valid tool for answering important research questions.

References

Armijo-Olivo S, Warren S, Fuentes J, Magee DJ. 2011. Clinical relevance vs. statistical significance: Using neck outcomes in patients with temporomandibular disorders as an example. *Man Ther.* 16(6):563–572.

Austin PC. 2011. An introduction to propensity score methods for reducing the effects of confounding in observational studies. *Multivariate Behav Res.* 46(3):399–424.

Barbosa FT, Castro AA, Sousa-Rodrigues CF. 2013. Neuraxial anesthesia for orthopedic surgery: Systematic review and meta-analysis of randomized clinical trials. *Sao Paulo Med J.* 131(6):411–421.

Buckley N. 1993. Regional vs general anaesthesia in orthopaedics. *Can J Anaesth.* 40(5 Pt 2):R104–R112.

---

* http://www.pcori.org/research-results/2015/practical-intervention-improve-patient-centered-outcomes-after-hip-fractures; accessed August 16, 2016.

Delaney JAC, Seeger JD. 2013. Sensitivity analysis. In: Velentgas P, Dreyer NA, Nourjah P, Smith SR, Torchia MM, editors. *Developing a Protocol for Observational Comparative Effectiveness Research: A User's Guide.* AHRQ publication no 12(13)-ehc099. Rockville, MD: Agency for Healthcare Research and Quality. Chapter 11, pp. 145–160.

Dreyer NA, Schneeweiss S, McNeil BJ, Berger ML, Walker AM, Ollendorf DA, Gliklich RE, Initiative G. 2010. Grace principles: Recognizing high-quality observational studies of comparative effectiveness. *Am J Manag Care.* 16(6):467–471.

Easterbrook PJ, Berlin JA, Gopalan R, Matthews DR. 1991. Publication bias in clinical research. *Lancet.* 337(8746):867–872.

Greenhalgh T. 1997. How to read a paper. Getting your bearings (deciding what the paper is about). *BMJ.* 315(7102):243–246.

Groenwold RH, Donders AR, Roes KC, Harrell FE, Jr, Moons KG. 2012. Dealing with missing outcome data in randomized trials and observational studies. *Am J Epidemiol.* 175(3):210–217.

Guay J, Parker MJ, Gajendragadkar PR, Kopp S. 2016. Anaesthesia for hip fracture surgery in adults. *Cochrane Database Syst Rev.* 2:CD000521.

Guyatt GH, Sackett DL, Sinclair JC, Hayward R, Cook DJ, Cook RJ. 1995. Users' guides to the medical literature. IX. A method for grading health care recommendations. Evidence-based medicine working group. *JAMA.* 274(22):1800–1804.

Hunt LP, Ben-Shlomo Y, Clark EM, Dieppe P, Judge A, MacGregor AJ, Tobias JH, Vernon K, Blom AW, National Joint Registry for England W et al. 2013. 90-day mortality after 409,096 total hip replacements for osteoarthritis, from the national joint registry for england and wales: A retrospective analysis. *Lancet.* 382(9898):1097–1104.

Ioannidis JP. 2005. Why most published research findings are false. *PLoS Med.* 2(8):e124.

Kaplan RM, Chambers DA, Glasgow RE. 2014. Big data and large sample size: A cautionary note on the potential for bias. *Clin Transl Sci.* 7(4):342–346.

Lin M, Lucas HC, Jr, Shmueli G. 2013. Research commentary—Too big to fail: Large samples and the *p*-value problem. *Inf Syst Res.* 24(4):906–917.

Luger TJ, Kammerlander C, Gosch M, Luger MF, Kammerlander-Knauer U, Roth T, Kreutziger J. 2010. Neuroaxial versus general anaesthesia in geriatric patients for hip fracture surgery: Does it matter? *Osteoporos Int.* 21(Suppl 4):S555–S572.

Macfarlane AJ, Prasad GA, Chan VW, Brull R. 2009. Does regional anaesthesia improve outcome after total hip arthroplasty? A systematic review. *Br J Anaesth.* 103(3):335–345.

Mazzali C, Duca P. 2015. Use of administrative data in healthcare research. *Intern Emerg Med.* 10(4):517–524.

Memtsoudis SG, Sun X, Chiu YL, Stundner O, Liu SS, Banerjee S, Mazumdar M, Sharrock NE. 2013. Perioperative comparative effectiveness of anesthetic technique in orthopedic patients. *Anesthesiology.* 118(5):1046–1058.

Neuman MD, Rosenbaum PR, Ludwig JM, Zubizarreta JR, Silber JH. 2014. Anesthesia technique, mortality, and length of stay after hip fracture surgery. *JAMA.* 311(24):2508–2517.

Neuman MD, Silber JH, Elkassabany NM, Ludwig JM, Fleisher LA. 2012. Comparative effectiveness of regional versus general anesthesia for hip fracture surgery in adults. *Anesthesiology.* 117(1):72–92.

Newhouse JP, McClellan M. 1998. Econometrics in outcomes research: The use of instrumental variables. *Annu Rev Public Health.* 19:17–34.

O'Hara DA, Duff A, Berlin JA, Poses RM, Lawrence VA, Huber EC, Noveck H, Strom BL, Carson JL. 2000. The effect of anesthetic technique on postoperative outcomes in hip fracture repair. *Anesthesiology.* 92(4):947–957.

Opperer M, Danninger T, Stundner O, Memtsoudis SG. 2014. Perioperative outcomes and type of anesthesia in hip surgical patients: An evidence based review. *World J Orthop.* 5(3):336–343.

Parker MJ, Handoll HH, Griffiths R. 2004. Anaesthesia for hip fracture surgery in adults. *Cochrane Database Syst Rev.* (4):CD000521.

Patorno E, Neuman MD, Schneeweiss S, Mogun H, Bateman BT. 2014. Comparative safety of anesthetic type for hip fracture surgery in adults: Retrospective cohort study. *BMJ.* 348:g4022.

Raghupathi W, Raghupathi V. 2014. Big data analytics in healthcare: Promise and potential. *Health Inf Sci Syst.* 2:3.

Rothman KJ, Greenland S, Lash TL. 2008. *Modern Epidemiology.* Philadelphia: Wolters Kluwer Health/Lippincott Williams & Wilkins.

Sharrock NE, Cazan MG, Hargett MJ, Williams-Russo P, Wilson PD, Jr. 1995. Changes in mortality after total hip and knee arthroplasty over a ten-year period. *Anesth Analg.* 80(2):242–248.

Chapter 5

Intelligent Healthcare: The Case of the Emergency Department

Shivaram Poigai Arunachalam, Mustafa Sir, and Kalyan S. Pasupathy

Contents

5.1 Introduction

The US healthcare system is often regarded as a complex, fragmented, and imbalanced system in the world, providing high-quality care to patients with advanced technological innovations and healthcare services, while accessible to only those who could afford such services with the high cost of care (Oster and Braaten 2016).

Thanks to the implementation of the Affordable Care Act, all Americans can at least give access to the basic healthcare service, which is considered as a significant progress in the history of healthcare reforms in the United States (Gonzalez 2013). No doubt, technological innovations, medical advancements, market conditions, use and analysis of electronic medical records (EMRs) and big data in clinical decision making, adoption of cloud computing, application of comparative effectiveness requirements for medicines, and evidence-based medicine have potentially created a convergent force that is effectively transforming healthcare (Ledbetter and Morgan 2001). In particular, the healthcare industry has seen significant changes in how clinical decisions are being made using actionable intelligence with the integration of various technological advancements to provide real-time solutions to specific patients in a timely manner. The ability to analyze clinical and cost data across all settings of care is essential for the future clinical and financial success of the healthcare industry.

Actionable intelligence is derived from raw healthcare data though collection, integration, analysis, and decision making that results in the desired response when acted upon (Wadsworth et al. 2009). The implementation of electronic health records has resulted in a rapid accumulation of data. Healthcare organizations can use business intelligence (BI) technologies to leverage the data and improve operational and clinical efficiency (LaRow 2007). The healthcare industry is now realizing that a BI framework yields meaningful and actionable knowledge about opportunities for improvement (Glaser and Stone 2008; Glaser and Tom 2008). BI supports evidence-based clinical decision making and assists the search for clinical evidence to support diagnoses, care plans development, and outcomes evaluation for patients (Wanless 2005). The demand for transformational changes in the healthcare industry motivates many hospitals and networks to adopt a healthcare analytics approach to ensure their survival and growth that requires investment in information technology (IT) for healthcare analytics. Healthcare advanced analytics uncovers trends, waste in terms of staff time and so on, and standardization of practice to reduce variability and other actionable insights; saves time; supports informed decision making; enables negotiations for greater savings both within and outside the department; and identifies utilization changes for improved quality of care. The shift to a healthcare analytics culture can reduce data silos and data ownership issues, creates an atmosphere of curiosity and collaboration, and finally allows organizations to see beyond what has already happened and begin to forecast what might happen next (Kankanhalli et al. 2016).

The adoption of electronic claims systems, laboratory information systems, radiology information systems, electronic health records, and other systems have created massive stores of clinical and financial big data that have the potential to drive significant healthcare performance improvement (Rahman and Slepian 2016). However, even with the abundance of healthcare data, challenges exist: a shortage of data scientists, trustworthiness of data to provide actionable intelligence, and resistance of the healthcare industry to changes spurred by the use of big data and the dynamic nature of big data that is highly variable, causing inconsistencies, duplications, and inaccuracies that often challenge the validity driven by the lack of global standards for collection, storage, and analysis of such big data. In short, the complexity of analyzing big data arises from its three dimensions, that is, variety, velocity, and volume (Gartner 2011).

Radio Frequency Identification (RFID) use in healthcare is quickly gaining traction especially in the supply chain for applications such as electronic chain of custody, sample tracking, drug tracking, and verification (Huang and Chu 2011; Pasupathy 2010; Pasupathy and Clark 2014; Wamba et al. 2013). Healthcare is considered to be the next home for RFID after manufacturing and retail. Generally, the healthcare industry has been investing extensively in IT to reduce operating costs and improve patient safety, and RFID is expected to become critical to healthcare organizations to achieve these two goals (Wang et al. 2006). Advanced RFID technology allows real-time visibility into healthcare operations and services that provide actionable intelligence to make decisions that can prevent fatal errors and is proving to be an excellent tool for improving accuracy and traceability while protecting patient data and brand authentication (Ajami and Rajabzadeh 2013). The use of RFID in healthcare has opened new avenues of research for actionable intelligence and has influenced many hospitals to improve the quality of service and care (Slack 2013). RFID data, which need advanced healthcare analytics tools and contribute to the growing big data in the healthcare setting (in turn facing similar challenges), are unique in many aspects.

The potential of RFID use has not been fully realized in the healthcare setting because of several factors that will be discussed in the following sections; nevertheless, its application is gaining importance in almost every department in the healthcare industry. The Emergency Department (ED) is discussed here as a case study. The ED's services are extremely important to provide immediate lifesaving care and many investigators have attempted preliminary research in RFID use in the ED to optimize care and improve healthcare delivery for ED patients. There is no doubt that RFID use can transform healthcare delivery in ED as an intelligent system that can provide optimal high-quality care and service in a very efficient and cost-effective manner. The goals of this chapter are as follows:

- Provide an overview of the current status and trends in the ED, and the traditional approaches used to improve services
- Provide an introduction to RFID and its application in healthcare and status of its use in the ED
- Provide future research directions by identifying potential gaps and challenges in the RFID use in ED that can motivate researchers in this field to optimize RFID data collection and transformation into actions that are both intelligent and optimal to improve the quality of ED care in a cost effective manner

The following sections will expand on the above goals.

5.2 Overview of the ED

The ED of the hospital is the major portal through which the community accesses time-sensitive and lifesaving complex care, and the ED is one of the most complex and busiest places in a hospital (King et al. 2006). EDs are a venue for unscheduled practices and typically have 24/7 operations. On a daily basis, EDs treat patients with accident injuries and/or acute sicknesses of different levels of medical needs that require immediate attention and must receive the most adequate treatment and care in the shortest possible time from the physicians and the nurses (Huang et al. 2010). ED service is delivered through an integrative collaboration among staff from various departments depending on the need and as the patient traverses through the system, including triage, registration, treatment, cashier, pharmacy, and admission for lifesaving care (Huang and Chu 2011).

ED crowding represents an international crisis that may affect the quality and access of healthcare (Hoot and Aronsky 2008). Commonly studied effects of crowding include patient mortality, transport delays, treatment delays, ambulance diversion, patient elopement, and financial effect. Commonly studied solutions of crowding include additional personnel and institution of observation units focusing on hospital bed access, nonurgent referrals, ambulance diversion, destination control, crowding measures, and queueing theory (Hoot and Aronsky 2008). Overcrowding has been shown to decrease by streaming of patients into groups of patients cared for by a specific team of doctors and nurses, and minimizing complex queues in ED by altering the practices in relation to the function of the hospital-specific triage scale (King et al. 2006). Patients with longer stays in the ED are less satisfied with ED service (Parker and Marco 2014).

Figure 5.1 shows an example of ED workflow in most hospitals where it begins with triage at the entrance adapted from Huang et al. (2010). For convenience, the workflow is partitioned into three domains: the examination center where most of the laboratory testing and radiology work is done; the ED comprising patients, physicians, nurses, all other healthcare providers, medical devices, and so on; and the pharmacy department where the patients receive their prescribed drugs and finally exit through appropriate discharge protocol. Once patients present at the ED, they are appropriately triaged based on the Emergency Severity Index (ESI); some hospitals have their own categorization of emergency levels, and all ED operations follow the triage assignments based on ESI and local codes. Based on the triage level, the sequence of operations slightly varies. A triage with a one- or two-level patient registration process is completed first, after which the patient is moved to the waiting room. However, for patients who need immediate lifesaving care, such as in level 3 or level 4 triage, they are directed to emergency care where physicians will give them the first line of care after completing registration.

While EDs in different hospitals are customized based on their setup and how other departments are integrated, EDs in general are organized as having emergency surgery, emergency internal medicine, and emergency pediatrics departments that

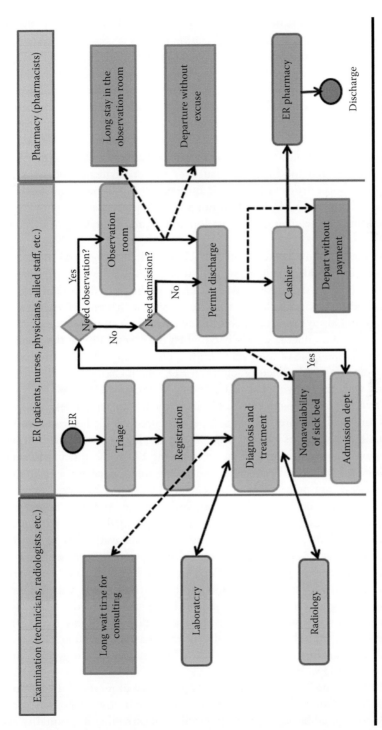

Figure 5.1 Representative example of a schematic showing ED workflow and potential procedural issues that compromise quality, cost, and suboptimal resource allocations. Challenges in the ED. (Adapted from Huang, Y. C., & Chu, C. P. (2011). RFID Applications in hospitals—A case study for emergency department. *Journal of Communication and Computer*, 8(7), 1–8.)

can provide urgent care to patients regardless of their condition, that is, including those involved in accidents. Once the registration process is completed, physicians make their initial diagnosis of the patient's condition; laboratory tests, radiography exams, and so on may be ordered, and the workflow between these units is bidirectional as indicated by the arrows in Figure 5.1. On the basis of the initial diagnosis and preliminary results, the decision of whether to admit the patient for further care or whether to keep the patient in the observation room to monitor progress (and to aid in making further clinical decisions) is made. Once the physician is convinced of the improved health status of the patient, a decision is made to discharge the patient and they exit the ED after insurance and/or payment processing and collect the prescription drugs as illustrated in Figure 5.1. Although the workflow appears to be well streamlined, it is often not a smooth process and may be highly chaotic depending on the emergency situation and is prone to negligence (Huang et al. 2010).

Based on the workflow demonstrated in Figure 5.1, five potential procedural workflow issues can be identified. First, long wait times incurred after triage and registration and before a diagnosis is made depend on the prioritization of patients with critical conditions, causing longer wait times for other patients. Since specialty consultants are not always present in the ED and patients can present any type of critical need, wait times fluctuate heavily based on the accessibility of the specialty physician. Hence, the issue of long wait times is an ongoing ED problem, which often arises from the unscheduled practices in ED, which change on a day-to-day basis. Second, with the growing use of observation units in EDs for patients who are not too sick but sick enough not to be discharged, they receive less attention as resources and staff are directed toward patients needing further care, leading to long wait times in the observation unit. Third, the long observation unit wait time triggers an ongoing ED issue of patients leaving ED without being formally excused, motivated by their dissatisfaction of being unattended for a long time. Fourth, since significant percentages of patients who present at EDs don't have the ability to pay, patients may leave without acknowledgement and this causes issues with costing and reporting. Finally, once the diagnosis is made on the patient and it is determined that the patient will be admitted, the nonavailability of sickbeds contributes to the longer wait times in EDs, resulting from overcrowding and large influx of ED patients on a continuous basis. In some hospitals, such wait times last for days, driving patient dissatisfaction and triggering ED exit without being discharged or paying; in most cases, the patient is moved back to the ED to wait for admission. EDs will continue to face these procedural workflow issues since such problems result from the nonavailability of resources and growing ED patient influx, which work against each other, and the ED management struggles to optimize this ill-posed ED workflow problem.

Hospital EDs in the United States face a large burden of responsibility for providing care to the injured, the very ill, the uninsured, and others who lack access to medical service in addition to the responsibility of providing high-quality and safe care, while keeping the patients satisfied (Wilper et al. 2008). EDs involve unscheduled practice that often requires optimal resource allocations to provide the urgent care needed as well as reducing the waiting time and time to provider based on the triage levels. Also, the increasing number of patients challenges ED workflow as well as staff and resource allocations as evident from the typical ED setup in Figure 5.1 and subsequently challenges the management in terms of keeping the operating costs at a reasonable level while providing high-quality emergency care. EDs, which are usually crowded and have long wait times, boarding times, and throughput times, have become a common access point for many patients who lack access to primary care or insurance, thereby compromising the service needs of ED. One of the key barriers in ED wait time improvement is the competition for providers' time and attention in the midst of human resource constraints (Willoughby et al. 2010). Liaw et al. (2002) reported on the early exit of ED patients that can be primarily attributed to excessively long wait time for diagnosis, time poverty, or unpleasant encounter with hospital personnel and total dissatisfaction. In general, the major factors contributing to prolonged patient stay for provisional observation in emergency rooms include excessively long wait times for available sickbeds, excessively long provisional observation times, understaffed medical personnel, and insufficient space (Huang et al. 2010).

5.2.1 Traditional Methods to Address ED Challenges

EDs present a challenging environment for workflow evaluation and measurement of the effect of information system interventions. Time-motion studies have been used in healthcare to gain insights into workflow issues, and they have been used in EDs to study task interruptions; advanced technical tools using synchronized ED data collection enable efficient implementation of such studies and analysis (Asaro 2003). A recent time-motion study in ED revealed that patients in the lesser priority areas (i.e., triage levels 2 and 3) waited longer before being assessed by staff. Patients requiring laboratory and imaging investigations have a prolonged length of stay (LOS), which varies depending on the specific tests ordered. Specialty consultation was associated with longer waiting times. A major bottleneck identified was waiting times for inpatient admission (Azzopardi et al. 2011). Advanced capacity management tools for EDs help address various ED challenges such as overcrowding, patient flow, and LOS in the ED, and help maintain and improve healthcare quality and patient safety (McCaughey et al. 2015). Many hospitals in the ED adopt flexible staffing as an option for high patient volume variability to address staffing issues in the ED (Cardello 1995). Several hospitals now adopt activity-based costing approaches in ED to use with Lean, Six Sigma cost–benefit analyses to address the increasing number of patients with below-cost to no-payment capability such as self-pay and public insurance who present at the ED for urgent care (Dyas et al. 2015).

Observation units have become an essential element for opening beds in EDs whose occupancy is determined for patients who are too sick to be sent home, but not sick enough to be admitted to full-fledged inpatient units (Schrock et al. 2010). The utilization of observation units has reduced some hospital admissions and 30-day readmission rates, although they do not completely fit the vision for which CMS had intended (Carlson 2013). Many hospitals adopt Point-of-Care Technologies (POCT) in EDs for quick throughput of laboratory results and other clinical data, which can play a key role in reducing LOS (Storrow et al. 2008).

A survey of ED administrators revealed that many hospitals have invested in EMRs, but most of them indicated that EMRs have not been worth the cost, that they did not reduce LOS and ED operation cost, and that they did not improve patient satisfaction (Schumacher Group 2010). The healthcare reform act is perceived to increase the burden while inadequate access to medical specialty services in EDs poses risks to patients. However, as mentioned before, EMR data in their raw form do not provide the necessary intelligence to make clinical decision making and need advanced analytics to provide actionable intelligence. The advent of RFID technology has indeed marked a new era in supply chain management, and its application in the healthcare industry has provided a new scope for workflow improvements especially in the ED. Section 5.3 reviews RFID and its potential to develop and implement an intelligent ED that can provide high-quality care at optimal cost with real-time feedback capability.

5.3 RFID in ED

5.3.1 RFID Overview and Its Application in Healthcare

RFID is a wireless automatic identification and data capture technology device that saves lives, prevents errors, saves costs, and increases security and therefore improves organizational performance (Wamba et al. 2013). RFID systems allow for the electronic tagging of assets, inventory, personnel, and patients by placing unique electronic identifiers on items in the form of stickers with electronic chips or on people in the form of bracelets or badges embedded with RFID chips (Pasupathy 2010; Pasupathy and Clark 2014). Tagged resources can be identified, tracked, and managed through a centralized database, and the technology assists in making more informed decisions regarding department resources in real time. There are two main types of RFIDs, namely, active and passive RFID. Active RFIDs contain a miniature battery and actively emit radio frequencies to the system while passive RFIDs contain no battery source, but instead draw the necessary power to emit a frequency through secondary "reader" devices such as handheld wands, which are called "interrogators" by industry vendors (Pasupathy 2010).

Five layers are used to describe the RFID's architecture: (1) the data capturing front end, which is made up of two different components such as the tag and reader; an RFID tag consists of a microchip that stores information and an antenna used to transmit data via radio waves and a reader sends out a signal that triggers a tag to transmit its stored data back to the reader; the transmitted data are then converted and forwarded to the middleware system; (2) the data-capturing and filtering layer, which refers to the middleware system, which is used to aggregate and filter data before they are routed to the database system and ensures data accuracy as well as reduces server loads; (3) processing modules, which refer to the database system's ability to store and monitor data; (4) the workflow layer, which is an integration interface that facilitates the integration of collected data with current systems; and (5) the applications layer, which allows users to use the integrated systems to perform operations (Pasupathy 2010). RFID gives managers timely, accurate information for the roles they oversee. Specifically, it provides real-time information about the physical location of people and equipment, overall movement profiles, utilization and status of locations, utilization of people resources, work queues for individual resources, and bottlenecks that may affect throughput (Wamba et al. 2013). Figure 5.2 shows the RFID data analytics that can provide new information in three different levels toward actionable intelligence. It can provide tracking and location of resources as well as automated information reporting on resources, and real-time advanced analytics provide actionable intelligence for real-time clinical decision making through triggers, alarms, and so on.

The use of RFID devices has been demonstrated to reduce healthcare costs and to improve patient safety and has been shown to provide an overall efficiency in process flow and healthcare delivery (Rousek et al. 2014; Wamba et al. 2013). Sales of RFID technology for supply chain applications are expected to grow from $94.6 million in 2013 to approximately $1.43 billion in 2019 with an expectation that RFID will reduce healthcare cost and management (Slack 2013). While there is a growing interest in the use of this technology in the healthcare setting, there

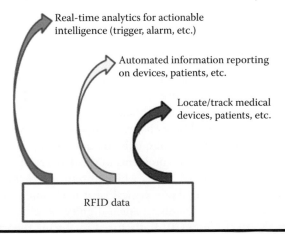

Figure 5.2 Application of RFID data in healthcare setting towards actionable intelligence.

are few studies performed in many departments to visualize the benefits associated with the use of this technology (Huang and Chu 2011). There are several factors that challenge the effective use of RFID in a healthcare setting, such as high implementation costs, substantial gap between technology implementation costs and the RFID-enabled benefits, lack of common standard of usage/data analysis, and low operational performance level in a harsh environment (Wamba et al. 2013). There are also serious concerns regarding privacy for patients as well as for the medical staff because patients will be monitored at all times as long as they are wearing the tags. Several human rights groups in the United States oppose RFID applications on patients for privacy reasons (i.e., through unauthorized RFID tracking), and some manufacturers in return respond with erasable tags (Huang and Chu 2011).

Technical difficulties may arise as well since the staff is required to handle this technology and keep it running with minimal issues. System interoperability is a major consideration in the adoption and operation of RFID systems in the supply chain (Slack 2013). An interesting yet practical barrier to RFID adoption in healthcare is the competition with other strategic health information technology (HIT) systems and initiatives (Slack 2013). New research is being attempted to better understand the business value generated in terms of the "quality of healthcare service" or "return on investment (ROI)" in the actual setting by using RFID-enabled technology within the healthcare value chain. Yet, the abovementioned challenges exist in actual implementation. There are recommendations to integrate RFID with hospital information systems and electronic health records and support it by clinical decision support systems to facilitate better healthcare workflow processes and reduce medical, medication, and diagnosis errors (Ajami and Rajabzadeh 2013). A recent study demonstrated the feasibility of implementing RFID technology within a 600-bed hospital as a financially viable decision with a 10.2-month payback period of the initial investment costs, and an expected 327% ROI within 3 years (Rousek et al. 2014).

5.3.2 RFID Application in ED

While there are potential applications of RFID in all different specialties in the hospital, the ED is one busy department where critical care is delivered for patients requiring urgent care and optimizing healthcare assets and services is highly desired. However, EDs face several workflow challenges discussed in Section 5.2. LOS is perceived as an important indicator of quality of care in EDs, and increased LOS at EDs may contribute to systematic problems in the delivery of efficient and high-quality medical care in the United States, which also means that patients wait longer to see ED physicians and to obtain critical treatments and test results (Karaca et al. 2012). ED crowding compromises patient dignity, privacy, and completeness of care (Boyle et al. 2012). Cesta (2013) discussed "queueing theory," according to which wait times and service delays increase exponentially as occupancy increases. Cesta (2013) stated that organizations have started to recognize the association between patient flow and quality care. There was more than a causal relationship between LOS and cost of care. The following has been shown to affect the care given: "Wrong medications or treatments, including over-utilization of medications and treatment; misuse of product or personnel resources; delays in care processes, including core measures" (Cesta 2013). Hospitals nowadays focus more on enhancing medical treatment quality, increasing patients' satisfaction toward hospitals, making more time available for emergency treatment, and enhancing EDs through the use of IT for optimal emergency care and patient satisfaction. Given these tangible problems in EDs, RFID technology can prove to be a handy resource to track medications, medical devices, patients, and healthcare providers and provide a platform to optimize resource use to improve ED care service in a timely fashion.

There is some literature on RFID adoption in EDs and many hospitals are attempting pilot studies to realize its benefits in their ED setting. Kuo et al. (2007) demonstrated the benefits of applying RFID in a pediatric emergency setting, indicating reduction in treatment time in the ED (–10%), reduction of waiting time in the ED (–45%), and improvement in patient satisfaction after RFID system implementation compared to before (+12%). Chen et al. (2005) observed a significant decrease in waiting time in acute bed admissions ($p = 0.014$) and ICU admissions ($p = 0.026$) between the two groups with and without RFID. There are also some studies that attempted to analyze the workflow benefits in EDs through simulation to demonstrate the feasibility of improved services with actionable intelligence by using RFID in the ED (Huang and Chu 2011).

There are numerous challenges with resource allocation based on the unscheduled practice nature in the ED. The application of RFID in the ED to the workflow shown in Figure 5.1 by tagging all devices, patients, and staff with RFID will result in the enhanced workflow process that can allow clinical decision making with actionable intelligence as shown in Figure 5.3. As evident from Figure 5.2, RFID not only can track or locate resources and provide automated information on them but also can provide real-time triggers or alarms to initiate actions to resolve the situation. For example, when a patient waiting for initial diagnosis crosses a predetermined threshold for wait time, a trigger or alarm could be sent to the staff to seek immediate attention. Alternative decision strategies such as dispatching additional staff or physicians based on the need is possible with such real-time wisdom that can be acted upon to address long waiting time before initial diagnosis.

Since observation units are now common in EDs, excessively long wait times can be monitored and acted upon with similar triggers and alarms to bring immediate attention to the attending staff. RFID data indeed provide real-time capability to mobilize the resources to specifically tackle long wait times in the ED. Also, triggers and alarms for early exit or exit without payment from ED can be addressed in real time by dispatching staff to the patient for immediate action. RFID can play an integral role in assigning sickbeds to patients on time without having to wait longer in the ED, since it can track the entry time of a particular patient into the ED, wait times, and the workflow and subsequently provide real-time information

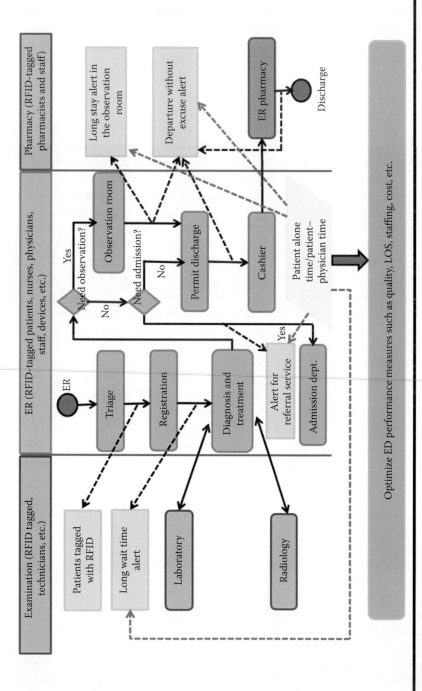

Figure 5.3 Representative example of an RFID-tagged ED workflow and potential for actionable intelligence to improve quality, cost, resource allocations, and so on. (Adapted from Huang, Y. C., & Chu, C. P. (2011). RFID Applications in hospitals—A case study for emergency department. *Journal of Communication and Computer*, 8(7), 1–8.)

on when and where the patient can be placed in a sickbed, thereby avoiding longer delays. While overcrowding in the ED is a current problem, RFID can track the number of patients entering the ED at any given time and can provide a priori information (and prediction) for the staff on whether or not they can take more patients and either redirect or route the patients to other close facilities for immediate care. Hence, RFID can play an integral role in capacity management for EDs by providing ED managers with actionable intelligence. As evident from Figure 5.3, RFID system and implementation can work in harmony with the ED workflow and offers a platform for continual improvement of healthcare delivery by providing opportunities for actionable intelligence. EMR data, RFID data, and laboratory data should be synchronized to provide the most valuable information that can provide real-time guidance for ED workflow with operational efficiency and improved quality of care. EDs with complete RFID tagging of triage station personnel, registration/cashier clerks, physicians, nurses, medical technicians/radiologists, pharmacists, patients, medical devices, and so on can as a whole provide a comprehensive status of the ED workflow, and ED managers should be tasked with an advanced RFID analytics team for intelligent decision making to optimize ED care. Hence, the question of whether ED can be transformed into an *intelligent* healthcare unit is not far from being answered, provided the implementation and analytics challenges with integrated and interoperable HIT systems are in place, which can indeed be a paradigm shift in the provision of lifesaving critical care.

5.3.3 Intelligent ED through Effective Teamwork and Communication with RFID and Sociometers

Sociometers from Sociometric Solutions, Inc. are wearable sensor devices equipped with an accelerometer, a proximity sensor with Bluetooth and infrared capabilities, and an audio recorder to capture and quantify social interactions. RFID and sociometers have the potential to improve the efficiency and safety of health systems by providing data-driven scheduling and resource utilization models and providing timely information to make intelligent clinical decisions for high-quality timely care and ensure patient safety (Clark and Pasupathy 2014; Wilper et al. 2008; Yu et al. 2015). Communication patterns within team members that see more engagement and maximize energy use are more successful (Pentland 2012). Sociometers play an integral role in capturing communication patterns and dynamics by recording speech patterns, body movements, user proximities, and face-to-face interactions and by capturing and storing the frequency and duration of these interactions (Blocker et al. 2016; Yu et al. 2016). Real-time analysis of such data provides insights into a macro-level perspective of medical staff interactions, quantifies behaviors, and identifies areas to intervene prospectively toward an intelligent system for real-time decision making. An efficient HIT architectural framework that integrates data from EMR, POCT, laboratory results, RFID, and sociometers can provide a comprehensive framework to provide data with actionable intelligence in

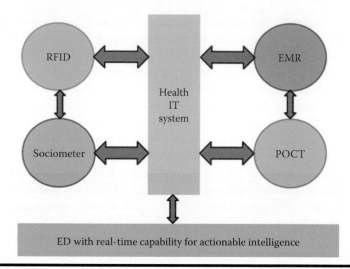

Figure 5.4 Framework for an ED with capability for actionable intelligence.

real time to provide lifesaving emergency care and to visualize an intelligent ED that is practically feasible as shown in Figure 5.4. Such an intelligent ED system will then be able to capture real-time human interactions during service delivery, identify workload levels, and predict future states to ultimately improve patient outcome and care delivery.

5.4 Future Research Directions

So how do healthcare delivery services meet the growing challenges and demand for optimal healthcare services for a decision-making process using healthcare data for actionable intelligence? While there is no one-stop approach for addressing these challenges, it is evident that multiple approaches need to be simultaneously taken to address this rapidly changing environment and to manage data to force an outcome that would result in actionable insight by the ultimate end user of the information (Brown et al. 2012). A universal and comprehensive approach is needed to address issues such as the acquisition of the highest-quality industry data, the warehousing and management of the data, which also provide dynamic access and control of the data with automatic provisioning to solutions and applications, and ultimately performance analytics. In short, organizations need trusted data that can be turned into actionable intelligence. Since the implementation of RFIDs and sociometers in the healthcare setting is still in its infancy stage and only a few hospitals have implemented them, developing a standard for universal data collection and healthcare analytics remains a far-fetched dream. However, vendors for these devices should follow a strategy to provide and analyze data that are interoperable within the current IT system of the hospital as a starting point, which later can culminate toward standardization, at least in the next decade. Also, strategies to store, retrieve, and analyze RFID big data and real-time streaming of sociometer data are essential (Slack 2013) to realizing intelligent healthcare systems.

Hospital inpatient care constitutes almost one-third of all healthcare expenditures in the United States (Gonzalez 2013). The universal metric for determining the success of various efforts, such as hospital cost containment, cost reduction, and alternative care delivery systems, is hospital LOS (Taheri et al. 2000). The authors note that substantial effort to reduce LOS has been made since the 1980s and there has been minimal or no cost reductions attributed to LOS reduction without compromising the quality of care. The LOS reduction problem has a totally different perspective; that is, "patient alone time" during care has never been explored thus far, mainly because of the unavailability of technological resources to track the patient–healthcare worker interaction time, which indeed could have significant impact on the LOS. RFIDs and sociometers offer the flexibility to track such complex interactions, which could be analyzed in terms of "patient alone time" and "patient–provider interaction time," and also their communication patterns, which has a direct impact on both the quality of healthcare provided and LOS, both of which can imply significant cost savings while achieving quality care (Yu et al. 2015). Future research to quantify these novel data is integral toward a totally different approach of analyzing RFID data. As seen from Figure 5.4, through appropriate data and process mining of RFID and EMR data, patient alone time and patient–provider time can be uniquely quantified, which can provide new insights into waiting time reduction strategy, LOS reduction toward improving ED workflow, and optimizing emergency care.

Also, further research is still needed in the RFID domain in general when applied to healthcare settings because it involves patients, and the needs of the patients come first. Wamba et al. (2013) pointed several noteworthy domains for RFID research that in particular are essential for applications in the healthcare setting, especially in the ED where unscheduled practice is common:

■ Novel advanced analytical methods for RFID big data analysis
■ Better mechanisms to address information security and privacy issues
■ Develop and analyze best RFID-enabled healthcare architecture
■ Analyze network effect of RFID technology within the entire healthcare value chain
■ Identifying key technical and business challenges of integrating RFID technology within the entire healthcare value chain
■ Assess benefits enabled by RFID technology when complying with healthcare laws and regulations

In addition, to fully realize the intelligent healthcare system, a flexible yet capable HIT that will resolve the barriers of implementation and can also operate at low cost is essential. Since it will take several years to break even with RFID implementation, the high HIT cost will prevent hospitals from using RFID to optimize healthcare service.

5.5 Conclusion

Advancement in technology and healthcare delivery services has imparted tremendous faith in patients for improved and optimal healthcare delivery in the future. To meet these demands, the healthcare industry is constantly presented with challenges in adapting and developing novel approaches for healthcare delivery, where healthcare analytics has proven to show significance in clinical decision making. While big data analytics has been the focus, several existing challenges are still unmet and there is a strict need to progress, in order to tap the information into actionable intelligence than can both serve optimal care and reduce healthcare costs.

While EMR provides patient-related data, large-scale intervention of data scientists is a necessity for actionable intelligence. EMR data cannot provide information on the process flow of healthcare services, which indeed has opened new avenues of research using RFID technology to optimize healthcare services. RFID can provide data on the use of medical devices, healthcare worker time, and patient alone time that can provide new information that can be transformed into actionable intelligence. Future research in the use of automatic identification and data capture technology devices such as RFID can yield invaluable information that can be deemed to be a paradigm shift in the domain of actionable intelligence. Application of RFIDs and sociometers in healthcare is still in its infancy, with very few hospitals having a fully realized RFID in their ED, which is the busiest unit in the hospital that provides emergency lifesaving care. A framework for an intelligent ED is presented, which is very practical, provided the barriers to its implementation can be resolved and guided by future research in several of the areas discussed. There is no doubt that RFIDs can revolutionize HIT framework, and real-time clinical decision making will be an integral part of healthcare services workflow with an ultimate goal of improving the quality of care at a lower operational cost.

References

Ajami, S., & Rajabzadeh, A. (2013). Radio Frequency Identification (RFID) technology and patient safety. *Journal of Research in Medical Sciences: The Official Journal of Isfahan University of Medical Sciences*, 18(9), 809.

Asaro, P. V. (2003). Synchronized time-motion study in the emergency department using a handheld computer application. *Studies in Health Technology and Informatics*, 107(Pt 1), 701–705.

Azzopardi, M., Cauchi, M., Cutajar, K., Ellul, R., Mallia-Azzopardi, C., & Grech, V. (2011). A time and motion study of patients presenting at the accident and emergency department at Mater Dei Hospital. *BMC Research Notes*, 4(1), 1.

Blocker, R. C., Yu, D., Hawthorne, H., Sir, M. Y., Hellmich, T. R., Hallbeck, S., Nestler, D. M., & Pasupathy, K. S. (2016). Application of sociometers in the emergency department. *Journal of Medical Devices*, 10(2), 020964.

Boyle, A., Beniuk, K., Higginson, I., & Atkinson, P. (2012). Emergency department crowding: Time for interventions and policy evaluations. *Emergency Medicine International*, 2012.

Brown, G. D., Patrick, T. B., & Pasupathy, K. S. (2012). *Health Informatics: A Systems Perspective*. Chicago, IL: Health Administration Press.

Cardello, D. (1995). Monitoring staffing variances and length of stay. *Nursing Management*, 26(4), 38–41.

Carlson, J. (2013). Observation care stirs ire. *Modern Healthcare*, 43(28), 8–9.

Cesta, T. (2013). Managing length of stay using patient flow—Part 1. *Hospital Case Management*, 21(2), 19–22.

Chen, C. I., Liu, C. Y., Li, Y. C., Chao, C. C., Liu, C. T., Chen, C. F., & Kuan, C. F. (2005). Pervasive observation medicine: The application of RFID to improve patient safety in observation unit of hospital emergency department. *Studies in Health Technology and Informatics*, 116, 311–315.

Clark, D. A., & Pasupathy, K. S. (2014). Process mapping and RFID: Complementarities. *Encyclopedia of Business Analytics and Optimization*, 1898–1909.

Dyas, S. R., Greenfield, E., Thotakura, S., Mary Hays DSN, R. N., Ivey, R., Spalding, J., & Phillips, R. (2015). Process-improvement cost model for the emergency department/practitioner. *Journal of Healthcare Management*, 60(6), 442.

Gartner. (2011). Gartner says solving 'Big Data' challenge involves more than just managing volumes of data. STAMFORD, Con. http://www.gartner.com/newsroom/id/1731916. Accessed June 1, 2016.

Glaser, J., & Stone, J. (2008). Effective use of business intelligence. *Healthcare Financial Management*, 62(2), 68–72.

Glaser, J., & Tom, F. (2008). The future of healthcare IT: What can we expect to see? *Healthcare Financial Management*, 62(11), 82–88.

Gonzalez, J. M. (2013). National Health Care Expenses in the U.S. Civilian Non-institutionalized Population, 2011. MEPS Statistical Brief No. 425. Rockville, MD: Agency for Healthcare Research and Quality. http://meps.ahrq.gov/data_files/publications/st425/stat425.pdf. Accessed April 18, 2016.

Hoot, N. R., & Aronsky, D. (2008). Systematic review of emergency department crowding: Causes, effects, and solutions. *Annals of Emergency Medicine*, 52(2), 126–136.

Huang, Y., Chu, C., Lin, Y., & Kuo, C. (2010). RFID applications in hospitals—A case study for emergency department. In *Proceedings of the 16th International Conference on Distributed Multimedia Systems*, 70–75.

Huang, Y. C., & Chu, C. P. (2011). RFID Applications in hospitals—A case study for emergency department. *Journal of Communication and Computer*, 8(7), 1–8.

Kankanhalli, A., Hahn, J., Tan, S., & Gao, G. (2016). Big data and analytics in healthcare: Introduction to the special section. *Information Systems Frontiers*, 18(2), 233.

Karaca, Z., Wong, H. S., & Mutter, R. L. (2012). Duration of patients' visits to the hospital emergency department. *BMC Emergency Medicine*, 12(1), 1.

King, D. L., Ben-Tovim, D. I., & Bassham, J. (2006). Redesigning emergency department patient flows: Application of Lean Thinking to health care. *Emergency Medicine Australasia*, 18(4), 391–397.

Kuo, F., Fu, C. J., Liu, L., & Jin, M. H. (2007). The implement of RFID in emergency medicine. In *2007 9th International Conference on e-Health Networking, Application and Services* (pp. 125–130). IEEE.

LaRow, M. (2007). Applying business intelligence to the needs of healthcare organizations. *Health Leaders News*, July 17.

Ledbetter, C. S., & Morgan, M. W. (2001). Toward best practice: Leveraging the electronic patient record as a clinical data warehouse. *Journal of Healthcare Information Management*, 15, 2, 119–131.

Liaw, S. J., Hu, P. M., & Liao, H. C. (2002). Patients who leave emergency departments prematurely. *Journal of Taiwan Emergency Medicine*, 4(2), 40–49.

McCaughey, D., Erwin, C. O., & DelliFraine, J. L. (2015). Improving capacity management in the emergency department: A review of the literature, 2000–2012. *Journal of Healthcare Management*, 60(1).

Oster, C., & Braaten, J. (2016). *High Reliability Organizations: A Healthcare Handbook for Patient Safety & Quality*. Indianapolis, IN: Sigma Theta Tau.

Parker, B. T., & Marco, C. (2014). Emergency department length of stay: Accuracy of patient estimates. *Western Journal of Emergency Medicine*, 15(2).

Pasupathy, K. S. (2010). Transforming healthcare: Leveraging the complementarities of health informatics and systems engineering. *International Journal of Healthcare Delivery Reform Initiatives (IJHDRI)*, 2(2), 35–55.

Pasupathy, K. S., & Clark, D. A. (2014). Increasing visibility through process mining. *Encyclopedia of Business Analytics and Optimization*, 1192–1202.

Pentland, A. (2012). The new science of building great teams. *Harvard Business Review*, 90(4), 60–69.

Rahman, F., & Slepian, M. J. (2016). Application of big-data in healthcare analytics—Prospects and challenges. In *2016 IEEE-EMBS International Conference on Biomedical and Health Informatics (BHI)* (pp. 13–16). IEEE.

Rousek, J. B., Pasupathy, K., Gannon, D., & Hallbeck, S. (2014). Asset management in healthcare: Evaluation of RFID. *IIE Transactions on Healthcare Systems Engineering*, 4(3), 144–155.

Schrock, J., Reznikova, S., & Weller, S. (2010). The effect of an observation unit on the rate of ED admission and discharge for pyelonephritis. *American Journal Emergency Medicine*, 28(6), 682–688.

Schumacher Group. (2010). Emergency Department Challenges and Trends. https://www.acep.org/uploadedFiles/ACEP/newsroom/NewsMediaResources/StatisticsData/schu2010surveyPDF.pdf. Accessed June 1, 2016.

Slack, C. (2013). Impact of radio-frequency identification (RFID) technologies on the hospital supply chain: A literature review. *Perspectives in Health Information Management*, 1.

Storrow, A. B., Zhou, C., Gaddis, G., Han, J. H., Miller, K., Klubert, D., Laidig, A., & Aronsky, D. (2008). Decreasing lab turnaround time improves emergency department throughput and decreases emergency medical services diversion: A simulation model. *Academic Emergency Medicine*, 15(11), 1130–1135.

Taheri, P. A., Butz, D. A., & Greenfield, L. J. (2000). Length of stay has minimal impact on the cost of hospital admission. *Journal of the American College of Surgeons*, 191(2), 123–130.

Wadsworth, T., Graves, B., Glass, S., Steve, H., Harrison, M. A., Donovan, C., & Proctor, A. (2009). Using business intelligence to improve performance. *Healthcare Financial Management*, 63(10), 68–72.

Wamba, S. F., Anand, A., & Carter, L. (2013). A literature review of RFID-enabled healthcare applications and issues. *International Journal of Information Management*, 33(5), 875–891.

Wang, S. W., Chen, W. H., Ong, C. S., Liu, L., & Chuang, Y. W. (2006). RFID application in hospitals: A case study on a demonstration RFID project in a Taiwan hospital. In *Proceedings of the 39th Annual Hawaii International Conference on System Sciences (HICSS'06)* (vol. 8, pp. 184a–184a). IEEE.

Wanless, S. (2005). Top 10 BI applications for clinical healthcare: Tidal wave of demand for clinical quality information. *DM Review*, 15(5), 62–79.

Willoughby, K. A., Chan, B. T., & Strenger, M. (2010). Achieving wait time reduction in the emergency department. *Leadership in Health Services*, 23(4), 304–319.

Wilper, A. P., Woolhandler, S., Lasser, K. E., McCormick, D., Cutrona, S. L., Bor, D. H., & Himmelstein, D. U. (2008). Waits to see an emergency department physician: US trends and predictors, 1997–2004. *Health Affairs*, 27(2), w84–w95.

Yu, D., Blocker, R. C., Hallbeck, M. S., Patel, A., & Pasupathy, K. S. (2015). Wearable sociometers in chaotic simulated environments. *Journal of Medical Devices*, 9(2), 020946.

Yu, D., Blocker, R. C., Sir, M. Y., Hallbeck, M. S., Hellmich, T. R., Cohen, T., Nestler, D. M., & Pasupathy, K. S. (2016). Intelligent emergency department: Validation of sociometers to study workload. *Journal of Medical Systems*, 40(3), 1–12.

Chapter 6

Network Analytics to Enable Decisions in Healthcare Management

Uma Srinivasan, Arif Khan, and Shahadat Uddin

Contents

6.1 Introduction

For most people, "healthcare system" often means the process of receiving treatment from a general practitioner (GP), a specialist, or the hospital. It is true that the main goal of a well-structured healthcare system is to provide the best possible care to its consumers; however, underlying the front-end service of hospitals, GPs, or other providers, an enormous network of people, organizations, funders, and stakeholders work together to keep the whole healthcare system running smoothly. All of these healthcare entities generate a large amount of data, which become valuable resources that help understand how the whole system is performing. As these entities and the data they generate are inherently connected, network analysis has a significant potential to offer insights into the hidden relationships across these data elements, which in turn can influence both cost and quality of healthcare. This chapter provides some basic network-based concepts and analytical measures that can be computed from healthcare data. It further describes some healthcare applications, where network analytics can provide insights to healthcare managers for evidence-based decisions.

In both public and private health sectors worldwide, health departments employ thousands of people who work together to deliver cost-effective high-quality healthcare services to people. At a broad level, based on their roles, the three main stakeholders in the health system are (a) healthcare consumers, (b) healthcare providers, and (c) healthcare funders and policy makers. We use the broader term healthcare *consumer*, rather than using other terms such as *patient*, to represent members of the community who use healthcare resources both outside the hospital in a primary care setting and within a hospital when they are admitted as inpatients for specific treatments. Healthcare *providers* include GPs, clinical specialists, pathology service providers, radiology and imaging providers, pharmacies, community healthcare centers, ambulance, public hospitals, private hospitals, aged care facilities, and ancillary health service providers such as dentists, physiotherapists, optometrists, dieticians, and so on. Basically, anyone who provides a healthcare service to a consumer in or outside hospitals is referred to as a service provider in the context of this chapter. Funders and policy makers are the other stakeholders in charge of administering, monitoring, and funding the whole healthcare system.

In the modern healthcare environment, large amounts of electronic health data are generated at every step of the process as the health consumer traverses through the health system. Healthcare service providers in the public and private sector, be they primary providers like GPs, or tertiary care providers like hospitals, store some aspects of health data in a computer system. The nature of electronic data varies depending on the needs of the providers. Examples of data collected and stored at a point of service include (i) patient demographics including location, (ii) details of service(s) provided, (iii) clinical notes about the health status of the patient, (iv) laboratory and radiology results, (v) drug prescription details, (vi) billing details related to costs of services often with specific billing codes, (vii) referral details, and (viii) other associated establishment costs, such as accommodation costs and theater charges. The level of detail can also vary significantly across providers.

In addition to the direct consumer health data, which are collected by service providers at every point of service, policy makers in both government and private health organizations assemble and analyze large amounts of data related to cost and quality of healthcare service delivery to make informed decisions on budgeting and resources allocation. A whole range of applications is designed to enable system-wide planning and assessment [1], analyze cost and service anomalies [2,3], and compute health determinants to support population and epidemiological studies [4]. Given the complex nature of the healthcare sector and the decisions that the stakeholders have to make, the key questions to consider are as follows: (a) Do healthcare consumers have all the information they need to make informed decisions about their healthcare choices? (b) Do service providers like doctors, hospitals, allied health workers, and so on have all the data that enable them to provide continuity of care to their patients? (c) Do health care funders like health insurers, government health departments, and health policy makers have a complete picture of the health status of the population to make informed decisions about healthcare costs and the quality of services provided?

As in other domains, health system managers use decision support systems based on statistical analysis and, more recently, predictive modeling techniques [5] built around health data repositories assembled from hospitals and health services administrative data sets. However, even sophisticated predictive modeling tools often do not consider nonparametric relationships that may exist among the variables within the data sets used. Given this context, network analysis offers a novel approach to detect and quantify hidden relationships among the variables in a data set. The variables we encounter in a healthcare data set include providers (represented by provider-ids), consumers/patients (patient-id), treatment(s) provided (indicated by treatment codes), associated costs of service, length of stay for a hospital episode of care, and health status indicators (e.g., readmission flag and smoking status).

Social network analysis can be used to compute objective metrics to understand the role and influence of providers, whose interaction and collaboration strategies could have an impact on the type of treatment provided, cost, and quality of care. For example, it can be utilized to analyze hidden relationships among chronic diseases or detect cliques or communities of practice that influence health outcomes.

Let us consider a few examples of information required by the three stakeholder groups, that is, the *consumers, providers,* and *funders,* to make informed decisions in the healthcare environment. In the case of a health *consumer,* information of where to go for a particular type of healthcare service or to find information about a specific service could readily be addressed by using online searches. However, to answer more complex queries such as "has this treatment worked for other people like me?" or "which doctor–hospital combination would give me the best quality of care?," online information sources or standard statistical reports would no longer be adequate. In such situations, network analytics and associated visualization can play an important role, as it can enable stakeholders to explore hidden relationships to make informed evidence-based decisions on choice of treatment and provider. For a service *provider,* network analysis can help understand the impact of a particular treatment on patients with a particular chronic condition such as diabetes, or the impact on the length of stay when his collaboration pattern or team size changes [3,6,7]. For the health *policy makers* in government or a private health insurance fund who need to balance cost and quality of care, network analysis can offer insights that can help them make informed decisions, in areas such as impact of team structure on cost and quality, disease progression and health trajectories of chronic disease patients [8], understanding and preventing waste, and the ability to plan and allocate resources to provide efficient services.

In the rest of this chapter, we describe how social network analysis can be used to reveal insights into each of the three stakeholder groups (i.e., healthcare *consumers, providers,* and *policy makers*), to make informed decisions that can influence both cost and quality of healthcare from their own perspectives. Social network analysis is commonly used to study relationships between individuals and communities as they interact with each other. One such classic example can be the analysis of Facebook connections to see how friendship evolves, community forms, ideas spread, trends set, and so on. In fact, virtual social networks, the physical world, society, and pretty much everything in them are connected in a complex dynamic system. Easley and Kleinberg's textbook [9] offers deep insight into the complexity of a connected world. Furthermore, a significant number of interesting and novel applications of network theory are reported in specialized domains [10–16].

Section 6.2 provides a theoretical foundation on social network analysis techniques. In order to design a network model, it is important to understand the semantics and the purpose of every data field in the health data set. This often requires explicit health domain knowledge of the attribute(s) as well as meaning associated with attribute values. For example, value of treatment codes such as MBS codes [17] or disease codes represented by the International Classification of Diseases (ICD) codes [18] can play a role in designing the nodes and edges represented in the network graph. Section 6.3 provides an overview on how healthcare data sets are originated, their differences in terms of source and focus, and how these different healthcare data sets can be utilized using network analytics. Section 6.4 describes a few specific applications where network analysis has been used to enable the stakeholders to make informed evidence-based decisions in the healthcare environment. Section 6.5 presents conclusions and future research directions.

6.2 Network Analysis Principles

6.2.1 Basic Concepts

In its simplest form, a network is presented as a graph of nodes and edges. Nodes represent objects and the edges connecting the nodes represent the relationships between the underlying objects. The objects could be individuals, social groups, organizations, and so on. The simplest network contains two nodes and one edge that links them. In the healthcare context, for example, node A and node B (see Figure 6.1a) can be two surgeons and the relationship that links them can be "performed surgery together on the same patient."

If they worked together on many patients, the edge can be represented as a thicker line indicating the strength of the relationship. This is an example of an undirected network. There can be instances where a particular information can flow from one node to another through an intermediary node. This will give directional property to the relationship and thus will produce a directed network as in Figure 6.1b.

Aside from their directionalities, relationships might be more than the sharing of an attribute or being in the same place at the same time. At the social level, for example, the fact that "A likes B" might lead to an exchange of ideas. Flows and exchanges can be very important in network analytics. In the network of Figure 6.1b, nodes A and C are connected through the intermediary node B. One can describe the network distance between two nodes in terms of the minimum number of steps or links between them. In this example, there are two steps between A and C; hence, the network distance between them is two. Network distance between nodes and how a network is structured affect the way nodes communicate. Figure 6.2 shows some particular macro-level network structures that are

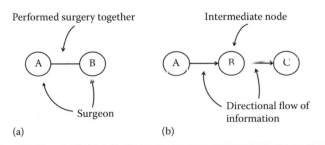

Figure 6.1 (a) An undirected network based on surgeon collaboration and (b) a directed network on information flow.

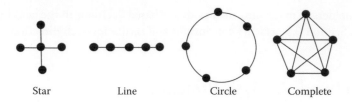

Figure 6.2   Different structures of communication network.

formed based on the way the nodes are connected. For example, the star network is formed by having a key central node that links all other nodes. The structure also affects the communication path; for example, for start network, all communication is through the central node.

The position of nodes in a network gives an indication of their participation in the network. Over time, researchers have proposed a variety of social network measures. Some quantify the structural characteristics of the entire network, while others emphasize the influence of individual nodes over the complete network. In the following sections, we describe the basic social network measures and classify them under the following three groups: (i) node-level measures, (ii) network-level measures, and (iii) measures for subgroup analysis. We have used node(s) and actor(s) interchangeably.

6.2.2 Node-Level Measures

Although there are many node-level social network measures, we focus mainly on centrality measures in this paper. Centrality is an important concept in the study of social networks. Conceptually, centrality measures how central an individual is positioned in a network [19]. There are three distinct measures for centrality: degree centrality, closeness centrality, and betweenness centrality.

6.2.2.1 Degree Centrality

Degree centrality is one of the basic measures of network centrality. For a node, it is the proportion of nodes that are adjacent to that node in a network. It highlights the node with the most number of links to other nodes in a network and can be defined by the following equation for the node (or actor) i in a network having N nodes [19]:

$$C'_D(n_i) = \frac{d(n_i)}{N-1} \tag{6.1}$$

where the subscript D denotes "*degree*" and $d(n_i)$ indicates the number of nodes with whom node i is connected. The maximum value for $C'_D(n_i)$ is 1 when node i is linked with all other nodes in the network. For an isolate node, its value is 0.

6.2.2.2 Closeness Centrality

Closeness centrality, another view of node centrality based on the distance, focuses on how "*close*" a node is to all the other nodes in a network [20]. The idea is that a node is central if it can quickly interact with all other nodes in a network. In the context of a communication network, such nodes need not rely on many other nodes for the relaying of information. For an individual node, it can be represented as a function of shortest distances between that actor and all other remaining actors in the network. The following equation represents the "*closeness centrality*" for an actor i in a network having N actors [19,20]:

$$C'_D(n_i) = \frac{N-1}{\sum\limits_{j=1}^{N} d(n_i, n_j)} \qquad (6.2)$$

where the subscript C denotes "*closeness*," $d(n_i, n_j)$ is the number of lines (or, links) in the shortest path between actor i and actor j, and the sum is taken over all $i \neq j$. A higher value of $C'_C(n_i)$ indicates that actor i is closer to other actors of the network, and $C'_C(n_i)$ will be 1 when actor i has direct links with all other actors of the network.

6.2.2.3 Betweenness Centrality

Betweenness centrality views an actor as being in a favored position to the extent that the actor falls on the shortest paths between other pairs of actors in the network. That is, actors that occur on many shortest paths between the other pair of nodes have higher *betweenness centrality* than those they do not [21]. The *betweenness centrality* for an actor n_i (i.e., $C'_B(n_i)$) can be represented by the following equation [19]:

$$C'_B(n_i) = \frac{\sum\limits_{j<k} \frac{g_{jk}(n_i)}{g_{jk}}}{[(N-1)(N-2)]/2} \qquad (6.3)$$

where $i \neq j \neq k$, $g_{jk}(n_i)$ represents the number of the shortest paths linking the two actors that contain actor i, and g_{jk} is the number of the shortest paths linking actors j and k. For the central actor of a star network, $C'_B(n_i)$ will take its highest value of 1; however, for any peripheral actor of a star, $C'_B(n_i)$ will take its minimum value of 0.

6.2.3 Network-Level Measures

Network-level measures quantify the structural characteristics (e.g., level of connectivity) of an entire network.

6.2.3.1 Network Size

The total number of participating nodes of a network is its *network size*. For example, if a network has 10 nodes, then its size is also 10.

6.2.3.2 Network Density

The *density* of a network represents the proportion of existing ties (or links) relative to the maximum number of possible ties among all nodes of that network [19]. The *density* for a network is 1 only when all nodes of that network are connected with each other. On the other hand, for a completely sparse network, the density value is 0, which indicates that there is no link between any two nodes of that network. For an undirected network of size N (i.e., it has N nodes), theoretically there are $[N*(N-1)]/2$ (i.e., $^{N}C_{2}$) possible links among its N nodes. If there are N_t links among its N nodes in that network, then, mathematically, *density* can be defined as [19]

$$\text{Density} = \frac{2*N_t}{N*(N-1)}. \tag{6.4}$$

6.2.3.3 Average Network Distance

Average network distance is an effective measure for capturing the aspect of how individuals are embedded in networks. For a network, it is the average value of the shortest distances between all pairs of actors [22], which is calculated by the following equation:

$$\text{Average Network Distance} = \frac{2*\sum_{i,j} d(i,j)}{N(N-1)} \tag{6.5}$$

where $d(i, j)$ is the shortest distance between actors i and j ($i \neq j$), and N is the number of actors of the network. In a given network, this measure computes the average amount of connections between any two members. The information about how far an actor is from all other actors in a network is very important for understanding its positional constraints and opportunities. Scott [23] argued that the distances among actors in a network may be an important macro-characteristic of that network. It may take a longer time for information to diffuse across a group of actors when distances among them are high.

6.2.3.4 Network Centralization

A centralization measure quantifies the range or variability of individual actor indices. There are three different types of centralization that are based on the three basic centrality measures.

6.2.3.4.1 Degree Centralization

The set of *degree centralities* (as in Equation 6.1), which represents the collection of *degree* indices of N actors in a network, can be summarized by the following equation to measure network *degree centralization* [20]:

$$C_D = \frac{\sum_{i=1}^{N} [C_D(n^*) - C_D(n_i)]}{[(N-1)*(N-2)]} \tag{6.6}$$

where $\{C_D(n_i)\}$ are the *degree* indices of N actors and $C_D(n^*)$ is the largest observed value in the *degree* indices. For a network with N actors, the *degree centralization* (i.e., C_D) reaches its maximum value of 1 when an actor chooses all other $(N - 1)$ actors and the other $(N - 1)$ actors interact only with this actor (i.e., the situation in a *star* graph). This index (i.e., C_D) attains its minimum value of 0 when all *degrees* are equal (i.e., the situation in a *circle* graph). Thus, C_D indicates the varying amount of the centralization of *degree* compared to both *star* and *circle* graphs.

6.2.3.4.2 Closeness Centralization

The set of *closeness centralities* (as in Equation 6.2), which represents the collection of *closeness* indices of N actors in a network, can be summarized by the following equation to measure network *closeness centralization* [20]:

$$C_C = \frac{\sum_{i=1}^{N} [C_C'(n^*) - C_C'(n_i)]}{[(N-1)*(N-2)]/(2N-3)} \tag{6.7}$$

where $\{C_C'(n_i)\}$ are the *closeness* indices of N actors and $C_C'(n^*)$ is the largest observed value in *closeness* indices. For a network with N actors, the *closeness centralization* (i.e., C_C) reaches its maximum value of 1 when an actor chooses all other

(N – 1) actors and each of the other (N – 1) actors has the *shortest distances* (i.e., geodesics) of length 2 to the remaining (N – 2) actors (i.e., the case of a *star* graph). This index (i.e., C_C) can attain its minimum value of 0, when lengths of the *shortest distances* (i.e., geodesics) are all equal (i.e., the case of a *complete* graph and *circle* graph). Thus, C_C indicates the varying amount of the centralization of *closeness* compared to *star*, *circle*, and *complete* graphs.

6.2.3.4.3 Betweenness Centralization

The set of *betweenness centralities* (as in Equation 6.3), which represents the collection of *betweenness* indices of N actors in a network, can be summarized by the following equation to measure network *betweenness centralization* [20]:

$$C_B = \frac{\sum_{i=1}^{N}[C'_B(n^*) - C'_B(n_i)]}{(N-1)} \tag{6.8}$$

where $\{C'_B(n_i)\}$ are the *betweenness* indices of N actors and $C'_B(n^*)$ is the largest observed value in the *betweenness* indices. Freeman [21] demonstrated that *betweenness centralization* reaches its maximum value of 1 for the *star* graph. Its minimum value of 0 occurs when all actors have exactly the same *betweenness* index.

6.2.4 Clique and Subgroup Analysis

6.2.4.1 Clique

A *clique* consists of a number of nodes or actors (i.e., more than two) having all possible ties (or links) present among themselves [24,25]. *Cliques* are often treated as social groups, and members of a *clique* interact with each other more regularly and intensely than with others in the same setting [23]. At the most general level, a *clique* is a subset of a network in which actors are more closely and intensely tied (or linked) to one another than they are to other members of the network. A *clique* can also be thought as a collection of actors, all of whom *choose* each other and there is no other actor in the network who also *chooses* and is *chosen by* all members of the clique [19,23]. That means a clique is a maximal fully connected subgraph. In Figure 6.3, actors A, B, C, and D form a *clique* as they are directly connected among themselves. Clique analysis can be very effective in understanding the attitude of actors in developing relationships with other actors in a network. For example, the presence of a higher number of cliques in a network indicates that actors of that network are likely to work in groups.

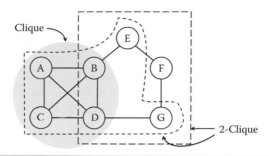

Figure 6.3   Illustration of Clique (i.e., ABCD) and 2-Clique (i.e., ABCDEG and BDEFG).

6.2.4.2 N-Clique

In order to make it more useful and general, the strict definition of *clique* (i.e., maximal fully connected subgraph) has been relaxed based on distances among nodes within a group. In this approach, nodes are considered as members of a clique if they are connected to every other member of the group at a distance greater than 1. Usually, the path distance of 2 is used. This corresponds to being "*a friend of a friend.*" Defining substructures in this way is called *N-clique*, where *N* stands for the maximum length of the path allowed to make a connection to all other members. A value of *N* = 2 indicates *2-clique*. In Figure 6.3, the actors *B*, *D*, *E*, *F*, and *D* form a *2-clique* as they are connected among themselves at a distance of 2. A *2-clique* is a subgroup in which all the group members are not required to be adjacent, but all of them would be reachable through at most one intermediary [19].

6.2.4.3 N-Clans

N-Clans, like *N-Cliques*, provide an alternative to the stricter *Clique* definition. It is possible for members of *N-Cliques* to be connected by nodes or actors who are not, themselves, members of the clique. In Figure 6.1, one of the two *2-Cliques* is *ABCDEG*. In this *2-Clique*, the node *E* is connected to the node *G* with a minimum distance of *2* through the node *F*, which is not a member of this *2-Clique*. For this reason, some researchers have suggested restricting *N-Cliques* by insisting that the total number of span or path distance between any members of *N-Cliques* also satisfy a condition. This approach is called *N-Clans* approach. In this approach, all ties among actors of an *N-Clique* occur through other members of the group. Although there are two 2-Cliques (*ABCDEG* and *BDEFG*), only one (i.e., *BDEFG*) satisfies the restriction of the *N-Clans* approach. That means, there is only one *N-Clans* in Figure 6.3.

6.2.4.4 K-Plexes

K-Plexes is another way to relax the strong assumption of *"maximal complete sub-group"* for *Cliques*. In this approach, actors may be members of a *Clique* even if they have ties to all but *K* other members of the *Clique*. A node is a member of a *Clique* of size *n* if it has direct ties to $(n - k)$ members of that *Clique*. With $K = 2$, there are 10 *K-Plexes* in Figure 6.3 (i.e., *ABCD, ABE, ADG, BCE, BDE, BDG, BEF, CDG, DFG*, and *EFG*).

6.3 Healthcare Data Sets

Healthcare providers and stakeholders collect large amount of data for record keeping and administrative purposes. The data collection, the regulatory policies, the health information coding standards, and the (electronic) health data transmitted and shared across information systems vary significantly across countries and depend on the organization structure, available resources, and implementation policy. Nevertheless, most developed countries have similar types of information stored in healthcare data sets.

We can broadly categorize healthcare data sets into four groups (see Figure 6.4) based on the ways they are collected. The **first** group is "medical records"; a medical record stores information related to a patient's medical condition including diagnosis and treatment. A medical record is created for each patient in most primary and tertiary healthcare settings and is mainly used by the providers. Each patient is given a unique identifier, for example, Medical Record Number or MRN, to link records created during subsequent consultations. As more countries start implementing some form of e-health, unified or shared medical records become a valuable resource to manage continuity of care so that the providers and emergency departments can have unified, updated, and consistent access to patients health records. The patient in turn can also have access to their complete medical history.

The **second** type of data set is the "administrative data set" that is collected for billing, quality assurance, auditing and other administrative purposes. Unlike "medical records," which mostly rest with individual providers, administrative data sets containing information on fees and charges, and a summary of services provided, are becoming a rich source of information that is shared across policy makers, funders, and providers involved in providing healthcare services. As a result, established policies and specifications are in place in most developed countries on what administrative data are collected and how they are stored and transmitted.

In Australia, as in several other countries, an important portion of administrative data consists of hospital admission and discharge details. Several applications that are illustrated in the following sections are based on data stored in such administrative records used in both public and private health sector in Australia. The administrative record of a hospital admitted patient contains patient demographics,

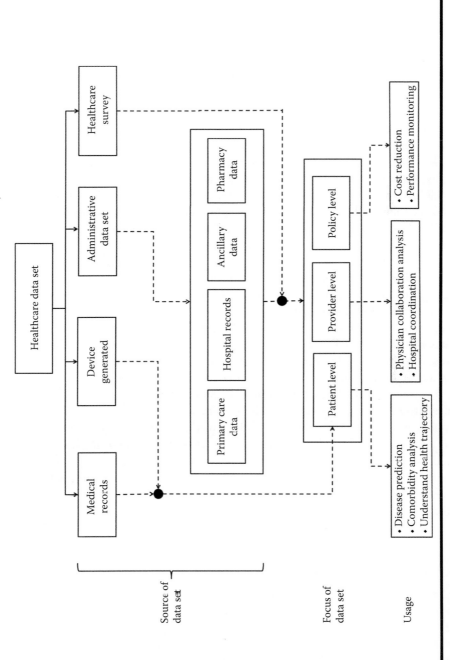

Figure 6.4 Organization of healthcare data.

patient's medical condition represented as principal and secondary diagnosis ICD codes [18], procedures performed represented as MBS [17] and ICD procedure codes, length of hospital stay, the total cost of care summarized as a DRG code [26], and itemized billing for costs of services provided (including accommodation and prosthetics). The billing information is of particular interest for private and public funders such as Medicare [27]. As the records also contain information about patient demographics, time and duration of stay, diagnoses and treatment, they can be used to understand the disease progression at a population level. Furthermore, the billing information in the administrative data also contains the provider information, that is, physicians and hospitals that have provided the treatment.

When we view it from a specific treatment or procedure perspective, the group of physicians who were involved in providing a particular type of treatment are available in the administrative data. This information can then be used to understand the collaboration pattern among the physicians within and across hospitals.

The **third** type of healthcare data set is "survey data" generated through systematic survey mostly conducted by researchers or other stakeholders to understand the trend in population level by tailoring specific questions. Specifically, chronic diseases incur long-term burden on healthcare as well as in the individual's quality of life. Therefore, many countries often maintain an active registry of database through longitudinal surveys of sections of the population. For example, "Diabetes Australia" keeps an active registry of diabetes patients under the "National Diabetes Services Scheme" [28] to monitor the prevalence of diabetes across Australia. Another example is the "45 and Up Study," which regularly surveys a large Australian population aged over 45 [29].

The **fourth** type of healthcare data set that is emerging as an important data set is "device-generated data," which are generated by electronic devices in an automated manner. For example, modern medical devices (e.g., ICU devices) may generate periodic vital statistics of patients that are often mined. Also, personal electronic devices (e.g., smartwatches, wristbands, and smartphone apps) generate and share real-time health statistics. Figure 6.4 shows a snapshot of the different types of healthcare data sets and their potential use by the different stakeholders.

6.4 Application Scenario

The applications described in this section are based on (Australian) hospital administrative data described in Section 6.3. Network analysis is used to explore administrative data from two perspectives: (i) to explore different aspects of collaboration among physicians, and (ii) to understand the health trajectory of chronic disease patients. These applications are explicitly designed to support informed decision making for the three stakeholder groups, namely, the consumer, the provider, and the policy maker.

6.4.1 Provider Collaboration Network

There is a large body of work that explores collaboration in the healthcare setting from different perspectives [30–35]. A comparative study of such research was made by Cunningham et al. [36] who reviewed 26 studies of professional network structures specifically to examine quality of care and patient safety.

The application described here explores collaboration that occurs in a hospital when surgeons and physicians work together to perform a specific surgery (e.g., hip replacement surgery) or treat a common set of patients who have had hip surgery. Figure 6.5 shows physician–patient interaction in a hospital. The black nodes represent physicians and the gray nodes represent patients. This graph basically illustrates that (a) multiple providers are involved in treating a patient, (b) some

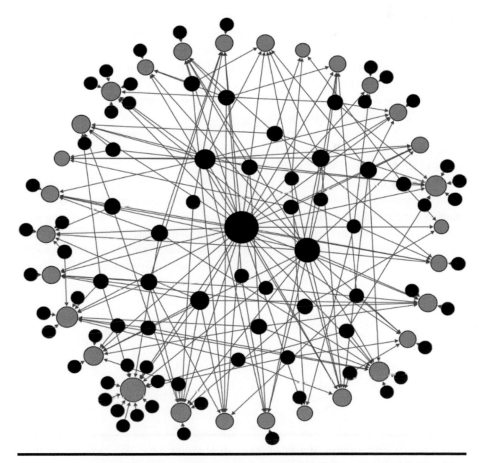

Figure 6.5   Illustration of a patient–physician network in a representative hospital of the research data set used in this study. Black nodes represent physicians and the gray nodes represent patients.

providers have more patients in common, and (c) some patients use more physician resources than others.

Over a period of time, as physicians start working together, both formal and informal collaborations begin to develop among physicians as they start treating a common set of patients. These collaborations can be modeled as social network graphs, with the nodes representing physicians and edges representing the common admitted patients they treat. The collaboration network can be different for different hospitals or even within the different units of a single hospital.

The application was developed to understand (a) the nature of collaboration among physicians who treat patients with a similar condition (e.g., hip replacement surgery) and (b) the impact of their collaborations on the cost of care for that condition.

We define a physician collaboration network (PCN) as a network that emerges among physicians during the course of providing treatment to shared patients. It can therefore be thought of as a "patient-sharing network among physicians." Figure 6.6 illustrates an example of the construction of such a PCN. In a hospital (say H1), patient Pat1 is visited by physicians Phy1 and Phy3; patient Pat2 is visited by physicians Phy1, Phy2, and Phy3. This is shown in the patient–physician network in Figure 6.6a. The corresponding PCN for this patient–physician network is shown in Figure 6.6b. The edge weight in this case is the common number of patients shared by the physicians. Therefore, in this network, the connection strength or edge weight between Phy1 and Phy2 is 1, that between Phy1 and Phy3 is 2, and that between Phy2 and Phy3 is 1.

Over a period of time, different types of PCNs evolve in a hospital as physicians treat patients for different conditions. For example, a PCN evolves among physicians treating patients who have had knee surgeries and another could evolve among physicians who treat patients with a cardiac condition. This particular study used data for total hip replacement patients from 85 different hospitals and correspondingly 85 PCNs were analyzed. Of these 85 PCNs, the study compared 5 PCNs with the highest readmission rate with 5 PCNs with the lowest readmission rate.

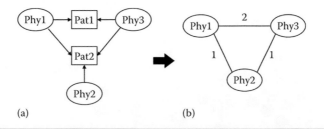

(a) (b)

Figure 6.6 **Construction of a PCN from an abstract data: (a) physician–patient links and (b) corresponding PCNs.**

In examining these PCNs, we considered two social network analysis measures— *degree centrality* and *betweenness centrality*. From the perspective of a PCN structure, a high *betweenness centrality* indicates that the PCN follows a *star-like* or *centralized* structure since *betweenness centrality* reaches its highest value of 1 for a *star* network. A *star-like* or *centralized* network has few actors with higher *betweenness centrality* values. This indicates that only a small number of actors play a major collaboration role. What is interesting about this finding is that it shows that a star-like network among providers reduces the value of the outcome variable—which in this case is the total *hospitalization cost*.

This analysis, therefore, offers some interesting insights to providers, hospital administrators, healthcare funders, and policy makers. Encouraging collaboration, with only one or two key people coordinating the communication (in other words, establishing a *star-like* or *centralized* PCN), can help in reducing the total *hospitalization cost*. On the other hand, a PCN with a flat network structure, where members have almost equal network participation, appears to have high a *hospitalization cost*.

6.4.2 Clique Analysis

In this example, we use the same administrative data set and consider 20 PCNs that evolved in 20 different hospitals, during the course of providing a specific hip replacement procedure. Based on the average hospitalization cost per patient, these 20 PCNs are categorized into two groups: (i) high-cost networks (with 10 PCNs) and (ii) low-cost networks (the remaining 10 PCNs). For the high-cost PCNs, the average hospitalization cost per patient is higher than \$32,798, and for the low-cost PCNs, the average cost is lower than \$17,713.

Next, we apply the three subgroup analysis approaches (i.e., *Clique*, *2-Clique*, and *2-Clan*) described in Section 6.2.4 to explore differences, in terms of structural differences in networks, between low-cost PCNs and high-cost PCNs. For a given network, each of the three subgroup analysis measures (i.e., *Clique*, *2-Clique*, and *2-Clan*) depends on the size of the network, that is, total number of actors within the network [19]. For this reason, we divide each of these three measures by the size of the corresponding PCNs in order to convert them into normalized values, so that they can be compared across different networks. Figure 6.7 shows a comparison of the average of these normalized values for *Clique*, *2-Clique*, and *2-Clan* for two sets of PCNs.

As can be seen in Figure 6.7, using normalized values (that indicate average number of subgroups), low-cost PCNs have high values for each of the three subgroup analysis measures. The *t*-test result shown in Table 6.1 confirms that these differences are statistically significant ($p < 0.05$). This indicates that in low-cost networks, physicians tend to work in smaller groups.

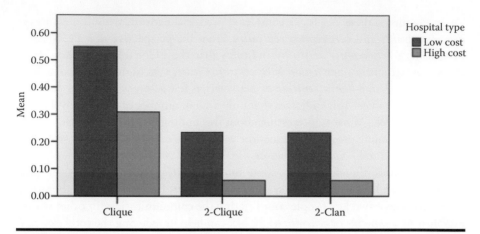

Figure 6.7   Comparison of average value of Clique, 2-Clique, and 2-Clan values between low-cost and high-cost PCNs.

Table 6.1   Statistical Significance of Low-Cost and High-Cost Cliques

Network Measure	Category	Mean	Mean Difference	t Value	Significance
Clique	Low cost	0.54	0.24	2.45	0.028
	High cost	0.3			
2-Clique	Low cost	0.23	0.18	4.13	0.002
	High cost	0.05			
2-Clan	Low cost	0.23	0.17	4.18	0.002

The healthcare policy makers could use the finding from this example to investigate further and make informed decision in regard to team size that is optimum for treating patients with different health conditions.

6.4.3 Team Composition

This application looks at a specific example of surgical teams who work together while performing knee surgeries and the potential impact of network relationships on the hospital length of stay [3].

The question we ask is: are there specific models of collaboration among a team of doctors who work together to perform knee surgeries? For example, does a knee surgeon prefer to work with the same anesthetist and assistant surgeon while performing all the knee surgeries, or does a surgeon work with many different anesthetists and associate surgeons? In this application, we explore the nature of collaboration among surgical teams and analyze the impact of team structure on healthcare quality and efficiency.

We constructed a tripartite graph to represent the collaboration among three types of providers—surgeon, assistant surgeon, and anesthetist, who form a team together that perform knee surgeries. This team composition is extracted from hospital administration data.

Figure 6.8 shows a network of providers where the three providers are represented by nodes of different colors: black (for surgeons), white-filled nodes with black outline (assistant surgeons) and gray (for anesthetists). The edges represent the common patients they treated during the same admission episode.

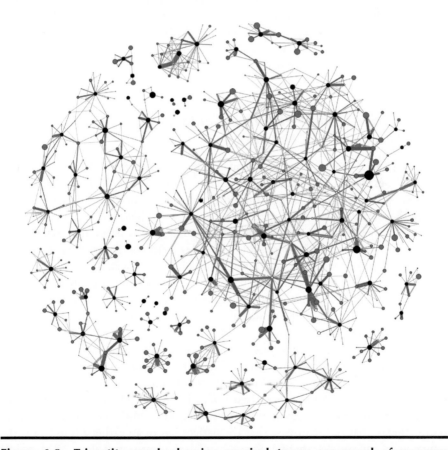

Figure 6.8 Tripartite graph showing surgical teams composed of surgeons (black), assistant surgeons (white-filled nodes with black outline), and anesthetists (gray).

The larger nodes indicate that these surgeons performed more surgeries. A thicker line between two nodes indicates that these two surgeons had more patients in common. The different clusters give an indication of how they operate as teams. As can be seen, there are some providers working with several teams, while some others work in smaller tightly knit teams as depicted by a single triangle. Analysis of the efficiency metrics of some of these team structures has given us some interesting insights into the nature of teams and their impact on performance. Team structures where one surgeon worked with larger number of teams appear to have a lower average length of stay, and in the case of tight cohesive teams, the readmission rate appears lower. Our results reported in Ref. [3] indicate that certain types of team structures have better performance over others.

Establishing a correlation between team structures and their performance metrics can enable hospital managers and doctors to plan ahead and assemble the right type of teams to improve quality of care and reduce healthcare costs, and when the performance of team compositions are measured in terms of healthcare matrices like average costs and length of stay, consumers can make an informed decision to choose the teams for their particular treatment regimens, which can translate into better health outcome.

6.4.4 Understanding Health Trajectory Using Disease Network

Here, we present an example application that leverages network analysis to analyze comorbidities that occur in patients with chronic conditions. Research shows that diseases, especially chronic or noncommunicable diseases, do not occur in isolation [37] as they share common risk factors based on an individual's genetic, environmental, and behavioral factors. Comorbidity analysis of a particular cohort (e.g., cohort of diabetic patients) can provide a high-level view of the disease progression, which in effect represents the health trajectory of that individual.

The application presented here is in the Australian healthcare context. It utilizes large and untapped longitudinal administrative data sets that contain ICD-10-AM disease codes that describe the principal and secondary diagnosis recorded during hospital admissions [8].

The first step of this application starts with modeling a *disease network* for an individual from hospital admission data. The network is designed in such a way that the nodes represent ICD codes present in any of the admissions for that patient. The relation between any two nodes indicates that the patient has progressed from one disease to another in two subsequent admissions. The relationship is directional; that is, the disease that the patient has in an earlier admission is the source node and the disease that occurs in a latter admission is the target node. If there are multiple diseases in any admission, then we consider all possible disease pairs. In cases where the patient has multiple diseases recorded in same admission, the relations are shown as bidirectional edges between possible disease pairs of the same admission. Every node and its edges have an associated *frequency* attribute that indicates the number of times that node (disease) or edge (indicating disease progression between two diseases) has been encountered in all of the admissions.

Mathematically, we can express the disease network for patient P_1 as a graph $N_p(V, E)$, where V is the set of nodes or vertices and E is the set of edges between any two nodes such as

$$V = \{v \mid v \in d_{a_i}, 1 \leq i \leq n\},$$

where P_1 has n admissions and d_{a_i} is the set of diseases or comorbidities that are recorded during ith admission a_i.

$$E = \left\{(v_1, v_2) \mid v_1 \in d_{a_i}, \ v_2 \in d_{a_j}, \ 1 \leq i \leq j < n, \ v_1 \neq v_2 \text{ when } i = j\right\}$$

that is, edge is an ordered set of two nodes that are present (a) in subsequent admissions where the source node is present in the former and the target node is present in the latter or (b) in the same admission as comorbidity. In the case where source and target nodes are the same in consecutive admissions, the edge will essentially be a self-loop.

Figure 6.9a provides an illustration of a disease network for an individual derived from ICD codes recorded over subsequent admissions. Now, taking this as a basis, we can generate a health trajectory of chronic disease patients that essentially shows the comorbidities, their prevalence, and progression. This is accomplished by first generating individual disease networks for patients who are diagnosed with a particular chronic disease. Then, we aggregate their disease networks by merging nodes and edges and adding up the frequencies of same nodes and edges when encountered across multiple disease networks. The resultant aggregated network can be termed as *baseline network*. The baseline network then becomes a representation of health trajectory of that particular disease. Figure 6.9b illustrates the baseline network that represents health trajectory of type 2 diabetes (T2D) patients. The baseline network is constructed by aggregating individual disease networks of T2D patients.

We then apply network centrality measures to understand which comorbidities are more prevalent. As mentioned earlier, every node in the baseline network represents a disease occurrence represented by its corresponding ICD-10 code. Both the node frequency and the weighted degree centrality measure can show the diseases that have occurred more frequently. Similarly, the edge frequency can indicate the patterns of progression that are more prevalent than others.

Once we construct the T2D baseline network, it works as the basis to predict the potential disease progression for new patients who could be at risk. We apply graph similarity matching techniques to compare the disease network of an

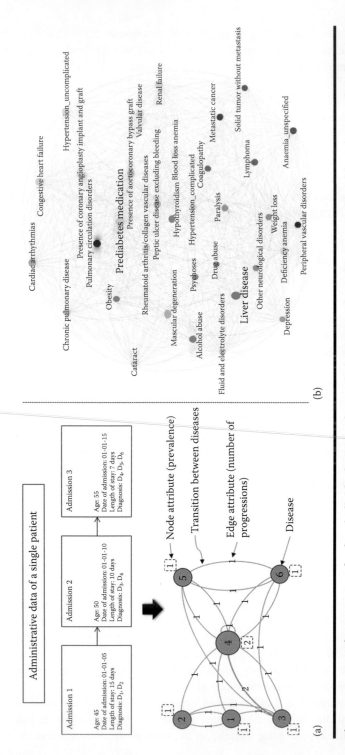

Figure 6.9 (a) Disease network of an individual patient from administrative data. (b) An actual health trajectory (baseline network) of chronic disease (type 2 diabetes) patients. Nodes indicate diseases or medical condition. Label size is proportional to prevalence. Proximity of the nodes is proportional to the comorbidity (i.e., closer nodes indicate that they occurred together more frequently).

Table 6.2 Summary of Actionable Insights

Applications	Policy Makers	Providers	Consumer
Provider collaboration network	• Visualize different types of collaboration models among providers and understand the impact on cost and quality	• Scenario analysis: Visualize the impact of different collaboration models on quality of care for treating patients with different health conditions	
Clique analysis	• Analyze the impact of team size on cost and quality of care • Plan and allocate resources based on optimum team size for different treatment regimens	• Scenario analysis: Visualize the impact of team size on quality of care and patient outcomes for different treatment regimens	
Team composition	• Understand the correlation between team composition and efficiency (cost and quality of care) • Plan and assemble the right team structure for acute care services	• Plan and assemble the right team structure for acute care services to enable better patient outcomes	• Ability to make informed decisions on choice of service providers for planned surgeries
Understanding health trajectory using disease network	• Planning and allocation of resources for proactive management of chronic diseases	• Patient education: Develop a new approach to patient education through powerful visualization of health trajectories	• Empower consumers to participate actively with their providers in managing their chronic disease

individual with network structures in the baseline network. The graph similarity method looks at the presence or absence of nodes and edges between two graphs. It also takes into account the frequency attributes to measure disease progression patterns of a patient's disease network. If the disease network of the individual matches a subgraph in the baseline network, it serves as an indication that the individual's health trajectory follows the trajectory of T2D patients. The more similar the two networks are, the more risky the patient is in terms of developing T2D, because we can see that the individual's health trajectory is following the trajectory of T2D patients' baseline network. We can further factor in the demographic effect (e.g., age, gender, etc.) and behavioral characteristics (e.g., smoking, which is also recorded in administrative data) to supplement the graph similarity scores that will result in better risk prediction.

Understanding disease progression or the health trajectory of a chronic condition such as diabetes can (a) enable governments to allocate appropriate resources to manage chronic disease progression, (b) enable providers to educate their patients to manage potential chronic disease onset in a proactive way, and (c) empower consumers with the information required to participate with their providers in managing their health.

In this section, we have discussed some network analytics–based applications that can be useful to different stakeholders, in discovering hidden relationships in health data. Table 6.2 provides a summary of actionable insights that can be gained from these applications by different stakeholder groups.

6.5 Discussions and Future Research Directions

The applications discussed in Section 6.4 illustrate the powerful capability of network analysis techniques to analyze and visualize information in new ways that can enable evidence-based decision making for stakeholders in the healthcare sector. We have shown that data items or variables available in health records can be analyzed using a network perspective and modeled as graphs. The examples illustrated different ways of modeling network graphs, using the same administrative data set. As illustrated, it is important to have a clear understanding of the problem definition. The task then is to carefully choose the appropriate healthcare entity as nodes and relationships as edges in order to model the problem. Network analysis offers several measures, both at the node level and at the network level, to understand nonparametric relationships within and across records in a data set. Measures of centrality, like closeness centrality and betweenness centrality in a collaboration network, give an indication of the relative importance and influence of the actors (or physicians in our case) in the context of their overall collaboration network. Network-level measures, such as density and network distance, can provide valuable understanding of the nature of connections or ties among the actors of the network and the time it would take to propagate a piece of information across the entire network. Subgroup analysis techniques, such as clique analysis, can provide ways of understanding the impact of microstructures or small groups within a larger community of providers.

Governments all over the world are shifting healthcare paradigms toward e-health–based systems. This means that data will be stored, transmitted, and accessed in ways that can open up new frontiers of data mining research, which can deliver best possible health outcomes to address the burden of chronic disease and an aging population. The tremendous potential of network-based analytics can be exploited in all of these new frontiers that are opening up with the availability of data, in formulating policies and delivering cost-effective, high-quality care.

References

1. Hollingsworth, B., Non-parametric and parametric applications measuring efficiency in health care. *Health Care Management Science*, 2003. **6**(4): 203–218.
2. Chandola, V., A. Banerjee, and V. Kumar, Anomaly detection for discrete sequences: A survey. *IEEE Transactions on Knowledge and Data Engineering*, 2012. **24**(5): 823–839.
3. Wang, F. et al., Application of network analysis on healthcare. In *Advances in Social Networks Analysis and Mining (ASONAM), 2014 IEEE/ACM International Conference on*. 2014. IEEE.
4. Koenig, W. et al., C-reactive protein, a sensitive marker of inflammation, predicts future risk of coronary heart disease in initially healthy middle-aged men results from the MONICA (Monitoring Trends and Determinants in Cardiovascular Disease) Augsburg Cohort Study, 1984 to 1992. *Circulation*, 1999. **99**(2): 237–242.
5. Srinivasan, U. and B. Arunasalam, Leveraging big data analytics to reduce healthcare costs. *IT Professional*, 2013. **15**(6): 21–28.
6. Uddin, S. et al., A study of physician collaborations through social network and exponential random graph. *BMC Health Services Research*, 2013. **13**(1): 234–247.
7. Landon, B.E. et al., Variation in patient-sharing networks of physicians across the United States. *JAMA: The Journal of the American Medical Association*, 2012. **308**(3): 265–273.
8. Khan, A., S. Uddin, and U. Srinivasan, Adapting graph theory and social network measures on healthcare data—A new framework to understand chronic disease progression. In *Australasian Workshop on Health Informatics and Knowledge Management*. 2016. Canberra: Australian Computer Society, Inc.
9. Easley, D. and J. Kleinberg, *Networks, Crowds, and Markets: Reasoning about a Highly Connected World*. 2010. Cambridge University Press.
10. Achacoso, T.B. and W.S. Yamamoto, *AY's Neuroanatomy of C. elegans for Computation*. 1991: CRC Press.
11. Adamic, L.A. and N. Glance, The political blogosphere and the 2004 US election: Divided they blog. In *Proceedings of the 3rd International Workshop on Link Discovery*. 2005. ACM.
12. Barnett, M.L. et al., Physician patient-sharing networks and the cost and intensity of care in US hospitals. *Medical Care*, 2012. **50**(2): 152–160.

13. Uddin, S., S.R. Atkinson, and L. Hossain, New directions in the analysis of social network dynamics. In *International Conference on Knowledge Discovery and Information Retrieval (KDIR)*. 2012. Barcelona, Spain: Springer.

14. Uddin, S. and L. Hossain, Disaster coordination preparedness of soft target organisations. *Disasters*, 2011. **35**(3): 623–638.

15. Uddin, S., L. Hossain, and K. Rasmussen, Network effects on scientific collaborations. *PLoS ONE*, 2013. **8**(2): e57546.

16. Uddin, S., A. Khan, and L.A. Baur, A framework to explore the knowledge structure of multidisciplinary research fields. *PLoS ONE*, 2015. **10**(4): e0123537.

17. *MBS Online: Medical Benefit Schedule*, http://www.mbsonline.gov.au/internet/mbsonline /publishing.nsf/Content/Home. 2016.

18. Marchesini, G., ICD code retrieval: Novel approach for assisted disease classification. In *Data Integration in the Life Sciences: 11th International Conference, DILS 2015, Los Angeles, CA, USA, July 9-10, 2015, Proceedings*. 2015. Springer.

19. Wasserman, S. and K. Faust, *Social Network Analysis: Methods and Applications*. 2003, Cambridge: Cambridge University Press.

20. Freeman, L., D. Roeder, and R. Mulholland, Centrality in social networks: II. Experimental results. *Social Networks*, 1979. **2**(80): 119–141.

21. Freeman, L., Centrality in social networks: Conceptual clarification. *Social Networks*, 1978. **1**(3): 215–239.

22. Chung, F. and L. Lu, The average distance in a random graph with given expected degrees. *Internet Mathematics*, 2004. **1**(1): 91–113.

23. Scott, J., *Social Network Analysis: A Handbook*. 2005, London: Sage Publications Ltd.

24. Luce, R.D. and A.D. Perry, A method of matrix analysis of group structure. *Psychometrika*, 1949. **14**(2): 95–116.

25. Harary, F., R.Z. Norman, and D. Cartwright, *Structural Models: An Introduction to the Theory of Directed Graphs*. 1965, New York: John Wiley & Sons.

26. *Australian refined diagnosis-related groups (AR-DRG) data cubes*, http://www.aihw .gov.au/hospitals-data/ar-drg-data-cubes/. 2016.

27. *Medicare: Looking after the health of Australians*, https://www.humanservices.gov.au /customer/dhs/medicare. 2016.

28. Australia, D., *The National Diabetes Services Scheme (NDSS)*. 2016 [cited 22-05-2016]; Available from: https://www.ndss.com.au/.

29. Institute, S., *45 and Up Study*. 2016 [cited 22-05-2016]; Available from: https://www .saxinstitute.org.au/our-work/45-up-study/.

30. Srinivasan, U. and S. Uddin, A social network framework to explore healthcare collaboration. *Healthcare Informatics and Analytics: Emerging Issues and Trends*, 2014: p. 44.

31. Hunt, J.S. et al., A randomized controlled trial of team-based care: Impact of physician-pharmacist collaboration on uncontrolled hypertension. *Journal of General Internal Medicine*, 2008. **23**(12): 1966–1972.

32. Arbuthnott, A. and D. Sharpe, The effect of physician–patient collaboration on patient adherence in non-psychiatric medicine. *Patient Education and Counseling*, 2009. **77**(1): 60–67.

33. Uddin, S., Exploring the impact of different multi-level measures of physician communities in patient-centric care networks on healthcare outcomes: A multi-level regression approach. *Scientific Reports*, 2016. **6**: 20222.

34. Uddin, S., L. Hossain, and M. Kelaher, Effect of physician collaboration network on hospitalization cost and readmission rate. *The European Journal of Public Health*, 2012. **22**(5): 629–633.

35. Uddin, S., M. Kelaher, and U. Srinivasan, A framework for administrative claim data to explore healthcare coordination and collaboration. *Australian Health Review*, 2015 (online first available).

36. Cunningham, F.C. et al., Health professional networks as a vector for improving healthcare quality and safety: A systematic review. *BMJ Quality & Safety*, 2012. **21**(3): 239–249.

37. Barabási, A.-L., Network medicine—From obesity to the "diseasome." *New England Journal of Medicine*, 2007. **357**(4): 404–407.

Chapter 7

Modeling and Analysis of Behavioral Health Data Using Graph Analytics

Rose Yesha and Aryya Gangopadhyay

Contents

7.1 Introduction

In the past decade, there has been a complete transformation in the type of data available on the Internet. Social media sites include web forums, photo and video sharing communities, and social networking platforms that offer combinations of all of these features. Particularly, there is an emphasis on the relationships among users within the community. Social media data have completely revolutionized the way in which human beings interact with one another. A recent survey in the United States found that 42% of the respondents use social media to search on healthcare-related issues, 25% discussed health-related experience online, and 20% are members of health communities or forums [1].

The prevalence of online social networks has enabled users to communicate, connect, and share content. Many of these networks serve as the de facto Internet portal for millions of users [2]. Because of the enormous popularity of these sites, the data about the users and their communications offer an enormous opportunity to analyze human behavioral on a large scale. When presented with unstructured data, such as that derived from raw forum data, the sheer volume of text makes the process seem impossible. This is where the role of text analytics takes the central stage. Text analytics seek to derive meaning from the text data. This task is very complex since human communication is so context dependent. This calls for well-designed text analytic techniques that are able to identify the major interactions between various terms on specific topics in big data platforms, and the ability to make sense of these data using prediction models and monitoring tools.

Social media can be used for healthcare in various ways including pharmacovigilance, patient recruitment for clinical trials, and outcomes research by providing an in-depth understanding of patient behaviors and experiences. This paper proposes the analysis of forum data for identifying behavioral health patterns, which aims to explain these techniques and their implications for behavioral health. The disorders explored in our methodology include posts from four various forums including OCD, Bluelight Marijuana, Substance Abuse, and suicide. This chapter proposes the analysis of social media data for identifying behavioral health patterns, which aims to explain these techniques and their implications for behavioral health. The rest of the paper is organized as follows: Related Work (Section 7.2), Methodology (Section 7.3), Results (Section 7.4), and Conclusion (Section 7.5).

7.2 Related Work

Mental health conditions affect a large percentage of individuals each year. Traditional mental health studies have relied on information collected through contact with mental health practitioners. There has been research on the utility of social media for depression, but there have been limited evaluations of other mental health conditions [3]. In the following part of this chapter, we will examine specific techniques that have previously been used to analyze forum data and define behavioral health and public health issues, and last, we will explore the implications that this research has for big data analytics.

7.2.1 Analysis of Social Media

In this part of the chapter, we will explore the various techniques that have been previously used to analyze the data found in social media sites. The rise of social media sites, forums, blogs, and other communications tools has created an online community of individuals who are able to socialize and express their thoughts through various applications [4]. Microblogging has become a very popular tool for communication among users. The individuals who write these messages blog about their lives, share opinions, and discuss current events. As more individuals participate in these microblogging services, more information about their messages becomes available. The massive amount of data in user updates creates the need for accurate and efficient clustering of short messages on a larger scale [5]. Certain research areas have been chosen to focus on the opinions and sentiments of these messages [6], community detection [7], politics [8], and user interests [9]. Techniques for clustering these data have included document clustering, topic modeling, sentiment analysis, and text mining.

7.2.1.1 Topic Modeling

Recent years have seen a surge in information that is both digitized and stored. As this trend continues, it has become increasingly difficult for users to find what they are looking for. Novel computational tools are needed to help organize, search, and comprehend these large amounts of data [10]. Currently, we are able to type keywords into a search and find documents that are related to them. However, there is a crucial element that is missing from this process. Specifically, it is important to utilize themes to explore specific topics. A thematic structure could serve as a portal through which users could explore and obtain knowledge about various topics. Topic modeling algorithms are statistical methods that analyze the words of the original documents and discover themes that occur. Furthermore, topic modeling analyzes how these themes relate to one another, and how they differ over time [11]. These algorithms do not need any previous annotations or labeling of the documents; these topics surface automatically from the analysis of the original texts. Blei [11] describes latent Dirichlet allocation (LDA), which is the simplest type of topic model. LDA is a statistical model of a collection of documents that tries to validate the intuition that documents exhibit multiple topics. The simple LDA model provides an effective and powerful way to discover and exploit the hidden thematic structures found in large amounts of text data.

7.2.1.2 Sentiment Analysis

Microblogging websites have developed into a source for varied types of information. Individuals post messages about their opinions, current events, complaints, and sentiments about products they use in their daily lives [12]. It is very often that companies study these user reactions on microblogging sites. The challenge then becomes how to build a technology that can detect and summarize an overall sentiment. A large amount of social media contain sentences that are sentiment based. Sentiment is defined as a personal belief or judgment that is not founded on proof or certainty [13]. Sentiment involves the use of Natural Language Processing (NLP), statistics, or machine learning methods to extract, identify, or characterize the sentiment content of a text source [12]. The automated identification of sentiment types can be beneficial for many NLP systems.

7.2.1.3 Text Mining

Text mining is the discovery of new information by automatically extracting information from a large amount of various unstructured textual resources [14]. Text mining can help an organization gain valuable insights from text-based content such as word documents, e-mail, and postings on social media sites like Facebook, Twitter, and LinkedIn [15]. Mining unstructured data with NLP, statistical modeling, and machine learning techniques can be challenging because natural language text is usually inconsistent. Unstructured data contains ambiguities caused by inconsistent syntax and semantics. Text analytics software can help by transposing words and phrases in unstructured data into numerical values, which can then be linked with structured data in a database and analyzed with traditional data mining techniques. By using text analytics, an organization can successfully gain insight into content-specific values such as emotion, sentiment, intensity, and relevance. Text mining techniques include methods for corpus handling, data import, metadata management, preprocessing, and the creation of term-document matrices. The main structure for managing documents in is a corpus, representing a collection of text documents.

7.2.2 Behavioral Health

Behavioral health can be classified into several different categories, depending on the type and severity of the mental health disorder. Mental healthcare practitioners rely on specific evaluation criteria, such as that contained in the *Diagnostic and Statistical Manual of Mental Disorders*, as well as data gathered from one-on-one sessions with the patient in order to reach a diagnosis for these disorders. Currently, more than 61.5 million Americans experience a mental illness in any given year. One in 17, about 13.6 million, has a serious mental illness such as major depression, schizophrenia, or bipolar disorder [16]. Approximately 60% of adults and almost one-half of youth ages 8 to 15 with a mental illness did not receive mental health services in 2013 [17].

7.2.2.1 Suicide

Many individuals at risk of suicide do not seek help before an attempt, and they do not remain connected to any mental health services after the attempt [18]. E-health interventions are now being defined as a means to identify individuals who are at risk, offer self-help, or deliver interventions in response to user posts on the Internet. Patterns found in users' social media usage can be especially indicative of suicide ideation. Research shows that there is some evidence to suggest that social media platforms can be used to identify individuals or geographical areas at particular risk for suicide. Specific language used in tweets can give practitioners and other Twitter users information about an individual's mental health status. Recent studies found specific tweets by users who both tweeted about suicidal ideations. One quote stated "people say 'stop cutting!' be happy with who you are. It's so much easier to say than do? I hate myself so much" [19]. Another tweeter posted, "I'm so sick of being bullied. Everyone cares about their problems and don't even bother to check on me. I'm going to kill myself!!" [19]. It is evident from these tweets that intervention is possible. The few studies done in this area have shown that it is possible to use computerized sentiment analysis and data mining to identify users at risk for suicide.

7.2.2.2 Depression

Many have begun turning toward online communities for help in understanding and dealing with symptoms. Nimrod [20] examined the content online forum discussion of depression in order to explore the potential benefits they could offer people with depression. Quantitative content analysis of 1 year of data from 25 top online communities was performed, using the Forum Monitoring System. Content analysis revealed nine main subjects discussed in the communities, including (in descending order) "symptoms," "relationships," "coping," "life," "formal care," "medications," "causes," "suicide," and "work." The results indicated that online depression communities serve as a place for sharing experiences and receiving techniques for coping [20]. Searching for online health information and searching within social media sites are both ongoing difficulties users face [21]. There are many reasons that these social media platforms are a valuable source of health information. For example, social media provides an important tool for people with health concerns to talk to one another. Also, these sites are well known as a source of tacit information, which is less common online. Wilson et al. [22] focused their study on a prevalent mental health issue, depression. Depression has increased substantially in developed and developing countries [23], and it is estimated to affect more than 350 million people [24]. Depression affects more than 27 million Americans and is believed to be responsible for more than 30,000 suicides every year [10,25]. Although discussing issues related to depression with others is seen to be an important facet of coping, personal factors discourage people from doing so in real life [26]. Therefore, social media sites provide an outlet for people to communicate with potentially millions of people, while reducing the consequences of real-life disclosure [27,28]. More users are choosing to share their thoughts and emotions that encompass their daily lives. The language and emotion used in social media posts may include feelings of worthlessness, helplessness, guilt, and self-hatred, which are all characteristic of depression. The characterization of social media activity can provide a measurement of depression symptoms in a manner that could help detect depression in populations. Choudhury et al. [29] examined the use of social media as a behavioral assessment tool. In contrast to behavioral health surveys, social media measurement of behavior captures social activity and language expression in a naturalistic setting [29].

7.3 Methodology

For this part of our research, we wanted to examine if we could detect some of the patterns simply by using visualization. We started by creating word clouds from Twitter data. Word clouds are one approach for visualization, and we will discuss other visualization techniques later in Section 7.4. Word clouds are one of the most popularly used visualization techniques for social media. Word clouds are effective for a very selective part of social media, for example, a few hundred tweets that are relevant to a certain answer for a specific question. However, creating a word cloud on a large scale is not going to yield significant results. We created two different word clouds by aggregating 10,000 tweets on each of two consecutive days.

7.3.1 Word Clouds

The purpose for this visualization was to be able to see which words were more prevalent than others. It can be seen that specific terminology such as "Andrew," "military," "Lydon," and "plz" occurred more frequently than other words. However, other words of little to no importance were also highlighted such as "http," "can," and "know." Most of the words in the cloud are visible, but many are also hidden in the background (Figure 7.1). Although this visualization technique gives us some information, it does not provide us with all the information.

Figure 7.1 Two word clouds of 10,000 tweets generated with hashtag "#ptsd" on two consecutive days.

7.3.2 Histograms

The analytic technique we used for analyzing social media data was the creation of histograms. Histograms provided us with a statistical representation of the data. This is the simplest type of statistical analysis that can be done. In the past, histograms have widely been used for text data. The histograms we created were able to give us information on the distribution of words depending on their occurrence. For our analysis, we analyzed 10,000 tweets and created histograms on two consecutive days. We repeated this process for more than 500 frequent terms, between 300 and 500 frequent terms, and between 200 and 300 frequent terms. The purpose of creating these different histograms was to analyze the distribution of words and see if any distinct patterns were beginning to emerge from this process.

From these histograms in Figure 7.2, we were able to see that there is some similarity and overlap. From this, it can be inferred that the most frequently occurring terms are "AMP," "620," and "Tahmoressi." AMP is an acronym for Attention Modification Program, which is used in individuals with general anxiety disorder. The term "620" has to do with house resolution 620, which calls for the release of Andrew Tahmoressi from Mexico. The final term, "Tahmoressi," referred to Andrew Tahmoressi, a marine sergeant who served two tours in Afghanistan and was honorably discharged from the service in November 2012. Looking at these frequently occurring terms, we were able to see that they were mostly related to either general or specific issues dealing with the military. This may give us a slightly better picture of the thematic structure, but once again, it does not provide us with all the information.

For these histograms in Figure 7.3, we used between 300 and 500 frequently occurring terms in 10,000 tweets. We saw that there were slightly different terms between these histograms. From these data, we can perhaps infer that the difference is due to the fact that these terms are not as frequent as others. Certain terms that were prevalent were 1791, which had to do with the 1791 think shop and 87 ideas workshop. These organizations advocate for Veterans who suffer from traumatic brain injury and posttraumatic stress disorder (PTSD). Again, we can see that there is a pattern of military terms here.

From these histograms in Figure 7.4, we were able to infer that that there were more generic terms that seem to occur for a smaller number of frequently occurring terms.

7.3.3 Term Associations

Term associations are another technique that we used to visualize the data. A major goal of text analysis is to extract, organize, and group the concepts that occur in the corpus. Mining significant associations from the corpus is key in this process. In the automatic classification of text documents, each document is a vector in a high-dimensional space, with each axis representing a term in the lexicon. Clustering

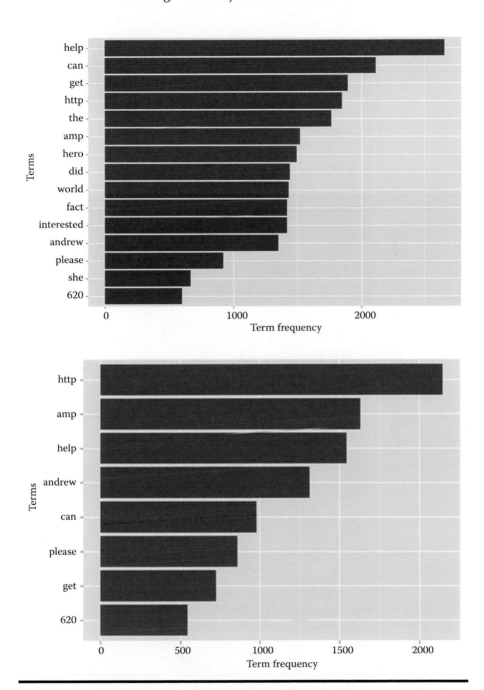

Figure 7.2 Histograms generated on two consecutive days for more than 500 frequently occurring terms with 10,000 tweets.

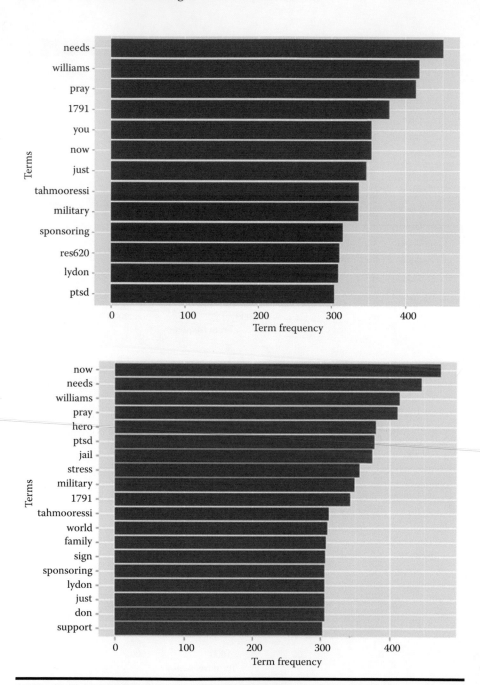

Figure 7.3 Histograms generated on two consecutive days for between 300 and 500 frequently occurring terms with 10,000 tweets.

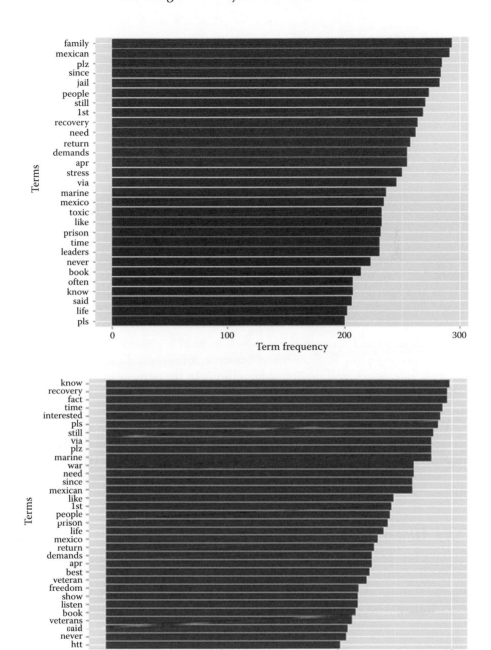

Figure 7.4 Histograms generated on two consecutive days for between 200 and 300 frequently occurring terms with 10,000 tweets.

	andrew
pray	0.50
1791	0.48
apr	0.39
demands	0.39
tahmooressi	0.39
return	0.38
1st	0.37
mexican	0.37
prayer	0.37
mexico	0.36
please	0.36
prison	0.36
since	0.36

	ptsd
researcher	0.33
med	0.31
study	0.31
pot	0.29
zones	0.25

(a)   (b)

Figure 7.5 Two term association charts expressing the percentage value as it relates to a specific term. (a) includes terms at least 25% related to the term "ptsd." (b) Includes terms at least 25% related to the term "Andrew."

significant terms and associations is shown to provide clusters that are purer in the concepts they yield. Raghavan and Tsaparas [30] presented two techniques for efficiently mining associations deemed significant by the measure of matrix mining and shortened documents. These experimental evaluations produced interesting associations and the algorithms performed well in practice.

For our research, term associations were performed using terms that were co-occurring with a specific term at least 25% of the time. For these visualization techniques, we used the terms "ptsd" and "Andrew" with 10,000 tweets (Figure 7.5).

These term associations may give us a better understanding of how to cluster the different themes together.

7.3.4 Hierarchical Clustering

Hierarchical clustering techniques are an important category of clustering methods. Agglomerative clustering techniques are the most common. This technique is done by starting with the points as individual clusters and, at each step, merging them to the closest pair of clusters. Hierarchical clustering is often displayed in a dendogram as shown below:

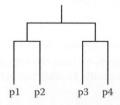

p1   p2   p3   p4

These dendograms display both the cluster–subcluster relationships and the order in which the clusters were merged. This approach is expressed more formally in the following Algorithm 1:

Algorithm 1: Basic agglomerative hierarchical clustering algorithm.

> **Input:** a proximity (similarity) matrix;
> **Initialization:** Put each data point in a separate cluster;
> **while** *there are more than one cluster* **do**
>> **Merge** the closest two clusters;
>> **Update** the proximity matrix to reflect the new clusters with the original clusters;
> **end**
> **Return** the clusters after each merge operation;

The analysis of basic agglomerative hierarchical clustering algorithm is straight-forward with respect to computational complexity. $O(m^2)$ time is necessary to compute the proximity matrix. Because of the additional complexity of keeping data in a sorted list, the overall time required for a hierarchical clustering is $O(m^2\log m)$. The space and time complexity of hierarchical clustering limits the size of data sets that can be processed.

Hierarchical clustering is a very standard technique. It is new in this context; there has been no research done on this for social media data. People have done hierarchical clustering for all kinds of applications, but relatively little work has been done with text data. It does give us some ideas of some of the topics automatically by looking at the terms.

These dendograms start to give us some information about different concepts. Out of the thousands of terms in these thousands of tweets, we were able to notice some semantic linkage. We could infer from these data that there are four major clusters that are emerging, and meaning has started to come about. The right large cluster in Figure 7.6a is related to military, jail, and Mexican prison. The last cluster in Figure 7.6b is related to getting veterans back to their families. We can see that the clusters differ from generic sentiments to more specific sentiments.

All methods of text clustering require many steps of preprocessing of the data. First, any nontextual information is removed from the documents. Then, stop words such as "I," "am," "and," and so on are also removed. Many text clustering algorithms rely on the *hierarchical algorithms* such as Single-Link or Average-Link [8]. *Scatter-Gather* [4] is a well-known algorithm, which has been proposed for a document browsing system based on clustering. It uses a hierarchical clustering algorithm to determine an initial clustering, which is then refined using the k-means clustering vector-space model. In this model, each text document d is represented by a vector of frequencies of the remaining m terms: To measure the

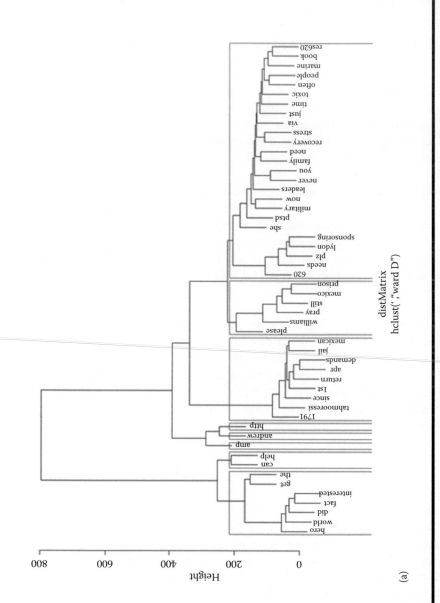

Figure 7.6 Two cluster dendograms were created on two consecutive days on 52 terms with 10,000 terms. (a) Hierarchical clustering of terms. *(Continued)*

Figure 7.6 (Continued) Two cluster dendograms were created on two consecutive days on 52 terms with 10,000 terms. (b) Hierarchical clustering of terms.

```
cluster 1: amp she http just people military recovery
cluster 2: help 620 amp needs sponsoring lydon plz
cluster 3: http can she andrew please get the
cluster 4: help can 620 get http need needs
cluster 5: time via now family recovery stress please
cluster 6: andrew http please pray 1791 williams tahmooressi
cluster 7: can did fact get help hero interested
cluster 8: ptsd need the marine can amp stress
```

```
cluster 1: can fact get help hero interested world
cluster 2: amp help http needs 620 sponsoring lydon
cluster 3: life http time military amp support war
cluster 4: http andrew please pray williams now help
cluster 5: stress recovery amp http help don time
cluster 6: 1st andrew apr demands jail since tahmooressi
cluster 7: htt ptsd need family war andrew time
cluster 8: can http help pls get 620 show
```

Figure 7.7   Clustering tweets with 10,000 tweets using hashtag #ptsd.

similarity between two documents d_1 and d_2 represented in the vector-space model, the cosine measure is used, which is defined by the cosine of the angle between two vectors.

A frequent item-based approach of clustering is promising since it provides a natural way of decreasing the large dimensionality of the document vector space. An experimental evaluation by Beil et al. [31] revealed that frequent term clustering yields a cluster quality comparable to that of state-of-the-art text clustering algorithms. Also, frequent term clustering generates a natural description for the clusters by their frequent term sets.

For our research, we selected the top seven terms in each cluster and this is what emerged (Figure 7.7). This is a very common technique in document analysis. Terms can be clustered in such a way, which indicates which terms are more prevalent. It is not possible to make sense of large amounts of data without an automatic technique. Our purpose is to try to establish that these techniques are applicable.

7.4 Results

7.4.1 Experimental Results of Twitter Data

Blondel et al. found in their research that the quality of the communities detected was very good, as was measured by the modularity [32]. This simple algorithm has several advantages. First, these steps are intuitive and easy to implement. Also, the algorithm is extremely fast; that is, computer simulations on large ad hoc modular networks suggest that its complexity is linear on typical and sparse data [10]. The accuracy of this method has been tested on ad hoc modular networks and is shown to be excellent as relative to other much slower community detection methods. For the purposes of our research, we partitioned graphs from terms gathered from Twitter data.

In Figure 7.8, two clusters (blue and red) with the top 21 terms were formed from the Twitter data. The top 21 terms were used because if the set was greater, then there would be too dense of a cloud.

In this approach, we determine whether it is possible to automatically detect themes using this method. It can be seen from the visualization that the blue cluster is related to generic issues such as PTSD and veteran issues. However, the red cluster is related to a particular veteran—Andrew Tahmooressi. Another significant feature of this particular graph partition is that AMP (Attention Modification Program) is the largest node, which means it has the maximum number of connections with other nodes. We are developing a method where a very large method of terms can be visualized. These clusters are based on interactions: if a node is blue, this doesn't mean that there is zero connection to the red nodes, but it does mean that it has many more connections to blue nodes. If we were to cut the blue and red communities, we would cut the minimum number of edges, which means that we are separating the nodes in the best way.

The terms are impossible to decipher just from the graph itself (Figure 7.9). The node is colored by the authority score. There are 263 nodes and 2466 edges. We could have used more than 4000 nodes, but the result would be a dark cloud and it would be discernable. This separates the clusters in a better way, and the number of interactions is much more than the number of nodes. However, it is still sparse and hard to follow.

There are four major partitions in Figure 7.10: red, blue, green, and yellow. This visualization applies the modularity algorithm to separate out the groups. These groups can be cleaned up by removing articles and propositions. It would be more sparse, but it would be easier to separate important terms. For our research purposes, we are looking at different clusters and seeing in what way they are different. From green to blue to red, the terms are getting more specific. The blue cluster seems to contain mostly generic sentiments, the green cluster is more specific to military and veterans, the red cluster deals specifically about Andrew Tahmooressi, and the yellow cluster is mostly Mexican (Spanish) tweets [33]. The algorithm is able to separate this nicely. We can identify the strong nodes by looking at the number of interactions between the nodes and the interactions with nodes outside of them. Another interesting feature is the sentiment analysis. It can be seen that there are more negative sentiments in the green cluster and more positive sentiments in the blue cluster. This was done without any linguistic analysis; the algorithm has no sense of semantics. This separation was done solely based on the interactions.

The red cluster is about Andrew Tahmooressi, a marine sergeant jailed in Mexico, who was subsequently released (Figure 7.11). House resolution 620 expressed the sentiment that the Government of Mexico should immediately release United

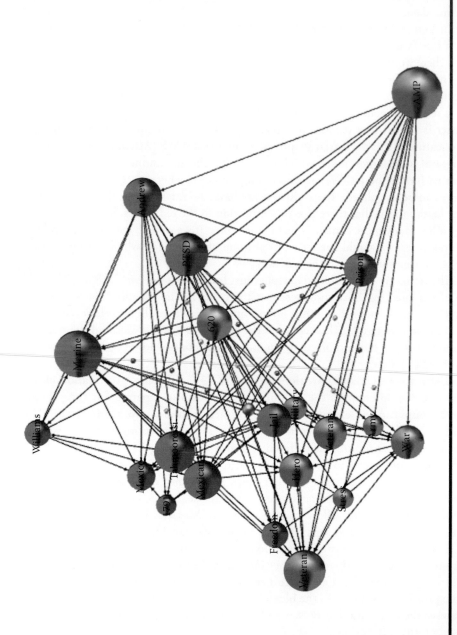

Figure 7.8 Graph partition of top 21 terms.

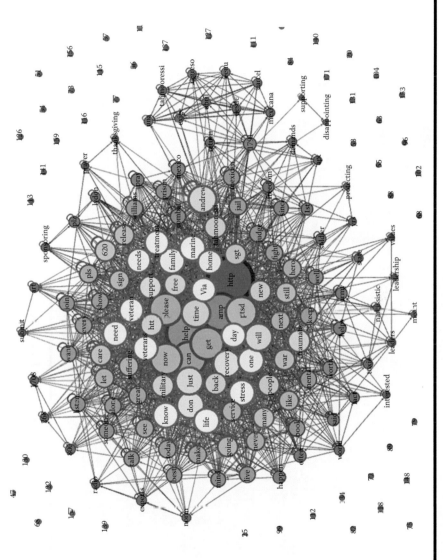

Figure 7.9 Graph with terms having a frequency of more than 100.

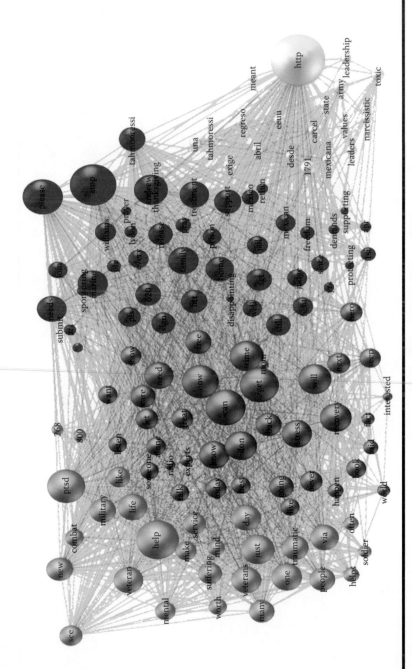

Figure 7.10   Graph partitioning with terms that have a frequency of more than 100.

Jill Tahmooressi retweeted
Ron Murphy @THETXEMBASSY · Nov 5
@Greta teaser #Tahmooressi
Looking forward to seeing it
Stand Tall Andrew
@JTahmooressi @ATahmooressi @HammarOlivia

   ↩   ↻ 30   ★ 31 ●●●   View more photos and videos

Jill Tahmooressi retweeted
Eva Maritza @EvaSolano2 · Oct 30
"@Montel_Williams: "@SandraAlabama: Please pray for Andrew
#BringBackOurMarine #MarineHeldInMexico Lord JESUS our...

   ↩   ↻ 27   ★ 22 ●●●   View more photos and videos

Figure 7.11 Tweets contained in red cluster.   *(Continued)*

Figure 7.11 (Continued)   Tweets contained in red cluster.

States Marine Sgt. Andrew Tahmooressi and provide for his swift return to the United States so that he can receive the appropriate medical assistance for his medical condition. Talk show host Montel Williams, as well as Andrew's mother, Jill Tahmooressi, sent multiple tweets on this.

> These tweets were primarily in Spanish and also expressed the sentiment that Andrew Tahmooressi should be freed from the Mexican jail and sent back home (Figure 7.12).

For Figure 7.13, we have parsed out the word "rip" from ptsd tweets in order to validate our research. This can help us find out where the connections are between the words. The connections can be seen in three major clusters: the yellow cluster seems to have a lot of French words, the green cluster seems to have words with positive sentiments (Figure 7.14), and the red cluster seems to have words with negative sentiments (Figure 7.15). We were able to separate themes automatically from the tweets. The algorithm was extremely capable of separating the terms based on their meanings. The size of the node is a score called the "authority" score. A node with a large size means that it is connected to nodes that are also important.

Figure 7.12 Tweets contained in yellow cluster.

Figure 7.13 Partitioned graph using hashtag #rip.

Brittany Murphy

Film actress

Brittany Murphy-Monjack, known professionally as Brittany Murphy, was an American film and stage actress, singer, and voice artist. Murphy, a native of Atlanta, moved to Los Angeles as a teenager, and pursued a career in acting. Wikipedia

Born: November 10, 1977, Atlanta, GA

Died: December 20, 2009, Los Angeles, CA

Spouse: Simon Monjack (m. 2007–2009)

Parents: Angelo Bertolotti, Sharon Murphy

TV shows: Sister, Sister, Boy Meets World, King of the Hill, More

Figure 7.14 The green cluster from the partitioned graph focuses on the death of Brittany Murphy who was remembered on her birthday (November 10).

Jet crash in Bahamas kills 9; prominent pastor Myles Munroe among the dead

By **Susanna Capelouto** and **Dave Alsup**, CNN
updated 7:02 PM EST, Mon November 10, 2014

FROM FACEBOOK

00:29 / 01:13

Source: CNN

STORY HIGHLIGHTS

• NEW: Police confirm Myles Munroe and his wife are among the victims of a plane crash

• The jet hit a crane and crashed into a junk site, police said

(CNN) -- A jet crashed Sunday near Freeport, on the island of Grand Bahama, killing all nine people on board, authorities said.

The aircraft hit a crane at the Freeport Ship Yard and crashed into a nearby "junk site," police said.

Figure 7.15 The red cluster from the partitioned graph focuses on the death of Myles Munroe who died in a plane crash with his daughter and wife on November 9, 2014.

7.4.2 Analyzing Forum Data

In this section, we describe our analysis of the Bluelight forum posts, which were downloaded for analysis in 2015. The purpose of the Bluelight forum is to educate the public about responsible drug use by promoting free discussion. The online blogs that were downloaded consisted approximately 5000 words. Figure 7.16 shows a snapshot of the Bluelight forum. The first step in our methodology consisted of data cleaning by removing stop words and other non-alphanumeric data. Next, a term document matrix (TDM) was created where each discussion thread was modeled as a document. The TDM was converted into a graph, which was analyzed further.

Figure 7.17 shows the graph of the TDM for the Bluelight forum. The graph had around 30,000 nodes connected by more than 120,000 edges. The average degree was 30, meaning that each term had 30 immediate neighbors on the average. The network diameter was 5, which indicates that any two nodes in the graphs are connected with a maximum of 5 hops. The average path length is 2, which is the average length of connection between any two nodes. Last, there were 938 connected components, which are disconnected subgraphs, many of which are singleton graphs. The color and size of the nodes correspond to node centrality measures. The node sizes in Figure 7.17 correspond to their degree. However, most centrality measures were highly correlated; thus, selecting any other centrality measure would have resulted in the same graph characteristics. Some of the nodes with the highest centrality were **anxiety**, **smoking**, **Xanax**, **Benzo**, **heart**, **marijuana**, **relaxation**, **cannabis**, and **documentary**. We divide these nodes into the following semantic groups: **experiential** (anxiety and smoking), **drug-related** (Xanax and benzodiazepine), **clinical** (heart and marijuana), **semi-religious** (relaxation and cannabis), and **social interaction** (documentary). All morphological varieties (such as smoke vs. smoking) were normalized to remove confounding patterns. In the following, we discuss the contexts of the above terms by using their immediate neighborhoods. Figure 7.18 shows the neighborhood of the node **anxiety**. This region of the graph deals with personal experiences and some recommendations including the Linden method for dealing with anxiety, panic attacks, and so on.

The next experiential concept was **smoking**. In this part of the forum, the user community discussed their individual experience of smoking marijuana and the differences among them.

The next two concepts are related to drugs such as **Xanax** and **Benzo**, which is a short form of **benzodiazepine**. These discussions are related to marijuana usage along with these drugs that are used to treat anxiety disorders, panic attacks, and anxiety-related depression. While still experiential, these discussions are related specifically to these drugs.

The next semantic group (clinical) has two related concepts: **relaxation** and **cannabis**. These discussions are rich in clinical contents. For example, one set of

Or hash for that matter

People with anxiety problems.

B00 -----> Cannabis Discussion

only if i'm smoking in a public/semi-public place...
if i'm at my dudes house or my house i feel fine.
im careful about where i light up tho

a lot of people actually. I thought there was a weed and anxiety mega thread because it was such a common topic. I think weed and social anxiety seem to be pretty common.

I got a really really bad anxiety 2years ago and i cant stop it. Everytime i smoke weed now i need to be alonebecause i cant even talk to my friends and im not talkative anymore even though in my head i wanted to talk to them but i just cant. So now I dont smoke weed anymore cuz my anxiety added paranoia.

Weed can cause anxiety in and of itself. Not just social anxiety. Physical anxiety is what I believe the problem to be, and that in turn causes the social anxiety.
You don't have to have "underlying issues" or any of that nonsense. I know the chillest people who smoke a joint and won't say a word, just freak out in their own minds so they don't touch the stuff. These are people who back in high school loved pot. If you get anxious while high but you're not when you're sober then point the finger at the chemical THC which is screwing with your brains and making you more anxious which is probably the most common side effect of the drug that is reported. Especially if you have been smoking too much, this can happen to veteran potheads and all of a sudden they can't smoke weed ever again. But are they going to quit? It's probably going to take them some time to figure it out, that there are no longer any positive effects and that the experience has been ruined by overdoing it. That's what happened to me it took forever to admit, since for the longest time before I started getting crazy anxious, I loved the herb.
Someone said people with anxiety problems get anxious when they are stoned. That's not always true. Sometimes people with genuine anxiety problems calm down when they smoke a bowl and get relaxed. Sometimes people with no anxiety issues whatsoever will go completely insane off the tiniest hit and be begging for mercy while heart is pounding out of chest. It can go either way. It doesn't depend on the strain, that's irrelevant. It depends on the individuals personal physical reaction to THC, among other things like their history of abusing/using the drug and for how long. Mainly personal neurochemistry.

The anxiety symptoms I always got from weed were physical in nature - my mind would race a bit but the root of the issue would be that I was uncomfortable with the physiological effects that weed had on my body. Not just the increase in heart rate, weed generally made me feel like complete shit. I believe that it actually messed directly or indirectly with the part of my brain that is responsible for "fight or flight" response, the amygdala or whatever...

I still smoked through the anxiety which was stupid, I am a person that does stupid things like that. For whatever reason I still smoked over an ounce a week because when I built up a tolerance then I didn't get anxious anymore. But then the anxiety would surface when I was sober, and I had previously never had sober anxiety before. So there was this conservation of anxiety thing going on... I couldn't escape from the weed anxiety. Either I smoked occasionally and my highs would be more like panic attacks, or I smoked day in day out, had a great time, loved my herb but then I had experience really bad withdrawals. The withdrawals would obviously include anxiety, due to the anxiety that I had always had smoking weed in the beginning. Smoking more weed wasn't just making that problem disappear - the problem that I shouldn't have ever touched weed to begin with since it's such a garbage drug for me with horrible side effects. I shouldn't have been smoking weed in the first place, due to the panic issues it caused me. But, the way it plays on the reward system of the brain is similar to opioids and cocaine and other psychologically addictive drugs. So I was hooked even though I thought it was a stupid drug basically. Which is weird, I got hooked fast too. Quicker and more seriously and intensely than with opioids, which I have no trouble controlling to a reasonable level when I use them for my chronic back pain. I've been sniffing bumps heroin for years due to my chronic pain and never have I experienced anything remotely like the intense cravings, obsessive thoughts, and physical withdrawal symptoms that I had with weed and I do use opioids daily. I wish I knew about them earlier in life... I would have thrown my bong in the garbage with a smile. Plus, I wouldn't have extreme anxiety right now because the opioid high doesn't have anxiety as a side effect.

Now I suffer from chronic extreme anxiety and panic disorder, which I never had before I smoked all that weed. There is an obvious correlation between the psychotic break that I had and how stoned I had been for many years. It surfaced when I quit blazing. No I wasn't self medicating with weed. As I explained, I was getting really high all day and

Figure 7.16 Snapshot of the Bluelight forum.

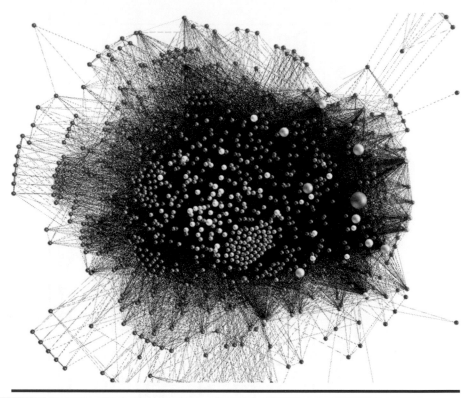

Figure 7.17 Graph of Bluelight forum.

discussion threads is related to the amygdala, which is a part of the brain used in decision-making, memory, and emotional reactions. This is part of the limbic system. An international group of researchers led by Vanderbilt University has discovered that there are cannabinoid receptors in the amygdala. A second set of discussion threads discuss the plant Sativa that has been used as a hallucinogenic, hypnotic, sedative agent.

The next semantic group discussed the chemical substance **entheogen** that has been used in religious, shamanic, and spiritual contexts and which may be synthesized from natural species. These are related to the practice of combining marijuana use with these semi-religious practices.

Finally, the last group is related to a BBC documentary about a story of an elderly lady's trials and tribulations after smoking marijuana.

7.5 Conclusion

The prevalence of online social networks has enabled users to communicate, connect, and share content. In this chapter, a method is presented for identifying these

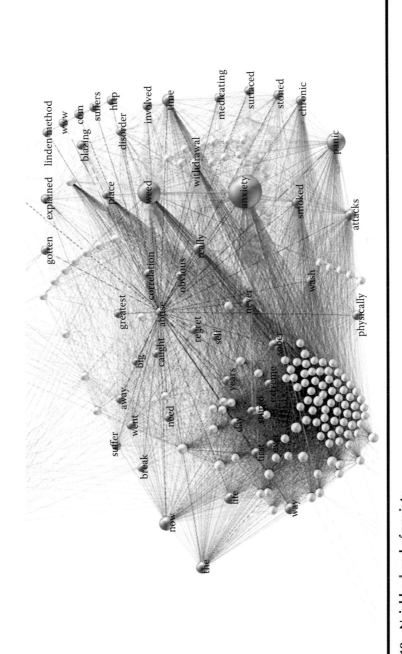

Figure 7.18 Neighborhood of anxiety.

themes and patterns within patient data. This methodology includes extraction of the main themes or patterns in the data and linking those themes back to the corpus from which they were generated. In our research, we partitioned graphs from terms gathered from Twitter and mental health forums. Our research objectives included identifying the topics being discussed in an online forum and tweets, identifying the set of topics that would allow us to differentiate between discussion forums on different behavioral health issues, determining similarities between discussion forums, and retrieving the most appropriate discussion forum data given a user query.

References

1. http://www.pwc.com/us/en/health-industries/publications/health-care-social-media.html. Accessed May 2016.
2. Statistic Brain. Twitter statistics, 2014. http://bit.ly/18KIwd2. Accessed January 5, 2016.
3. Jan-Are K. Johnsen, Jan H. Rosenvinge, and Deede Gammon. Online group interaction and mental health: An analysis of three online discussion forums. *Scandinavian Journal of Psychology*, 43(5):445–449, 2002.
4. Georgios Paltoglou and Mike Thelwall. Twitter, myspace, digg: Unsupervised sentiment analysis in social media. *ACM Transactions on Intelligent Systems Technology*, 3(4):66:1–66:19, September 2012.
5. Zhiyuan Chen and Bing Liu. Topic modeling using topics from many domains, lifelong learning and big data. In Proceedings of the 31th International Conference on Machine Learning, ICML 2014, Beijing, China, June 21–26, 2014, pp. 703–711, 2014.
6. Jianfeng Si, Arjun Mukherjee, Bing Liu, Sinno Jialin Pan, Qing Li, and Huayi Li. Exploiting social relations and sentiment for stock prediction. In Proceedings of the 2014 Conference on Empirical Methods in Natural Language Processing, EMNLP 2014, October 25–29, 2014, Doha, Qatar, A meeting of SIGDAT, a Special Interest Group of the ACL, pp. 1139–1145, 2014.
7. Mark Newman. Fast algorithm for detecting community structure in networks. *Physical Review*, 2004.
8. Andranik Tumasjan, Timm Oliver Sprenger, Philipp G. Sandner, and Isabell M. Welpe. Predicting elections with twitter: What 140 characters reveal about political sentiment. *ICWSM*, 10:178–185, 2010.
9. Huayi Li, Arjun Mukherjee, Bing Liu, Rachel Kornfield, and Sherry Emery. Detecting campaign promoters on twitter using Markov random fields. In 2014 IEEE International Conference on Data Mining, ICDM 2014, Shenzhen, China, December 14–17, 2014, pp. 290–299, 2014.
10. CDC. Available online at http://nccd.cdc.gov/sbroker/WEATSQL.exe/weat/freqyear.hsql.
11. David M. Blei. Probabilistic topic models. *Communications of the ACM*, 55(4):77–84, April 2012.
12. Bing Liu. *Sentiment Analysis and Opinion Mining. Synthesis Lectures on Human Language Technologies*. Morgan & Claypool Publishers, San Rafael, California, 2012.

13. Dmitry Davidov, Oren Tsur, and Ari Rappoport. Enhanced sentiment learning using twitter hashtags and smileys. In COLING 2010, 23rd International Conference on Computational Linguistics, Posters Volume, August 23–27, 2010, Beijing, China, pp. 241–249, 2010.
14. Charu C. Aggarwal and Cheng Xiang Zhai, editors. *Mining Text Data*. Springer, New York, 2012.
15. Maria-Evgenia G. Rossi, Fragkiskos D. Malliaros, and Michalis Vazirgiannis. Spread it good, spread it fast: Identification of influential nodes in social networks. In Proceedings of the 24th International Conference on World Wide Web Companion, WWW 2015, Florence, Italy, May 18–22, 2015—Companion Volume, pp. 101–102, 2015.
16. Mark Matthews, Saeed Abdullah, Geri Gay, and Tanzeem Choudhury. Tracking mental well-being: Balancing rich sensing and patient needs. *IEEE Computer*, 47(4):36–43, 2014.
17. Byron W. Keating, John A. Campbell, and Peter Radoll. Evaluating a new pattern development process for interface design: Application to mental health services. In Proceedings of the International Conference on Information Systems, ICIS 2013, Milano, Italy, December 15–18, 2013, 2013.
18. Amayas Abboute, Yasser Boudjeriou, Gilles Entringer, Jerome Aze, Sandra Bringay, and Pascal Poncelet. Mining twitter for suicide prevention. In Natural Language Processing and Information Systems—19th International Conference on Applications of Natural Language to Information Systems, NLDB 2014, Montpellier, France, June 18–20, 2014. Proceedings, pp. 250–253, 2014.
19. Scott Burton, Christophe Giraud-Carrier, and Carl Hanson. Tracking suicide risk factors through twitter in the US. *Crisis*, 35(1), 2014.
20. Galit Nimrod. From knowledge to hope: Online depression communities. *International Journal on Disability and Human Development*, 11(1):23–30, 2012.
21. Ryen W. White and Eric Horvitz. Cyberchondria: Studies of the escalation of medical concerns in web search. *ACM Transactions on Information Systems*, 27(4), 2009.
22. Robert S. Wilson, Ana W. Capuano, Patricia A. Boyle, George M. Hoganson, Loren P. Hizel, Raj C. Shah, Sukriti Nag, Julie A. Schneider, Steven E. Arnold, and David A Bennett. Clinical–pathologic study of depressive symptoms and cognitive decline in old age. *Neurology*, 83(8):702–709, 2014.
23. BBC, 2013. Available online at http://www.bbc.com/news/health-23192252.
24. WHO. Available online at http://www.who.int/mentalhealth/prevention/suicide/wspd/en/.
25. Georgios Paltoglou and Mike Thelwall. Twitter, myspace, digg: Unsupervised sentiment analysis in social media. *ACM Transactions on Intelligent Systems Technology*, 3(4):66:1–66:19, September 2012.
26. Jason B. Luoma, Catherine E. Martin, and Jane L. Pearson. Contact with mental health and primary care providers before suicide: A review of the evidence. *American Journal of Psychiatry*, 159(6):909–916, 2002.
27. Mitja D. Back, Juliane M. Stopfer, Simine Vazire, Sam Gaddis, Stefan C. Schmukle, Boris Egloff, and Samuel D. Gosling. Facebook profiles reflect actual personality, not self-idealization. *Psychological Science*, 21(3):372–374, 2010.
28. Miles Efron and Megan Winget. Questions are content: A taxonomy of questions in a microblogging environment. In Proceedings of the 73rd ASIS&T Annual Meeting on Navigating Streams in an Information Ecosystem—Volume 47, ASIS&T '10, pp. 27:1–27:10, Silver Springs, MD, USA, 2010. American Society for Information Science.

29. Munmun De Choudhury, Michael Gamon, Aaron Ho, and Asta Roseway. "Moon phrases": A social media facilitated tool for emotional reflection and wellness. In 7th International Conference on Pervasive Computing Technologies for Healthcare and Workshops, PervasiveHealth 2013, Venice, Italy, May 5–8, 2013, pp. 41–44, 2013.
30. Prabhakar Raghavan and Panayiotis Tsaparas. Mining significant associations in large scale text corpora. Proceedings IEEE 2002 International Conference on Data Mining, 2002.
31. Florian Beil, Martin Ester, and Xiaowei Xu. Frequent Term-Based Text Clustering. SIGKDD '02, Alberta, Canada, 2002.
32. Vincent D. Blondel, Jean-Loup Guillaume, Renaud Lambiotte, and Etienne Lefebvre. Fast unfolding of communities in large networks. *Journal of Statistical Mechanics*, 2008.
33. Alexander Pak and Patrick Paroubek. Twitter as a corpus for sentiment analysis and opinion mining. In Proceedings of the International Conference on Language Resources and Evaluation, LREC 2010, May 17–23, 2010, Valletta, Malta, 2010.

Chapter 8

The Heart of the Digital Workplace: Intelligent Search Moves the Measure from Efficiency to Proficiency for a Fortune 50 Healthcare Company

Jay Liebowitz and Diane Berry

Contents

8.1 Introduction

While the digital workplace conjures up images of working from the beach via mobile apps or viewing holographic analytics in a shared office space, according to the research firm Gartner in a recent report, the digital workplace constitutes an "ongoing, deliberate approach to facilitating an agile response to workplace changes by delivering a more consumer-like computing environment" [1]. The report, "Digital Workplace Organizational Change Imperatives," further states that the digital workplace "delivers a more social, mobile, accessible and data-driven work environment that is better able to exploit changing business conditions."

Social and mobile are important form factors of the "accessible, data-driven work environment." It is the very data that makes possible the digital workplace that also creates significant roadblocks to its success, regardless of the interaction channel. Whether coined Big Data, information, knowledge. or just plain data, it comes in all shapes and sizes and in all forms, and the vast majority of it is unstructured. It has become too large and fast-changing to leverage in the ways of the past—system integrations, data migrations, and master data management programs that required years of effort and millions of dollars to enact.

What matters for the digital workplace, particularly for healthcare companies, is how quickly, securely, and relevantly data and information can be incorporated into everyday work to help people become more agile in response to change: to learn faster and to work smarter and better to serve customers, consumers, and patients. To understand how healthcare companies (who by definition are heavily reliant upon knowledge) are evolving to a digital workplace and the role of intelligent search in that effort, interviews were conducted with employees of several companies, including a highly diverse Fortune 50 Healthcare Company. This excerpt of the study focuses on the Fortune 50 Healthcare Company, which requested its name be withheld as its transformation to a digital workplace, including its use of Intelligent Search, is considered to be a strategic competitive differentiator.

8.2 The Ecosystem of Record Meets Systems of Insight

Employees are already overwhelmed by information. Sixty-five percent of executives surveyed rated the overwhelmed employee an urgent or important trend in a recent Deloitte research report, *Global Human Capital Trends: Engaging the 21st Century Workforce*. Knowledge workers find the information they need to do their jobs only 56% of the time, although they spend 36% of their time searching for and consolidating it, according to the June 2014 IDC (idc.com) report, "The Knowledge Quotient: Unlocking the Hidden Value of Information." The same IDC report states that 61% of knowledge workers regularly access four or more systems to get the information they need to do their jobs, and 13% access 11 or more systems. The digital workplace creates abundantly more data, at higher rates, and places significantly greater value on its access—while at the same time opening up new systems, too. Access to the most relevant data becomes the primary challenge.

Technologies that enable the digital workplace are undergoing transformation. According to Microsoft CEO Satya Nadella, "…we are at the dawn of a new generation of business systems. With the ability to reason over data, we now can build these systems of intelligence…. Only when businesses create a culture that empowers everyone to have access to data and insight that drive action will they be positioned to truly transform."*

What enables such systems of intelligence (or cognitive systems) is a combination of search, analytics, and machine learning. Enterprise search had been generally understood as providing better and faster ways of finding information in organizational databases and varied information systems. The value provided by such systems was considered to be gains in efficiency from finding information faster. Now termed "Insight Engines" by Gartner [2], "Cognitive Search" by research firm Forrester [3], and Intelligent Search by technology providers such as Coveo, these highly advanced technologies enable companies to virtually unify data from within their entire "ecosystems of record," create structure where none existed before (in unstructured information), and uncover relationships among data from vastly different systems. Perhaps most importantly, the technology also understands and promotes relationships between those data and the context of employees, customers, and partners—anywhere and anytime. Understanding how people interact with information via analytics provides machine learning algorithms with the data to continuously learn and present ever more relevant information to people, often without an explicit search being conducted. As an example, intelligent search can "know" what an employee is working on that created success for other employees with similar needs, and simply show the information that will help, without any explicit search being done. The search is conducted in the background: each individual's interaction with each piece of data is analyzed and recorded via analytics, while the machine learning automatically learns and tunes what is presented. Of course, active searches are also enabled and interactions are captured. When working with search terms, the technology begins to understand intent based on what each user does with the information presented, over time.

Such technology can be grouped under the broad category Cognitive Systems, which unsurprisingly is projected to grow to $31.2 billion in spending globally by 2019, according to IDC, a market intelligence firm. Healthcare companies are reported by the same firm as among the top three consumers of Cognitive Systems (at 18%, with Banking at 20% and Retail at 17%) [4].

---

* Satya Nadella, Microsoft CEO, speaking at the Microsoft Convergence Conference in 2015.

Although efficiency and the ensuing increase in productivity are important, clearly such spending indicates even greater returns for the digital workplace. Clearly, this includes a move toward "proficiency" in near real time and the value that more knowledge brings to organizations, from better outcomes for patients to faster time to market for new products. "Upskilling" employees with contextually relevant information provides significant value to the organization. In fact, UpSkill America (upskillamerica.org), supported by President Obama, was established in 2014 as a public/private partnership. Today, it includes several government agencies and more than 100 companies. According to UpSkill America, as well as Bersin by Deloitte (home.bersin.com) recent research, upskilling refers to the skills development and training of employees for enhancing skill sets of employees to provide better performance in their current positions, equipping employees with the skills and opportunities required to advance to higher paying positions, and meeting the increasing need for higher-level skills to support higher value-added activities in the economy. As automation more often handles more repetitive and lower-level tasks, the workforce requires higher-level and more adaptive skills.

If people and knowledge are determined to be the key assets to the organization, then there should be improved ways to connect the two in meaningful ways, to allow employees, customers, and partners to become more proficient, productive, and agile in their daily work. In fact, crowd-sourced knowledge management is being advocated by many companies like Lithium (lithium.com) and Coveo (coveo.com), in terms of letting the users define what is needed and utilized through involving them and their digital conversations.

With the more consumer-like experience of the digital workplace, applications will become even more fragmented and specialized; organizations will favor best-of-breed technologies and will continue moving to the cloud at a rapid pace. According to our interviews, IT executives and business leaders are realizing that the "system of record" model has failed and instead they are embracing the full "ecosystem of record," defined as all of the legacy applications of the past, and new, consumer-like cloud sources containing all of an organization's work and intellectual capital, mapped to organizational know-how. Gartner refers to the "portfolio of digital workplace tools and services, which is applied to customers, partners and employees," [1] as part of the Digital Workplace. Organizations are applying this model to consolidate information via secure, unified indexing technology, and success requires relevance, contextual accuracy, high levels of security, and value for the end user accomplishing a task.

The digital workplace better engages and leverages digital literates and information assets. If companies live on knowledge, then connecting the right information with the right person at the right point in time via intelligent search is at the heart. The current transformation of search—including analytics and machine learning—will connect everyone with the information they need to do their work, everywhere, and regardless of form factor. Intelligent search should have a personalized approach to knowing the user's patterns and preferences—and those of similar people—so that predictive analysis capabilities can recommend the information to help the user in solving their tasks and achieving their goals.

Companies like Coveo, Logitech (Logitech.com), Amazon (amazon.com), and others are applying such technology to connect relevant insights from the systems of record to the systems of engagement (consumerism), with the effect of moving from efficiency to proficiency—all centered on increased customer engagement. Injecting content into the context of the employees, partners, and customers then enables the promise of the digital workplace.

8.2.1 A Fortune 50 Healthcare Company Story: Capitalizing on Search Innovation

Within the highly regulated Healthcare industry and reliant upon knowledge, expertise, and agility for innovation, this Fortune 50 Healthcare Company is in the beginning stages of its journey toward a digital workplace; however, it exhibits many of the characteristics of such agile, engaged workplaces—including consumer-like experiences. The organization's bottom-up approach to deployment and broad, secure connectivity leverage intelligent search techniques to help employees to better connect and innovate. Growing to a $3 billion company, one division of the company's mission is to "reduce time to market, increase R&D productivity, innovate and create differentiated products, leverage IT for competitive advantage, and provide flexibility to support different business needs." Over recent years, the vision has grown from being a single-product company to one that encompasses its area of healthcare in greater totality.

Going back to 2011, the Research and Development Division (R&D) within the group realized that easy and quick access to knowledge assets was critical to enabling innovation—assets that were dispersed across more than 30 different systems. An intelligent search tool based on Coveo technology was created by the R&D team to allow their highly skilled engineers and scientists to work in more meaningful ways through moving from "search and navigate" to ultimately creating enriching discussions among scientists and engineers, increasing collaboration across functional silos.

Currently, there are 1500–1600 users of the tool, and there is potential to broaden to even more employees throughout the division, plus additional divisions of the Fortune 50 company. As of this writing, four additional divisions have deployed the Coveo technology.

Before having Intelligent Search, employees report that it was extremely difficult to find information necessary to do their work. The Executive Sponsor of the program and former Vice President of R&D, said:

> Before, 18% of R&D time was spent just looking for information (let alone actually finding what was needed). The infrastructure hadn't kept up with growth. There was no way to access information. You would

have people seeking a particular document created by someone, who may have left the company, and they would go from person to person—it would take weeks to find a single document. Intelligent Search gave us a huge advantage that we could just connect all of our 30+ systems easily and fast. The tool permeates nearly everything we do.

In today's environment, innovation and reducing time to market are critical goals.

Companies must be able to work in "smarter" ways even as complexity grows, another tenet of the digital workplace, as this executive points out:

Increases in complexity are exponential, it's not just two times, it's a factor of times more complex. In the past, we would have 50 to 75 people working on a single product in the early stages. Today, you can't have that many. You need to do more with less, and intelligent search allows us to do that.

He adds:

Intelligent Search helps people understand what a particular scientist has been working on, his or her research agenda, so they can better approach them for a discussion and collaborate with them, with confidence. The best discoveries come from engagement, when people are comfortable connecting and sharing ideas.

As evidenced by these quotes, organizations such as this Fortune 50 Healthcare Company division can apply these types of search technologies to transform the way they do work. For example, according to the Intelligent Search Program Lead, the tools allow for the "integration of knowledge and know-how into computational systems in order to access and solve complex problems normally requiring a high level of human intervention and expertise." Specifically, it can allow insights to be developed across functional areas by capturing, sharing, applying, and generating knowledge from the Intelligent-Search produced contents. The Program Lead further states that

With 34 sources/systems of information, 5 million documents, and 10 billion relations, our tool is bringing all these together in a "smart" fashion. For example, finding specific information previously would take 1–2 months with multiple SMEs (Subject Matter Experts), and now only takes 1–2 minutes through using it.

Of course, as pointed out in the Spring 2015 MIT Sloan Management Review article, "Minding the Analytics Gap," a gap often exists between the ability to produce analytics results and the ability to apply them effectively in business issues. Senior executives at the company wanted to be sure that the program was producing business value. To help in this regard, a Return on Investment Estimation for Intelligent Search was calculated starting in 2013. One approach used a query-based method whereby queries were classified as "basic search," "informational search," "investigational search," and "re-creation of information" buckets; the total hours saved amounted to approximately $6.1 million to the organization annually. However, as the team agrees, this remains a measure of "efficiency." They firmly believe the results are much higher, especially related to increases in proficiency and the ensuing benefits. Anecdotal evidence: Fewer recalls (thanks to better knowledge use at all stages of product development), a better ability to meet regulatory requirements on first attempts, and the ability to innovate and go to market faster speak to much greater dollar impact.

The North America IT R&D Director and Intelligent Search IT Partner at the organization describes the impact on revenue enhancement and cost avoidance: "The output of individuals increases in part with this technology and access to prior work… even a one-day reduction in the time to market can mean hundreds of millions of dollars for a blockbuster product."

8.2.2 Staying in "the Flow"

Of course, key to a digital workplace is improving proficiency as people work—in Knowledge Management circles, this is termed as being "in the flow of work." The former VP R&D expressed how such learning, via Intelligent Search, increased proficiency, which then provided "confidence building" and "engagement" in this regard:

> For new (especially younger) employees, it is hard to approach more experienced people. Our intelligent search accelerates the confidence level of people in the organization by helping them to understand what a particular scientist has been working on (and confidence drives engagement, communication, and innovation).

One of the end users, a Compliance Assessor and Trainer, expressed how Intelligent Search helped her to "learn at the point of need":

> We can relate code names to what a clinical study actually is. We use so many code names for different studies that it's difficult to remember. For example, what "Lucy" was—now we can just plug in the word Lucy and see exactly what it is (so the system automatically uncovers the ontology used in an organization and relates concepts and words together). With new products coming out, I need to know for planning purposes what each of them are, including their characteristics so I can plan for audits.

Even beyond having the information in the flow of work, and the associated agility and upskilling benefits, healthcare organizations also find that intelligent search technologies reduce risks of delay in going to market with new products. Stringent regulations regarding document control can mean months to years of delay if even a single, validated document from the product development and testing process cannot be found. The Compliance Assessor and Trainer noted:

> If we cannot find a validated document it is non-conformant. We'd need to figure out why we had a document control issue and document that and fix it. If that happens, then we can't even simply recreate the document, we need to follow the process and even retest to ensure the findings are replicable, and the paperwork that proves it was tested to "X" standard. This is why people would spend weeks or months trying to find a certain document versus recreating it.

The Search Administrator cites this as a proof-point when the program was initially launched:

> In one case, we were about to re-do a study, because we could not find a particular document. We just plugged it into the first roll-out of Intelligent Search and there it was—saving months and months of work.

Clearly, when the knowledge that matters is recommended based on context to the employee, proficiency increases through use of that relevant information. The Fortune 50 Healthcare Company also reports that this increases the satisfaction and engagement of its highly educated workforce: "People feel more rewarded when they are learning constantly," said the program administrator.

Such ability to increase proficiency in the flow of work has far-reaching impact in the digital workplace. According to Sonus Networks, employee and customer proficiency is an important area of focus in terms of allowing their employees to "upskill" in the flow of work, and allowing their customers to become more savvy through Sonus' ability to provide them with more intelligent, informative customer portals. "Our definition of 'customer' has evolved," said Sonus CIO Bill Parks, to include "external customers—direct—large partners and distributors, indirect partners and all of their end customers. We needed the capability to understand all of them and to satisfy all of their varied needs."

Just as with the Fortune 50 Healthcare Company, adoption of these new, intelligent technologies makes sense to line managers and employees, who welcome the consumer-like experience.

8.3 Viral Employee Engagement

A tenet of the digital workplace is engagement, via consumer-like experiences with data. The Fortune 50 Healthcare Company's experience in implementing this new technology was a departure for the organization, relying on viral adoption versus top-down mandates. A Senior Manager of Controls Automation and the Intelligent Search IT Administrator described the approach:

> We planned to let 80 people start using it initially, and it ended up being 110 because people heard about it. Others saw what was going on and also wanted it. When we wanted to expand, we just had the people talk—everyone said we want this, you can't take it away! Management really appreciated that kind of adoption and return. It wasn't that they were saying here's a new system and you have to use it—it was the people, the engineers and scientists saying, we want to use this!

This division of the Fortune 50 Healthcare Company, along with its sister-companies, is well positioned to capitalize on using approaches such as Intelligent Search to transform the way its employees work. In the near term, the program's developers would like to also incorporate the people expertise-finding features of the technology with the corporate HR system, as well as to take advantage of the user analytics and machine learning capabilities of Coveo. The expertise-finding feature will allow the potential for increased connections between experts to stimulate collaboration and innovation, as well as taking advantage of analytics for predictive modeling. Also, to further increase the penetration of Intelligent Search, the User Support Group at the division stimulates interest in the program among like-minded professionals.

8.3.1 Agility: Hallmark of the Digital Workplace

As the Fortune 50 Healthcare Company found, in today's digitally enabled workplace, it is possible—even required—to do more with less, and key to enabling such employee agility is providing contextually relevant knowledge in the flow of work. More empowered, engaged employees are better able to rapidly respond to and even uncover trends before they start.

Real-time gains in proficiency increase the agility of the organization as well as its customer bases. As customers gain proficiency and their interactions are handled via self-service, support analysts and engineers are freed of repetitive tasks, as described by Sonus Technologies. With the information they need at their fingertips, they become able to handle higher-level work more accurately and more quickly—increasing employee engagement and satisfaction (and therefore retention) and reducing time to productivity.

More agile companies can go to market faster, in entirely new ways. Sonus' Bill Parks discussed the ability to go to market faster after acquisitions: "Following M&A, the ability to assimilate data from multiple sources is so valuable to get to market faster. Our industry is still in a period of transition, and understanding where that evolution is going, having the ability to move as quickly as possible, getting there before anyone else, Coveo helps extensively."

Agility in the intelligent search deployment, management, and continuous improvement also supports digital workplace success. The Fortune 50 Healthcare Company reported its ability to quickly create connectors to all of their 34 different systems across their "ecosystem of record."

The Executive Sponsor of the program noted the importance of easily leveraging all of the company's systems:

> The beauty of this technology is that it forms an umbrella over all of your systems, you can leverage what's in legacy systems and you can leverage what's in newer systems. We tried to do something like this two or three times in the past, but by the time we implemented and moved information into a new infrastructure, it was obsolete, people wouldn't use it, and we'd have to change. Now with this technology, we can simply add sources to our infrastructure over time and it never becomes obsolete.

Sonus' Program Manager notes that his organization had a working cloud solution in place with single sign-on and guided search across five different information sources in less than a month after its acquisition: "This was an important, quick win right away," he said, and was instrumental in the technology's adoption by the sales department, in addition to support.

8.3.2 The Analytics of Experience

Important to both agility and quality, the ability to tune the relevance of results and the transparency of that relevance seem to be the most important factors for adoption and success of intelligent search. As with all technology, if it doesn't provide value, people will not adopt it, and search without superb relevance falls flat. Particularly in the digital workplace, relevance is required for employee engagement via a consumer-like experience. In order to tune relevance, one must understand user experience and behavior with content, visible through analytics, which track the clickstream of all data interactions. The ability to review analytics and manually adjust relevance is in common use within sophisticated search platforms. However, for organizations to become the "Amazons" of support and all operations, it's important to automate the tuning of relevance, through applying machine learning to usage analytics. This capability is employed by customers of Coveo, reducing both effort associated with managing search and reliance upon deep data classification programs.

With the use of analytics on the actual content, and people's interaction with that content, organizations are able to apply knowledge discovery techniques for predictive modeling and proactive insights. This allows for the creation of early warning systems to predict possible customer problems, and prescribe training paths and webinars that may be relevant for the customer. Because the system is constantly learning, changes in seasonality, products, terminology, and usage are all automatically incorporated.

Such ability to know what information matters, to whom, and when, enables organizations to engage employees and customers in a much more agile manner— and to place customer needs at the center of operations. These types of intelligent search technologies support and enable business and digital transformation.

8.3.3 Recommendations for Healthcare Organization Success with Intelligent Search for the Digital Workplace

The digital transformation, covering both digital business and the digital workplace, creates increased risk of disruption, as well as increased opportunities for gain. Each of the companies interviewed for this study has an increased risk of "switching"— if customers are not engaged and if the customer experience isn't as expected or desired, it is much easier to change providers than at any time in the past. The Fortune 50 Healthcare Company division has more competition today than at any time in the past, and any reduction in innovation and its market leadership would surely see its customers defecting. This organization has chosen a knowledge transformation for its digital workplace success, utilizing intelligent search to connect the dots between all of their information assets and their employees.

Based on this company's experiences, what can be learned for organizations to be able to compete in the digital workplace? First, look at the "meta-effects" of search technologies. Improved search and findability not only can lead to improvement in employee satisfaction and experience but also can increase customer engagement, when utilized in self-service portals, by increasing their proficiency with a company's products. This meta-effect works in terms of improving the "proficiency" of both customers and employees, whether transforming the way employees work through acquiring new skills from working in smarter ways to providing increased customer proficiency through more tailored interactions in self-service portals.

Second, knowledge management has now progressed from managing and curating knowledge to crowd curation and access, thanks in large part to machine learning and analytics. Organizations need to recognize this knowledge management transformation in order to keep up with their competition. Analytics, as applied to knowledge management and predictive modeling, enables crowd curation of knowledge based on crowd behavior, and the auto-tuning of relevance possible with the application of machine learning will also continue to be a growing trend in the future and key to engagement with knowledge. Of course, particularly for heavily regulated industries such as healthcare, curated/validated content will continue to be critical, along with the less formal, crowd-curated content.

Third, organizations can create economic value from the information ecosystem, as well as calculate a measurable return on investment through KPI (Key Performance Indicator)-driven analytics and reporting. The various vignettes in this case study–focused chapter discussed how those organizations are achieving impactful results based on broadly utilizing the new ecosystem of record.

Last, organizations must also take advantage of "learning at the point of need" in the flow of work. With our growing workforce of digital literates, they expect to be able to learn "just in time," when they need to do so.

Acknowledgment

The authors greatly appreciate the support of the employees from each of these companies who were interviewed for this study, as well as the support from Coveo.

References

1. Elise Olding, Matthew W. Cain, and Mike Gotta. Gartner, Inc. Digital Workplace Organizational Change Imperatives, October 27, 2014, G00270161.
2. Whit Andrews, Hanns Koehler-Kruener, and Tom Eid. Gartner, Inc. 'Insight Engines' Will Power Enterprise Search That Is Natural, Total and Proactive, December 8, 2015.
3. Rowan Curran and Mike Gualtieri. Forrester, Brief: Cognitive Search Is Ready to Rev Up Your Enterprise's IQ, May 2, 2016.
4. IDC, *Industry Spending on Cognitive Systems Soars*, May 5, 2016, Infographic (http:// www.idc.com/promo/thirdplatform/innovationaccelerators/infographics/cognitive -systems).

Chapter 9

The Promise of Big Data Analytics—Transcending Knowledge Discovery through Point-of-Care Applications

Lavi Oud

Contents

9.1 Introduction

Big data is becoming exponentially prevalent across all facets of healthcare, with increasing accessibility by clinicians, investigators, and policy makers. While often considered in reference to populations, the breadth and complexity of modern healthcare increasingly affords big data attributes to individual patients. Indeed, on a purely volume-based appraisal, the electronic health record (EHR) data of a typical middle-aged person can approximate the collected works of Shakespeare.[1]

The potential of big data–driven analytics to transform healthcare has been outlined in a recent report by the Institute of Medicine titled "Best Care at Lower Cost: The Path to Continuously Learning Health Care in America." The report stated that "achieving higher quality care at lower cost will require fundamental commitments… that foster continuous learning, as the lessons from research and each care experience are systematically captured, assessed, and translated into reliable care."[2]

This initiative was complemented by a recent call by President Obama for a Precision Medicine Initiative.[3] Followed by the recent National Institutes of Health's Precision Medicine Initiative Cohort Program, it aims to achieve "the right treatment at the right time to the right person" by tapping on an unprecedented scale the intersection of human genetics, environmental exposures, and lifestyle choices, allowable with the evolving contemporary big data analytics.[4]

Many inroads were already made to help realize the full potential of big data in patient care. Moreover, from a fiscal perspective, a report by McKinsey Global Institute suggests that creative and effective use of big data in US healthcare could create more than $300 billion in value annually, with two-thirds of this value being a result of reduced healthcare expenditures.[5]

However, while data sources and methods for generating medical evidence are changing radically, the explosive growth of big data has exposed an incremental strain when measured against the pace of expansion of big data analytics to point-of-care applications and targeted knowledge discovery.

When appraising the progress to date and future directions in big data analytics–based applications, the care of patients in an intensive care unit (ICU) and the specialty of critical care medicine can provide a unique prism to examine the aforementioned strain and promise of big data analytics in healthcare.

It is estimated that more than 5.7 million patients are admitted annually to the ICU in the United States,[6] accounting for nearly half of total hospital charges,[7] and nearly 1% of the national gross domestic product.[8] The data product associated with care of the critically ill embodies key elements of big data, generating even for individual patients high data volume, of remarkable variety and, importantly, at comparatively high velocity. Decision-making involving care of critically ill patients involves routinely time-sensitive, high-stakes elements and is uniquely suited to benefit from real-time targeted clinical decision support (CDS) tools.

However, as is the case with big data analytics, critical care medicine appears increasingly at a crossroad, affected substantially by big data–related constraints.

Thus, uncertainties involve basic systemic issues, including the actual number of available ICU beds in the United States,[8] the number of affected patients,[7] and the optimal organization of care delivery.[9] In addition, uncertainties remain about who should or should not be admitted to the ICU, with remarkable variation of utilization transcending case mix.[7,10]

The approach to care of critically ill patients often involves syndrome-based classification, with some of the more common syndromes of varying or uncertain validity and relevance to point-of-care application.[11–13] While the majority of patients admitted to the ICU survive hospitalization, it has been increasingly recognized that survivors commonly sustain substantial and often persistent physical, cognitive, and mental health–related disability,[14] frequently requiring transition to post-acute care facilities and high longitudinal utilization of healthcare resources.[15] However, the underlying mechanisms of these long-term sequelae, and thus means for prevention and remedy remain elusive.

At the same time, strain has become evident between the documented expansion of ICU bed infrastructure,[16] a projected shortfall of critical care physicians,[17] and concomitant suggestions of rather excessive and inappropriate ICU bed capacity and need to close many of the existing ICU beds.[18,19]

Each of the aforementioned critical care–related areas stands to benefit from both broad and targeted applications of big data–driven analytic approaches applied at the bedside, healthcare system level, and policy making.

This chapter (1) provides an overview of some of the commonly used big data repositories employed in critical care–related study and describes select big data analytics–enabled promising initiatives involving point-of-care applications and knowledge discovery, as applied to critical care medicine; (2) outlines future directions in bedside and research applications; and (3) addresses key contemporary and future challenges facing big data analytics.

9.2 Select Big Data Repositories Used in Critical Care Research and Point-of-Care Applications

A recent unprecedented growth in published critical care studies was fueled in part by broader use of large secondary data sets to answer novel questions. Secondary data are generally defined as data gathered for a specific reason (i.e., routine clinical care, clinical trial) and subsequently employed for a different goal. The available secondary data repositories with application to critical care vary substantially in the richness of clinical data, accessibility, and cost.

9.2.1 Administrative Data Sets

Administrative data sets usually provide limited clinical detail and are generally based on utilization claims. At their most basic form, these data repositories include patient demographics, use of select hospital resources, costs or charges, coded data on diseases and procedures, and key disposition outcomes.

The National Inpatient Sample (NIS) is the largest national administrative data repository of hospitalized patients in the United States and is based on representative annual sampling.[20] The State Inpatient Databases (SID) provides information on nearly 100% of nonfederal hospital stays in participating individual states.[21] Both NIS and SID provide de-identified patient data and are highly accessible to investigators at relatively low acquisition charges.

The Premier Healthcare database is administered by Premier Research Services and represents the largest inpatient drug utilization data set in the United States, based on more than 700 hospitals, adding more than 5 million inpatient discharges annually.[22] In addition, the data set includes time-stamped information on diagnostic studies and procedures. Although used in multiple studies to date, accessibility is relatively limited and has high costs, in excess of $50,000–$100,000.

9.2.2 Benchmarking and Quality Improvement Data

Available data sets contain richness of clinical detail on ICU-managed patients, thus allowing investigators broad insights when exploring links between structure, process of care, and patient/unit-level outcomes.

The APACHE data set was originally created to derive serially revised severity of illness scoring systems for critically ill patients, and is currently owned by Cerner.[23] The data set includes patient data from ICUs in voluntary hospital participants and provides APACHE-based risk adjustment. The data set has low accessibility, requiring partnership with Cerner.

A more recent resource of clinically rich data is available through the eICU Research Institute. The data originate from Philips eICU, currently the largest vendor of ICU telemedicine in the United States. The data set comes from more than 400 non-federal voluntary hospital participants and includes more than 3 million ICU patient-days.[24] As is the case with the APACHE data set, accessibility remains low.

9.2.3 Electronic Health Records

EHR would be an ideal source of clinically rich individual patient data to address a broad range of questions spanning patient, population, healthcare system, and policy-making levels. However, as noted later, substantial challenges remain in realizing EHR's full potential.

The Multiparameter Intelligent Monitoring in Intensive Care (MIMIC) database, currently in its third iteration (MIMIC III), is a highly detailed de-identified repository of more than 58,000 ICU admissions from 2001 to 2012 in the Beth Israel Deaconess Medical Center.[25] The data set includes patient demographics, code status, ICD-9 codes, hourly nurse-verified vital signs, severity of illness scores, ventilator settings, clinical laboratory data, detailed time-stamped medication records, fluid boluses, free text reports of imaging, ECGs, nursing and respiratory therapy notes, and discharge summaries. A separate high-resolution waveform data are available, but the latter are not linked to the MIMIC III clinical data base. The MIMIC data set has been among the most extensively studied ICU-specific data repositories for clinical research and point-of-care applications. The access to the data is free.

The Department of Veterans Affairs (VA) maintains an EHR-based data set of all VA inpatients in more than 100 hospitals. This data repository has been created to improve care in VA facilities under the Inpatient Evaluation Center.[26] The data set provides rich clinical detail and includes an excellent VA-specific risk-adjustment tool. The access to the data set is relatively limited and use requires partnering with VA investigators.

9.2.4 Completed Nationally Funded Studies

The National Heart, Lung, and Blood Institute maintains the Biologic Specimen and Data Repository Information Coordinating Center (BioLINCC).[27] The repository includes data from completed clinical trials and epidemiological studies. The data are highly and freely accessible to investigators.

9.3 Point-of-Care Applications of Big Data Analytics

Numerous recent reports described application of big data–derived analytics to bedside care of critically ill patients. The point-of-care–focused initiatives outlined below address areas spanning basics of data representation and use, through care decisions and prognostication (Table 9.1).

Effective care of critically ill patients commonly requires time-sensitive, high-stakes decisions. These decisions routinely require clinicians to review high-volume, often complex, data to identify key elements to guide decision-making. It has been

Table 9.1 Select Reported Point-of-Care Applications Based on Big Data–Derived Analytics in Critical Care

- Reduction of information overload, improvement of data utilization, and reduction of care errors[34–36]
- Guidance in patient triage[37]
- Improved efficiency in serial diagnostic testing[38]
- Advanced monitoring-based prediction of in-ICU clinical deterioration[39–42]
- Enhancement of efficacy and safety of therapeutics with narrow risk–benefit margins[43]
- Refinement of targeted resuscitative therapy[44]
- Refinement of outcome prediction during early care phases of care of critically ill patients[45–49]

recently estimated that the care of critically ill patients generates a median of 1348 individual data points per patient per day,[28] often with more than 120 data points per hour during the initial 10 h in the ICU.[29] In addition, the care of an ICU patient was found to involve, on average, 178 processes of care daily, requiring clinician oversight.[30] This magnitude of data would readily qualify as big data from the perspective of bedside clinicians engaged daily in complex analytical processes, as part decision-making for patient care.

Moreover, this volume, velocity, and complexity of critical care–related data load can be mentally demanding, time consuming, and associated with increased propensity for care errors. Not unexpectedly, a study by Rothschild and colleagues found on average 149.7 serious errors per 1000 patient-days in the ICU.[31]

Given this background, the introduction of EHR was expected to facilitate ready access to data, enhance care efficiencies, and improve patient outcomes. However, contemporary EHR-based data remain scattered and some studies reported increased time demands among ICU physicians after the introduction of EHR,[32] and a recent systematic review found no evidence for a positive impact on resource utilization or ICU or hospital morality.[33]

Because clinicians routinely seek patient-specific, relevant data elements, the practically value-neutral, scattered data, as generally presented in the contemporary EHR, may hinder time-sensitive critical decision processes. To examine the impact of an alternative approach to data access, retrieval, and decision-making in the ICU, investigators at the Mayo Clinic created a new platform of data representation that provided ICU physicians with real-time, high-value data, bundled into discrete packets.[34] When examined in a simulated environment, including several critically ill patients, the new platform led, when compared in a randomized, crossover study to the existing EHR interface, to sharp reduction in the number of median data points requiring review per patient (102 vs. 1008), with a lower cognitive load index. In addition, the new data representation platform resulted in a markedly shorter time to complete care tasks and reduced the number of errors per physician.[35] After live launch into a multi-ICU environment, the new data representation system reduced time of data gathering by 25% per patient and enhanced efficiency of data access, which was perceived to be significantly less difficult and demanding.[36]

Patients are commonly admitted to the ICU in the United States for monitoring, with many never requiring life-support interventions. Thus, clinicians' ability to reliably identify those "too well" to benefit from ICU admission can inform more efficient resource allocation and enhance availability of ICU beds for critically ill patients. A recent preliminary report by Vranas et al. described use of unsupervised machine learning technique trained on a multicenter cohort in California and found that approximately 23% of ICU patients could be "too well" to benefit from ICU care.[37] The potential to apply these findings to individual patient triage requires further study.

Diagnostic studies are commonly repeated in ICU patients as part of clinicians' efforts to identify evolving deterioration. However, many of these repetitive tests do not affect prevention or care, though they can be associated with high costs and, at times, adverse effects. Using the MIMIC data set, Cismondi et al. developed predictive models to inform clinicians whether a laboratory test has changed significantly since last determination in patients admitted for gastrointestinal bleeding.[38]

ICU patients undergo routinely broad continuous and intermittent monitoring, in part to help prevent deterioration, well before reaching an overt, consequential stage. However, catastrophic events can occur unexpectedly. Clinicians' ability to identify such patients early can lead to effectively targeted preventative and interventional measures and improve patient outcomes. A recent study by Moss et al. using a large data set of vital signs and waveforms from a time series resulted in identifying unique signatures for respiratory failure and hemorrhage up to 24 h before such events across different ICUs.[39] Broader applications of predictive cardiopulmonary monitoring were reported by Pinsky et al., showing both the ability of machine learning algorithms to identify and "clean" artifacts versus true alerts[40] and the capability to identify patients developing cardiorespiratory insufficiency over 48 h before actual events.[41,42]

Practice patterns vary substantially among critical care clinicians, in part because of lack of adequate high-quality guiding data. This practice variability often involves interventions with a narrow risk–benefit margin. Data-rich analytics were used by Ghassemi et al. to optimize use of heparin during ICU stay,[43] and by Fialho et al. to model fluid responsiveness in critically ill patients.[44] Both studies demonstrate the potential to achieve better targeted therapy with reduced risk of adverse effects.

Accurate prognostic estimates for critically ill patients are a key part of ICU clinicians' choices of intervention and goals of care discussions with patients and their healthcare proxies. Available severity of illness scoring systems, commonly based on initial select patient attributes, show markedly improved outcome prediction in critically ill populations. However, the performance of these scores remains unsuitable for predictions for individual patients. Several recent initiatives have explored the impact of big data–based modeling on refining prognostic estimates among critically ill patients. Lehman et al. have demonstrated, using switching vector autoregressive framework to study vital signs, that the prognostic performance of the first 8 h of blood pressure time series is similar to that of the SAPS-I severity of illness scores.[45] These findings support the hypothesis that latent dynamic studies can produce more timely prognostic insights, as compared to snapshot-based severity of illness scores. Similar findings were noted by Mayaud et al., who found that data interrogation during hypotensive episodes among septic patients outperformed the prognostic capability of traditional severity of illness scores.[46] Finally, Lehman et al. demonstrated the feasibility of incorporating unstructured data (nurses' notes) into prognostic modeling of critically ill patients using hierarchical Dirichlet processes to automatically discover specific "topics." Combining data from nurses' notes during the first 24 h of ICU care with a traditional severity of illness score (SAPS-I) markedly improved the predictive performance of SAPS-I alone.[47]

The scalable capacity of EHR-based prediction models was recently reported by Mayhew et al.[48,49] Using supervised machine learning algorithms, the investigators studied a cohort of more than 165,000 patients in California with possible sepsis. They demonstrated robust time-dependent mortality signatures as early as 3 h into an emergency department stay. The findings showed that the models were robust to the computational requirements of large EHR-based data sets.

The highlighted big data–driven point-of-care applications underscore the rapid progress made in the use of innovative analytics methods. However, the reported studies were based for the most part on single-center data sets, and the generalizability of these findings to other care settings, patient populations, and data platforms has not been examined.

9.4 Knowledge Discovery and Big Data Analytics

The rapid expansion of accessible digitized secondary data repositories has led to exponential growth in reported discovery in critical care medicine. The following examples represent select highlights of recent reports driven by big data analytics.

The negative results of numerous clinical trials in patients with sepsis and acute respiratory distress syndrome (ARDS), two of the most common syndromes leading to critical illness, may reflect the heterogeneity of studied populations. Varying response to study interventions among enrolled patients may have masked interventions' benefit in specific patient subtypes that could not be identified a priori. Several recent reports support these concerns and may guide future targeted investigations.

A recent study by Wong and colleagues used unsupervised learning approach to examine genome-wide expression profiles in an observational cohort of pediatric septic shock and have identified distinct subtypes based on specific glucocorticoid receptor signaling, with distinct response to systemic steroids and different risk of death.[50] These preliminary findings provide support to further study the currently controversial corticosteroid therapy in septic shock patients.

Recombinant activated protein C (rAPC) was pulled off the market by the manufacturer several years ago after lack of clinical benefit in patients with septic shock and severe sepsis. However, in a hypothesis-generating post hoc analysis using whole-genome scans, investigators have identified patient subtypes with differential response to rAPC, defined objectively based on the presence of specific gene markers with absolute risk reduction of death >12.5%.[51] These findings affirm the limitations of the current syndrome-based patient enrollment criteria in clinical trials.

In a more recent post hoc study by Calfee and colleagues, using clinical and biological data from two prior ARDS Network studies, the investigators used latent class analysis to identify unique ARDS endotypes. Two distinct endotypes were identified with both divergent clinical outcomes and different response to mechanical ventilation with high PEEP, with one endotype benefiting from high PEEP, while the other showing detrimental effect.[52] The defining covariates for each endotype were not previously considered in ARDS trials and thus likely has contributed to prior negative reports.

Sepsis has been well known to be associated with high risk of long-term sequelae among hospital survivors. However, there has been uncertainty whether these observations reflect intrinsic long-term impact of sepsis or rather that of patients' baseline comorbidities. In a recent propensity-matched cohort study by Prescott and colleagues, using data from the US Health and Retirement Study, the investigators linked data on patients' baseline outpatient state, hospital data, and data on subsequent clinical course, to examine the absolute adjusted contribution of sepsis to long-term mortality. The study has demonstrated for the first time that even after extensive adjustment for baseline and other covariates, sepsis confers marked increase in long-term mortality among survivors, as compared to nonhospitalized patients, those hospitalized with an infection, but without sepsis, or those with systemic noninfectious inflammatory states.[53] These findings can help target further investigations into the underlying mechanisms of sepsis-mediated adverse effects in order to identify preventative and therapeutic interventions to mitigate its long-term sequelae.

As noted earlier, practice variability is commonplace in the care of critically ill patients, often coupled with uncertainty about actual benefit of used interventions. In two recent studies based on data from 139 ICUs in the United States compiled by Project IMPACT, the investigators demonstrated remarkable variability in use of arterial catheters, often in patients with a mortality risk of 2% or less.[54] Importantly, in a propensity-matched cohort analysis of the same population, this group found that arterial catheters were not associated with improved hospital mortality of medical patients undergoing mechanical ventilation, while use of arterial catheters was actually associated with increased risk of death among the subset of patients receiving vasopressors, namely, the subgroup most expected to benefit from such invasive monitoring.[55]

Finally, in a recent report by Wallace and colleagues,[56] the investigators examined regional versus national growth patterns in the number of ICU beds in the United States, given the noted substantial growth.[16] The study demonstrated that a 15% national growth in ICU bed numbers between 2000 and 2009 masked substantial regional variability, with 25% of hospital referral regions accounting for 75% of bed growth, with markedly variable population-adjusted regional changes in bed number (interquartile range –3.8 to +5.9 ICU beds per 100,000).[56] As previously noted, the actual "appropriate" number of ICU beds in the United States and the public health impact of noted growth remain debated.[17–19]

9.5 Future Directions

The initiatives described earlier, designed to inform clinicians at the point of care, demonstrated for the most part proof of concept. Leveraging the evolving capabilities of analytic tools to realize the full potential of big data would be geared to achieve real-time, patient- and context-specific accurate decision support. Termed by some as Dynamic Clinical Data Mining,[57] the envisioned system will continuously aggregate the full scope of individual patient's healthcare data during course of care. Clinicians will be presented with automated and query-responsive decision support on diagnosis, triage, intervention, and prognosis, based on continuously updated population-level data analytics on similar patients.[57] Fully operational, this type of system could bring unprecedented precision to individual care decisions.

When examining knowledge discovery, the randomized controlled trial (RCT), though considered the standard approach to examining therapeutic interventions, has increasingly acknowledged shortcomings. These include the following: (a) high costs and difficulties in conducting trials; (b) both lack of adequate applicability of findings to individual patients owing to average treatment effects being unrepresentative of a given individual, and for others, lack of population generalizability owing to study settings and populations not representing general practice; (c) discomfort among patients and physicians with randomization; and (d) prevalent long time lag to incorporation of RCT results into clinical practice. The challenges involved in the conduct of RCTs have led in part to recent widely cited analysis by Ioannidis titled provocatively "Why most published research findings are false."[58] The challenges associated with the conduct of high-quality RCTs may explain the current estimate that 80%–90% of medical decisions have no RCT-based evidentiary support.[59] This knowledge gap accounts for a substantial part of the observed clinical practice variability.

Big data has currently relatively low cost of acquisition and its high-value attributes would be considered a logical alternative to addressing the aforementioned concerns about RCTs. However, the key drawback of big data, as currently employed in knowledge discovery and clinical practice, is lack of capacity for causal inference of derived findings. Regardless of its size, detail of measurements, and sophisticated adjustment for covariates, common big data–based approaches cannot eliminate unmeasured factors that could explain apparent differential outcomes between intervention and control.

Nevertheless, building on the complementary strengths of RCTs and big data, a recent proposal by Angus advocates the fusion of the two to meet the goal of a self-learning health system.[60]

The proposed approach includes EHR-based patient screens for trial eligibility to broaden and ease enrollment, and capitalize on existing data capture of EHR for study-specific data acquisition, to ease the burden of data collection. In addition, it has been proposed to consider broadening the randomization unit when a study involves a full healthcare system, using randomization by cluster (i.e., randomizing a whole ward).

In order to address the realities of clinical practice, where comparisons of therapeutic effect commonly involve multiple rather than single alternatives, often conditional on other exposures, adaptive trial strategies can vary enrollment criteria over time, adding and dropping interventions over time.[61] Thus, to generate both broad (i.e., generalizable) estimates of an intervention's effect and narrower answers (i.e., addressing heterogeneity in treatment response), extremely broad enrollment would be required to address the whole breadth of a disease or syndrome. As noted by Angus, using the latter approach, embedding an RCT into the EHR would be not only efficient but also essential to meet scientific goals.[60]

Finally, in order to facilitate timely integration of RCT findings into clinical practice, Angus has proposed a new approach to trial design termed randomized, embedded, multifactorial, adaptive platform (REMAP). An example of such trial would be enrolling all willing patients in a healthcare system. Enrolled patients would then be preferentially assigned to the best-performing therapy regimens, essentially consistent with the principles of continuous quality improvement. With this approach, playing on the strengths of both RCTs and big data–driven analytical approach, the healthcare system would become self-learning, based on causal inference, with practically simultaneous knowledge generation and translation.[60]

Other evolving trends to facilitate knowledge discovery branched to an "open data" movement, recently spearheaded by the pharmaceutical industry. Examples include the creation of ClinicalStudyDataRequest.com website where, as of this writing, data of more than 900 completed studies have been posted by 13 pharmaceutical companies.[62]

Capitalizing on the open data movement, other proposed innovative approaches to knowledge discovery in healthcare include crowdsourcing (i.e., large groups of qualified individuals working asynchronously toward a common problem)[63] and "hackathons" or "datathons" (bringing together a large group of individuals with diverse but potentially complementary and synergistic skills and knowledge to collaborate toward a clinical problem).[64,65]

Given the often unrecognized biases and assumptions of individual investigators, which in turn can affect reported results, it is hoped that shared explorations of big data can provide all involved with inherent feedback and improve validity of new discoveries.

9.6 Contemporary and Future Challenges

The remarkable inroads made in bringing big data analytics to the forefront of patient care and the resultant innovative approaches to knowledge discovery and translation remain tempered by numerous systemic and external barriers. The challenges outlined below, spanning from science and methodology-related factors through both demonstrated and potential transformation of human behavior, both individually and at the societal level, remain to be effectively addressed in order to realize the full potential of big data to positively transform public health and individual patient care (Table 9.2).

While increasingly ubiquitous, the generated healthcare data remain, for the most part, scattered and segregated across individual practices, hospitals, healthcare systems, and state and federal agencies. Combined with prevalent lack of interoperability of contemporary commercial data platforms, the current state of big data continues to hinder assessment of the external validity of created local/regional solutions to point-of-care and quality measurement, and presents considerable challenges to knowledge discovery and translation.

At the clinical point of care, the contemporary CDS tools have shown, often counterintuitively, a potential to adversely affect patient care. The later risk stems from the often ubiquitous, context-free alerts, especially for prescription of therapeutics. The result has been, in turn, an "alert fatigue," where clinicians were found in one study to ignore 46% to 96% of alerts, thus risking missing important patient-specific messages.[66] In addition, end users often cannot turn off or change settings of CDS-based alerts because of liability concerns of vendors, though proposals have been made to address the latter.[67]

In addition, the promise of EHR in general and that of targeted, context-specific CDS to address clinicians' needs across the full continuum of patient care remains tempered by what is seen by many as a dehumanizing[68] and increasingly time-consuming[69] force on the current EHR-driven practice. The potential to effectively

Table 9.2 Contemporary and Future Challenges of Big Data–Derived Analytics

- Data scatter and segregation
- Inadequate interoperability
- Imbalance in development of data platforms between regulatory requirements and those related to priorities of end users
- Indiscriminate, context-free clinical alerts
- Limited use of unstructured data
- Inadequate data security
- Uncertain level of control of errors in source data
- Unpredictable impact of unquantifiable domains of individual and organizational healthcare-related operations
- Adversity between data generators and secondary users
- Potentially adverse impact of precision medicine-driven improvement in individual-level prognostic and predictive capabilities on healthcare financing, clinical practice, personal health-related coping and decision-making, and societal responses
- Disparate access to benefits of big data resources and related analytics capabilities among low-resource countries

address these concerns, highlighted in recent reports,[70,71] demonstrates opportunities to remedy the current state.

On the opposite side, educators voiced concerns that medical trainees may develop so-called automation bias and come to extensively rely on CDS tools in decision-making, rather than apply patient-specific, critical, independent thinking.[72] The validity of these concerns remains uncertain, but will require further examination as CDS systems become more broadly and effectively deployed.

Importantly, the ability of vendors of health information technology to systematically focus on improving the performance of available data platforms appears to be substantially hindered by lingering needs to prioritize compliance with vast regulatory requirements.[73] The aforementioned challenges may explain, as noted earlier, the finding of a recent systematic review showing the lack of positive impact of the EHR on resource utilization costs and mortality among critically ill patients.[33]

Although substantial progress has been shown in big data applications involving structured data (i.e., waveform), the promise of harnessing information from unstructured data (i.e., free text clinical documents and media files [e.g., pathology and radiology imaging]) remains largely untapped. While access to unstructured data in big data repositories is increasingly available, it is hoped that evolving sophistication of techniques for natural language processing will allow clinicians and researchers to tap the vast information locked in unstructured data.[74]

The transition of paper-based health data into large digitized data repositories was not matched with commensurate data security. The result has been, in turn, increased capacity for unauthorized access, leading to large-scale health data breaches, often with criminal intent. A recent study by Liu and colleagues on the "epidemiology" of health information breaches in the United States involving 500 or more individuals reported 949 data breaches, affecting 29 million records between 2010 and 2013, with the number of reported breaches rising over time.[75] These events, often reported in lay media, can in turn adversely affect patients' willingness to entrust their health information to clinicians and may lead to adverse health effects.[76] The breadth of data compromise can further rise with expected improvements in interoperability of data platforms and creation of national data repositories. Effective measures to assure data security remain an urgent target.

A key concern with the increasing availability of big data and its expanding application to clinical care, data discovery, and expected incremental impact on policy making has been the need to assure the veracity of unsupervised data gathering. Aptly warning against the risk of naïve use of big data, Zak Kohane of Harvard Medical School noted that "You really need to know something about medicine. If statistics lie, Big Data can lie in a very, very big way."[77] The latter concern has fueled an ongoing debate between proponents of evidence-based medicine (EBM) and those of big data applications. The key point of contention has been EBM's emphasis on explicit control of biases in both data collection and analysis, to maximize internal validity and to allow inferences on causality versus the common lack of specific protocol-guided approach in big data collection and analysis, aiming to

maximize precision and external validity. The concerns of traditional EBM proponents have been that algorithm-guided machine learning can identify patterns in
vast data sets, while the findings may not fully capture the clinical context, with
inability to address whether a finding is true, spurious, or affected by bias. A collaborative effort, building on the complementary strengths of each approach, holds
a potential to safely and effectively advance healthcare.[1,60]

Because provision of healthcare, both at the bedside and at a system level, is
inherently a human enterprise, even a perfectly accurate capture and analysis of
contemporarily collected clinical and institutional data cannot reliably identify the
multitude of intangible factors affecting differential practice and outcome patterns.
Thus, while data modeling can readily cluster analyses by individual facilities or
practitioners, available reports demonstrate that patient outcomes can vary, not
surprisingly, through otherwise undocumented communication patterns among
caregivers,[9,78] staffing variability,[9] and domains of organizational values and goals,
senior management involvement, and problem solving and learning.[78] Of note,
mere availability and use of protocols and specific processes of care often do not
differentiate varying performance in patient outcomes.[78] The lessons from these
studies suggest the need for caution when introducing big data–based findings to
clinical practice, quality assessment, and policy making, and underscore the importance of complementary tools to address inherent limitations of big data.

The human nature aspects in examination of the barriers to advancing the promise of big data were further highlighted after a recent proposal by the International
Committee of Medical Journal Editors that authors should be required to share
clinical trial data.[79] A recent editorial brought up the substantial animosity by some
investigators who create data sets, toward what they perceived as "research para-
sites," namely, other researchers using created data for other questions or for verification of the original findings.[80] While markedly beneficial, collaborative efforts
between primary data creators and new investigators continue to be reported,[81]
solutions to foster collegial and beneficial use of secondary data are sorely needed.

The recent enthusiasm about big data as a platform to drive the long-sought
goal of precision medicine, allowing truly individualized care, can lead to a much
needed positive impact on patient care. Nevertheless, with a reality of finite fiscal
resources for healthcare, big data–derived insights into unique individual traits in
response to therapy should not detract from the need to consistently apply cost–
benefit analyses to ever smaller subtypes of illness in the population, in order to
assure a balanced view against overall public health goals.

The repercussions of the envisioned unprecedented progress through ever more
sophisticated and broad application of big data analytics in healthcare cannot be
adequately considered without careful examination of the impact of such progress
on broader human dimensions of resultant realities. Importantly, considerations
of a potential for unintended consequences of sought goals of big data analytics
on broader economical, clinical, and societal areas are often missing in the contemporary discourse. While unlikely to be realized in the near future, the big data

promise in precision medicine may lead to an unprecedented ability of clinicians to have near-certainty or complete certainty about an individual person's propensity to develop or manifest specific illness in the long term and to have similar prognostication ability about short-term mortality outcomes and morbidity trajectories of an acute illness.

Past experience has shown that our ability to prognosticate (at least for groups or population subsets) precedes medicine's capacity to effectively intervene to prevent illness or cure/reverse its course, once developed. A transition from the current probabilistic uncertainties to near-certainty or complete certainty for individuals on a population scale would be expected to have immediate repercussions on the approach taken by payers for healthcare to support or withhold funding for both long-term and short-term care of specific patients, as discretion based on theoretical risk/benefit would be all but eliminated for practical purposes.

Unprecedented certainties about individual patient prognosis or response to available therapy may in turn force clinicians to face new challenges related to potentially narrowing decisional discretion and expected loss of applicability of the traditional type of clinical practice guideline, geared to address care of a heterogeneous population with specific illness or specific risks. Indeed, progress in precision medicine may require physicians to reexamine the role of "art" in the well-honored tenet of art versus science in the practice of medicine. Moreover, changing prognostic certainties would drive reexamination of the application to daily practice of the contemporary bioethics concepts of beneficence, maleficence, and justice. In addition, the present concept of rationing of medical care, at the societal, fiscal, and clinical levels, will also require substantial reexamination, with a need to achieve a clearer societal compact.

From an individual's perspective, a key part of a patient's (and the family's) ability to cope with a prospect of future illness (i.e., dementia) or an existing one has been driven by the inherent uncertainty about individual-level outcomes, thus providing, at its core, an ongoing measure of hope. The potential of precision medicine to introduce near-certainties or complete certainties about future outcomes can profoundly and possibly adversely affect coping ability, follow-up on clinical counseling, and choices of care and lifestyle.

Future progress in realizing the key goals of big data analytics in terms of advancing the concept of precision medicine is likely to be driven in part by substantial progress in "omics" areas. Such advances and the potential for adverse effects outlined earlier may give rise to propositions from health professionals and the lay public to capitalize on achieved progress by simply "eliminating" illness, perhaps at the pre-gestational level, a concept envisioned as a warning prospect in popular entertainment media.[82,83] Past repeated surges of the allure of various versions of eugenics should serve as further warning to carefully consider unintended repercussions of big data–driven, healthcare-related advances.

Finally, the pursuit of big data and its applications in healthcare has been restricted for the most part to high-resource countries. As the cost of acquisition and storage of digitized data continues to drop, careful consideration should be given to needs and potential benefits of big data applications in the more prevalent resource-limited areas. Importantly, applicability of bedside solutions and knowledge discovery are bound to differ when considered on a more global scale and thus will need to be carefully examined.

9.7 Conclusions

The revolution brought to all facets of healthcare by the widespread availability of big data repositories, and innovative, rapidly improving analytic applications stand to bring beneficial transformation to the full spectrum of the healthcare system, spanning individual patient care through system structure and policy making. The preceding overview highlights the many opportunities and challenges that, when properly addressed, can allow realization of the big data promise.

References

1. Sim, Ida. Two way of knowing: Big data and evidence-based medicine. *Ann Intern Med* 164, no. 8 (2016):562–3.
2. Institute of Medicine, Committee on the Learning Health Care System in America. *Best Care at Lower Cost: The Path to Continuously Learning Health Care System in America*. Washington, DC: The National Academies Press; 2012.
3. The precision medicine initiative. The White House. Available at https://www.white house.gov/precision-medicine
4. About the precision medicine initiative cohort program. Precision medicine cohort program. National Institutes of Health. Available at https://www.nih.gov/precision -medicine-initiative-cohort-program
5. Manyika, James, Chui, Michael, Brown, Brad et al. Big Data: The Next Frontier for Innovation, Competition, and Productivity. McKinsey Global Institute, 2011.
6. Critical Care Statistics. Society of Critical Care Medicine. Available at http://www .sccm.org/Communications/Pages/CriticalCareStats.aspx
7. Barrett, Marguerite L., Smith, Mark W., Elixhauser, Anne, Honigman, Leah S., Pines, Jesse M. Utilization of Intensive Care Services, 2011. HCUP Statistical Brief #185. December 2014. Agency for Healthcare Research and Quality, Rockville, MD. Available at http://www.hcup-us.ahrq.gov/reports/statbriefs/sb185-Hospital-Intensive -Care-Units-2011.pdf
8. Halpern, Neil A., Pastores, Stephen M. Critical care medicine beds: Use, occupancy, and costs in the United States: A methodological review. *Crit Care Med* 43, no. 11 (2015):2452–9.
9. Checkley, William, Martin, Greg S., Brown, Samuel M. et al. Structure, process, and annual ICU mortality across 69 centers: United States Critical Illness and Injury Trails Group Critical Illness Outcomes Study. *Crit Care Med* 42, no. 2 (2014):344–56.

10. Chen, Lena M., Render, Marta, Sales, Anne, Kennedy, Edward H., Wiitala, Wyndy, Hofer, Timothy P. Intensive care unit admitting patterns in the Veterans Affairs health system. *Arch Intern Med* 172 no. 16, (2012):1220–6.
11. Vincent Jean-Louis. The Berlin definition met our needs: Not sure. *Intensive Care Med* 42, no. 5 (2016):651–2.
12. Singer, Mervyn, Deutschman, Clifford S., Seymour, Christopher Warren et al. The third international consensus definitions for sepsis and septic shock (Sepsis-3). *JAMA* 315, no. 8 (2016):801–10.
13. Deutschman, Clifford S. Imprecise medicine: The limitations of Sepsis-3. *Crit Care Med* 44, no. 5 (2016):857–8.
14. Needham, Dale M., Davidson, Judy, Cohen, Henry et al. Improving long-term outcomes after discharge from intensive care unit: Report from a stakeholders' conference. *Crit Care Med* 40, no. 2 (2012):502–9.
15. Hua, May, Gong, Michelle Ng, Brady, Joanne, Wunsch, Hannah. Early and late unplanned rehospitalizations for survivors of critical illness. *Crit Care Med* 43, no. 2 (2015):430–8.
16. Halpern, Neal A., Pastores, Stephen M. Critical care medicine in the United States 2000–2005: An analysis of bed numbers, occupancy rates, payer mix, and costs. *Crit Care Med* 38, no. 1 (2010):65–71.
17. US Department of Health and Human Services, Health Resources and Services Administration. *Report to Congress. The Critical Care Workforce: A Study of the Supply and Demand for Critical Care Physicians*. May 2006. Available at http://bhpr.hrsa .gov/healthworkforce/reports/studycriticalcarephys.pdf
18. Gooch, Rebecca A., Kahn, Jeremy M. ICU bed supply, utilization, and health care spending: An example of demand elasticity. *JAMA* 311, no. 6 (2014):567–8.
19. Rubenfeld, Gordon D. Does the United States need more intensivist physicians? No. *Chest* 149, no. 3 (2016):625–8.
20. HCUP NIS Database Documentation. Healthcare Cost and Utilization Project (HCUP). Agency for Healthcare Research and Quality, Rockville, MD. Available at https://www.hcup-us.ahrq.gov/db/nation/nis/nisdbdocumentation.jsp
21. HCUP SID Database Documentation. Healthcare Cost and Utilization Project (HCUP). June 2016. Agency for Healthcare Research and Quality, Rockville, MD. Available at www.hcup-us.ahrq.gov/db/state/siddbdocumentation.jsp
22. Premier Research Services. Available at https://www.premierinc.com/transforming -healthcare/healthcare-performance-improvement/premier-research-services/
23. APACHE Outcomes. Cerner. Available at http://www.cerner.com/Solutions/Hospitals _and_Health_Systems/Critical_Care/APACHE_Outcomes/
24. Philips eICU Research Institute. Available at http://www.usa.philips.com/healthcare /solutions/enterprise-telehealth/eri
25. Medical Information Mart for Intensive care (MIMIC). Available at https://mimic .physionet.org/
26. Quality, Safety, and Value. US Department of Veterans Affairs. Available at http:// www.qualityandsafety.va.gov/
27. Biologic Specimen and Data Repository Information Coordinating Center (BioLINCC). National Heart, Lung, and Blood Institute. Available at https:// biolincc.nhlbi.nih.gov/home/

28. Manor-Shulman, Orit, Beyene, Joseph, Frndova, Helena, Parshuram, Christopher S. Quantifying the volume of documented clinical information in critical illness. *J Crit Care Med* 23, no. 2 (2008):245–50.

29. Herasevich, Vitaly, Litell, John, Pickering, Brian. Electronic medical records and mHealth anytime, anywhere. *Biomed Instrum Technol* Suppl (2012):45–8.

30. Donchin, Yoel, Gopher, Daniel, Olin, Miriam et al. A look into the nature and causes of human errors in the intensive care unit. *Crit Care Med* 23, no. 2 (1995):294–300.

31. Rothschild, Jeffrey M., Landrigan, Christopher P., Cronin, John W. et al. The critical care safety study: The incidence and nature of adverse events and serious medical errors in intensive care. *Crit Care Med* 33, no. 8 (2005):1694–700.

32. Carayon, Pascale, Wetterneck, Tosha B., Alyousef, Bashar et al. Impact of electronic health record technology on the work and workflow of physicians in the intensive care unit. *Int J Med Inform* 84, no. 4 (2015):578–94.

33. Thompson, Gwen, O'Horo, John C., Pickering, Brian W., Herasevich, Vitaly. Impact of the electronic medical record on mortality, length of stay, and cost in the hospital and ICU: A systematic review and metaanalysis. *Crit Care Med* 43, no. 6 (2015):1276–82.

34. Pickering, Brian W., Herasevich, Vitaly, Ahmed, Adil, Gajic, Ognjen. Novel representation of clinical information in the ICU: Developing user interfaces which reduce information overload. *Appl Clin Inf* 1, no. 2 (2010):116–31.

35. Ahmed, Adil, Chandra, Subhash, Herasevich, Vitaly, Gajic, Ognjen, Pickering, Brian W. The effect of two different electronic health record user interfaces on intensive care provider task load, errors of cognition, and performance. *Crit Care Med* 39, no. 7 (2011):1626–34.

36. Pickering, Brian W., Dong, Yue, Ahmed, Adil et al. The implementation of clinician designed, human-centered electronic medical record viewer in the intensive care unit: A pilot step-wedge cluster randomized trial. *Int J Med Inform* 84, no. 5 (2015):299–307.

37. Vranas, Kelly, Jopling, Jeffrey, Ramsey, Meghan, Sweeney, Timothy E., Escobar, Gabriel J., Liu, Vincent. Estimating the proportion of patients "too well" to benefit from critical care: A machine learning approach. *Am J Respir Crit Care Med* 193 (2016):A3632.

38. Cismondi, Federico, Celi, Leo Anthony, Fialho, Andre S. et al. Reducing unnecessary lab testing in the ICU with artificial intelligence. *Int J Med Inform* 82, no. 5 (2013):345–58.

39. Moss, Travis J., Lake, Douglas E., Calland, Forrest J. Signatures of subacute potentially catastrophic illness in the ICU: Model development and validation. *Crit Care Med* (2016), doi: 10.1097/CCM.0000000000001738.

40. Chen, Lujie, Dubrawski, Artur, Wang Donghan et al. Using supervised machine learning to classify real alerts and artifact in online multisignal vital sign monitoring data. *Crit Care Med* 44, no. 7 (2016):e456–63.

41. Pinsky, Michael R., Clermont, Gilles, Hravnak, Marilyn. Predicting cardiorespiratory instability. *Crit Care* 20 (2016):70.

42. Ogundele, Olufunmilayo, Claremont, Gilles, Sileanu, Florentina, Pinsky, Michael R. Use of derived physiologic variable to predict individual patients' probability of hemodynamic instability. *Am J Respir Crit Care Med* 187 (2013):A5067.

43. Ghassemi, Mohammad M., Richter, Stefan E., Eche, Ifeoma M., Chen, Tszyiw W., Danziger, John, Celi, Leo Anthony. A data-driven approach to optimized medication dosing: A focus on heparin. *Intensive Care Med* 40, no. 9 (2014):1332–9.
44. Fialho, Andre S., Celi, Leo Anthony, Cismondi, Federico et al. Disease-based modeling to predict fluid response in intensive care units. *Methods Inf Med* 52, no. 6 (2013):494–502.
45. Lehman, Li-wei, Nemati, Shamin, Adams, Ryan P., Moody, George, Malhotra, Atul, Mark, Roger G. Tracking progression of patient state in critical care using inferred shared dynamics in physiological time series. *Conf Proc IEEE Med Biol Soc* 2013 (2013):7072–5.
46. Mayaud, Louis, Lai, Peggy S., Clifford, Gari D., Tarassenko, Lionel, Celi, Leo Anthony, Annane, Djillali. Dynamic data during hypotensive episode improves mortality predictions among patients with sepsis and hypotension. *Crit Care Med* 41, no. 4 (2013):954–62.
47. Lehman, Li-wei, Saeed, Mohammed, Long, William, Lee, Joon, Mark, Roger. Risk stratification of ICU patients using topic models inferred from unstructured progress notes. *AMIA Annu Symp Proc* 2012 (2012):505–11.
48. Mayhew, Michael B., Sales, Ana, Greene, John D. et al. Identifying time-dependent mortality signatures in cases of suspected infection using scalable predictive models. *Am J Respir Crit Care Med* 193 (2016):A2714.
49. Sales, Ana, Mayhew, Michael B., Greene, John D. et al. Modeling patient subpopulations improves sepsis mortality prediction. *Am J Respir Crit Care Med* 193 (2016):A6149.
50. Wong, Hector R., Cvijanovich, Natalie Z., Lin, Richard et al. Identification of pediatric septic shock subclasses based on genome-wide expression profiling. *BMC Med* 7 (2009):34.
51. Man, Michael, Close, Sandra L., Shaw, Andrew D. et al. Beyond single-marker analyses; mining whole genome scans for insights into treatment responses in severe sepsis. *Pharmacogenomics J* 13 (2013):218–26.
52. Calfee, Carolyn S., Delucchi, Kevin, Parsons Polly E., Thompson, B Taylor, Ware, Lorraine B., Matthay, Michael A. Subendotypes in acute respiratory distress syndrome: Latent class analysis of data from two randomized controlled trials. *Lancet Respir Med* 2 no. 8 (2014):611–20.
53. Prescott, Hallie C., Osterholzer, John J., Langa, Kenneth M., Angus, Derek C., Iwashyna, Theodore J. Late mortality after sepsis: Propensity matched cohort study. *BMJ* 353 (2016):i2375.
54. Gershengorn, Hayley B., Garland, Allan, Kramer, Andrew, Scales, Damon C., Rubenfeld, Gordon, Wunsch, Hannah. Variation in arterial and central venous catheter use in the United States. *Anesthesiology* 120, no. 3 (2014):650–64.
55. Geshengorn, Hayley B., Wunsch, Hannah, Scales, Damon C., Zarychanski, Ryan, Rubenfeld, Gordon, Garland, Allan. Association between arterial catheter use and hospital mortality in intensive care units. *JAMA Intern Med* 174, no. 11 (2014):1746–54.
56. Wallace, David J., Angus, Derek C., Seymour, Christopher W., Barnato, Amber E., Kahn, Jeremy M. Critical care growth in the United States: A comparison of regional and national trends. *Am J Respir Crit Care Med* 191, no. 4 (2015):410–6.
57. Ghassemi, Marzyeh, Celi, Leo Anthony, Stone, David J. State of the art review: The data revolution in critical care. *Crit Care* 19 (2015):118.

58. Ioannidis, John PA. Why most published research findings are false. *PLoS Med* 2, no. 8 (2005):e124.

59. Mills, Edward J., Thorlund, Kristian, Ionnidis, John. Demystifying trial networks and network meta-analysis. *BMJ* 346 (2013):f2914.

60. Angus, Derek C. Fusing randomized trials with big data: The key to self-learning health care system? *JAMA* 314, no. 8 (2015):767–8.

61. Berry, Scott M., Connor, Jason T., Lewis, Roger J. The platform trial: An efficient strategy for evaluating multiple treatments. *JAMA* 313, no. 16 (2015):1619–20.

62. Clinical Study Data Request. Available at https://www.clinicalstudydatarequest.com/

63. Celi, Leo Anthony, Ippolito, Andrea, Montgomery, Robert A., Moses, Christopher, Stone, David J. Crowdsourcing knowledge discovery and innovations in medicine. *J Med Internet Res* 16, no. 6 (2014):216.

64. Badawi, Omar, Brennan, Thomas, Celi, Leo Anthony et al. Making big data useful for health care: A summary of the inaugural MIT critical data conference. *JMIR Med Inform* 2, no. 2 (2014):e22.

65. Aboab, Jerome, Celi, Leo Anthony, Charlton, Peter et al. A "datathon" model to support cross-disciplinary collaboration. *Sci Transl Med* 8, no. 333 (2016): 333ps8.

66. van der Sijs, Heleen, Aarts, Jos, Vulto, Aarnold, Berg, Marc. Overriding of drug safety alerts in computerized physician order entry. *J Am Med Inform Assoc* 13, no. 2 (2006):138–47.

67. Kesselheim, Aaron S., Cresswell, Kathrin, Phansalkar, Shobna, Bates, David W., Sheikh, Aziz. Clinical decision support systems could be modified to reduce 'alert fatigue' while still minimizing the risk of litigation. *Health Aff* 30, no. 12 (2011):2310–6.

68. Verghese, Abraham. Treat the patient, not the CT scan. *New York Times*. February 26, 2011. Available at http://www.nytimes.com/2011/02/27/opinion/27verghese.html?_r=0

69. Block, Lauren, Habicht, Robert, Wu, Albert W. et al. In the wake of the 2003 and 2011 duty hours regulations, how do internal medicine interns spend their time? *J Gen Intern Med* 28, no. 8 (2013):1042–7.

70. Frankel, Richard, Altschuler, Andrea, George, Sheba et al. Effects of exam-room computing on clinician-patient communication: A longitudinal qualitative study. *J Gen Intern Med* 20, no. 8 (2005):677–82.

71. Frankel, Robert M. Computers in the examination room. *JAMA Intern Med* 176, no. 1 (2016):128–9.

72. Tierney, Michael J., Pageler, Natalie M., Kahana, Madelyn, Pantaleoni, Julie L., Longhurst, Christopher A. Medical education in the electronic medical record (EMR) era: Benefits, challenges, and future directions. *Acad Med* 88, no. 6 (2013):748–52.

73. Halamka, John. Making a difference. Health System CIO. Available at http://health systemcio.com/2016/06/02/making-a-difference/

74. Iwashyna, Theodore J., Liu, Vincent. What's so different about big data? A primer for clinicians trained to think epidemiologically. *Ann Am Thorac Soc* 11, no. 7 (2014):1130–5.

75. Liu, Vincent, Musen, Mark A., Chou, Timothy. Data breeches of protected health information in the United States. *JAMA* 313, no. 14 (2015):1471–3.

76. Agaku, Israel T., Adisa, Akinyele O., Ayo-Yusuf, Olalekan A., Connolly, Gregory N. Concern about security and privacy, and perceived control over collection and use of health information are related to withholding of health information from healthcare providers. *J Am Med Inform Assoc* 21, no. 2 (2014):374–8.

77. MIT editors. Business report: Data-driven health care. *MIT Technol Rev* 117 (2014):1–19.
78. Curry, Leslie, Spatz, Erica, Cherlin, Emily et al. What distinguishes top-performing hospitals in acute myocardial infarction mortality rates? A qualitative study. *Ann Intern Med* 154, no. 6 (2011):384–90.
79. Taichman, Daren B., Backus, Joyce, Baethge, Christopher et al. Sharing clinical trial data: A proposal from the International Committee of Medical Journal Editors. *JAMA* 315, no. 5 (2016):467–8.
80. Longo, Dan L., Drazen, Jeffrey M. Data sharing. *N Engl J Med* 374, no. 2 (2016):276–7.
81. Dalerba, Piero, Sahoo, Debashis, Paik Soonmyung et al. CDX2 as a prognostic biomarker in stage II and stage III colon cancer. *N Engl J Med* 374, no. 3 (2016):211–22.
82. Gattaca. Available at http://www.imdb.com/title/tt0119177/
83. Jabr, Ferris. Are we too close to making Gattaca a reality? *Scientific American*, October 28, 2013. Available at http://blogs.scientificamerican.com/brainwaves/are-we-too-close-to-making-gattaca-a-reality/

Chapter 10

Predictive Analytics and Machine Learning in Medicine

L. Nelson Sanchez-Pinto and Matthew M. Churpek

Contents

10.1 Introduction

Clinical prediction models have existed for decades,[1,2] but they are just now attracting a wider interest in medicine.[3,4] Given the complexity and abundance of clinical information, the limited ability of clinicians to accurately prognosticate outcomes, and the plethora of prediction problems that clinicians face daily, it is not surprising that there is a growing interest in the field of prediction research. Unfortunately, while many models have been developed, few are appropriately validated, and almost none are routinely used in clinical practice.[5,6] This paradigm will likely change drastically in the next few years given the intersection of four major forces: (a) the growing complexity and cost of patient care, (b) the advent of Big Data in medicine, (c) the adoption of machine learning methodology in biomedical research, and (d) the development of the digital infrastructure in healthcare.

The convergence of biomedical Big Data (as the fuel), machine learning (as the engine), and prediction research (as the scientific framework) is defined as predictive analytics in medicine.[7] Biomedical Big Data refers to the thousands of petabytes of data being generated by electronic medical records (EMRs), biomedical "multi-omics" data, physiologic signals, medical images, financial transactions, hospital operations, and so on, much of which is being captured and stored electronically.[8] Machine learning overlaps with other constructs, such as artificial intelligence and data mining, and is defined as the science of how computers learn from data.[8,9] Machine learning, in turn, falls under the auspices of data science, which is the scientific discipline that brings together computer science, statistics, informatics, and domain expertise to gain knowledge and insight from large amounts of complex data[10] (Figure 10.1).

The digital infrastructure in healthcare represents the most significant facilitator of predictive analytics.[11,12] Gone are the days when the majority of clinical data were kept in paper records and prediction models focused on simplicity and ease of use so that clinicians could calculate predictions by hand.[2] The digital infrastructure makes EMRs and other information systems the backbone of the medical data universe, and it allows the digitalized information of patients to be coupled with complex computational algorithms in a way not possible even a few years ago.[11,12]

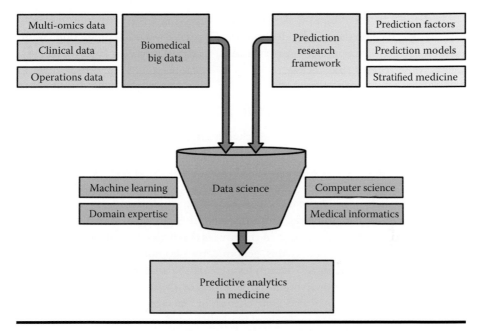

Figure 10.1   Conceptual model of Predictive Analytics in Medicine.

More importantly, the actionable knowledge that these algorithms produce can then be served back to patients and providers through this same digital platform in the form of decision support tools, therefore closing the data loop and potentially achieving the goal of improving care and reducing cost.[8,11,13,14]

In this chapter, we will review the principles of prediction research as the scientific framework of predictive analytics and the emergence of machine learning methods as the key tool set in this field. We will also discuss how to build a prediction model with a step-by-step guide that goes from the formulation of the prediction problem all the way to the validation and implementation of the model using examples to illustrate the process.

10.2 Prediction Research in Medicine

Prediction research—also called prognosis research—is the investigation of the statistical relationship between future outcomes or clinical events among people with a given health status.[4,6] The goal of this research is to improve health by effectively using the insights gained by the prediction models to prevent or treat diseases early in their course. As discussed above, prediction research that utilizes large amounts of medical data and machine learning methods is more commonly referred to as predictive analytics.[7]

As defined by the Prognosis Research Strategy Group, the prediction research framework can be further subdivided into three areas of study: (a) prediction factor research, (b) prediction model research, and (c) stratified medicine.[4] We will briefly discuss those areas of study below.

10.2.1 Prediction Factor Research

In prediction factor research, the researcher attempts to elucidate which variables (or predictors) in the data are associated with a specific outcome. More fundamentally, however, prediction factor research is the area of study that focuses on the discovery of new predictors.[8,15] These predictors are often directly related to the underlying pathobiology of the disease process being studied and can be found in biological, pathological, imaging, clinical, or physiologic signal data sets. Perhaps the most exciting avenue of research in this area is the discovery of novel biomarkers using biomedical "omics" data, that is, genomic, transcriptomic, proteomic, metabolomics, or microbiomic data.[15] Examples include the analysis of gene-expression microarrays to uncover new biomarkers of sepsis or the modeling of genetic networks of clinical significance into gene clusters or "metagenes."[16,17] It is important to note that there is a significant body of work dedicated to uncovering new predictors in other types of medical data. An example of this is the study of the morphological characteristics of breast tumor samples in pathology images using machine learning–based image analysis to predict long-term mortality[18] or the study of the heart rate variability in electrophysiologic signals to predict sepsis.[19]

Developing prediction models utilizing one or a few of these novel predictors has become the norm in this field of research,[15] but it is worth noting that the performance of such models is usually inferior to those that use these novel predictors and biomarkers along with other clinical variables that provide a more holistic representation of the patient's health state.[8] This is probably attributed to the fundamental reality that diseases are rarely explained by a single mechanistic pathway and are instead a result of the perturbation of several homeostatic systems.[20] This perturbation and its trajectory can rarely be measured with a single biomarker, let alone a single biomarker at a single point in time.[17]

10.2.2 Prediction Model Research

Prediction model research is the central component of prediction research, and we will explore the development of a prediction model in detail in the Section 10.3. However, it is important to highlight that beyond the technical process of model development, there are questions that are important to explore in prediction model research.[6] These are questions such as the following: What makes a good prediction model? What clinical problems are and are not suited for prediction modeling? What is the best way to validate a model? How can we study the clinical impact of a model? What is the best way to analyze the cost–benefit ratio of a model? How does the attitude of clinicians affect the impact of a prediction model? We will attempt to answer some of these questions in this chapter.

10.2.3 Stratified Medicine

Stratified medicine refers to the targeting of treatments according to the biological or risk characteristics shared by subgroups of patients.[21] Such targeted treatments can be pharmacological, such as the use of trastuzumab in women with HER-2–positive breast tumors,[21] or nonpharmacological, such as increased vigilance in patients at high risk of clinical deterioration in hospital wards.[22] Oncologic research has contributed significantly to the field of stratified medicine, both with examples of stratification based on absolute risk and stratification based on biological subtypes, and has achieved tremendous success.[23] There is no reason to believe that other areas in medicine will not stand to benefit from this type of approach, and promising work in sepsis, asthma, and cardiovascular diseases is emerging.[24–26]

Similar constructs, such as "precision medicine" or "personalized medicine," are closely related to stratified medicine, especially when the stratification is based on the underlying molecular and cellular pathobiology of the disease processes studied.[21] Another related concept, popularized by the biologist Leroy Hood, is P4 medicine, where the four "Ps" stand for predictive, preventive, personalized, and participatory medicine.[20] What P4 medicine preaches is (a) using a systems biology approach to understanding disease; (b) measuring clinical variables and novel biomarkers to estimate the state of the patient's different biological systems, stratify patient subtypes, prognosticate clinical trajectories, and predict treatment responses; (c) preventing clinical deterioration and unfavorable outcomes by using targeted interventions; and (d) engaging patients to actively participate in their own care and wellness, recognizing that patients are at the center of their own health and need to be involved in a two-way relationship with the healthcare system. The promise of this approach is that it will shift the current healthcare system paradigm from a *reactive* healthcare, where we wait for diseases to happen before we start empirical treatments, to a *proactive* healthcare, where patients are stratified, clinical trajectories and treatment responses are predicted, and targeted interventions are used.[20]

10.3 How to Build a Prediction Model

Although there are many machine learning methods used in the field predictive analytics in medicine, in this section, we will focus on the application of supervised statistical learning algorithms to predict clinical events. Supervised learning is performed to uncover the relationship between the candidate predictors and outcome when the outcome is known in the training data set.[27] These algorithms are being increasingly used to develop risk prediction models in the medical literature.[3,8,22,28,29] Unsupervised learning, in contrast, is performed to uncover patterns in the data, without using a specific outcome. For interested readers, there is a growing body of research pertaining to the use of unsupervised learning algorithms for stratification, for example: phenotype and endotype profiling[25,26] or patient similarity for mortality prediction.[30]

In this section, we will review the steps that are important to develop a valid and useful prediction model. It should be used as a general guideline and it is not intended to be prescriptive or all-inclusive. Additional details for developing clinical prediction models and on using machine learning methods in general can be found in several excellent specialized texts.[27,31,32]

10.3.1 Defining the Prediction Problem and Model Requirements

Probably the best way to start designing a prediction model is to first identify the prediction problem and envision how the prediction model will be used clinically. This process will inform the type of output you want from the model and the data that will be needed to develop it. There are many informational needs that clinicians face daily that could become prediction problems. Questions such as the following: What antibiotic should I start on this hospitalized patient? What is the risk of a central venous catheter infection on this patient? Which of the patients in the hospital ward are most likely to deteriorate in the next 24 hours? In the example of antibiotic choice you might have several requirements, such as appropriate antimicrobial coverage (e.g., >90%) for the top three most likely pathogens, tailored to the institutional microbial resistance patterns. Using these requirements, you can define the type of output you would want from your model, such as a multiclass ranking of different bacterial pathogens in order of likelihood, based on the patient's phenotype and clinical course. The top three pathogens could then be linked by simple rule matching with the antibiotics that would provide >90% coverage based on institutional antibiograms. These requirements would also inform you of the data that you need to train the model (e.g., patient clinical data, institutional antibiograms, etc.) and even the algorithms most likely to be successful, such as a random forest, in this case, which performs well in multiclass problems.[33]

10.3.2 Study Design and Data Collection

The most common type of data used for clinical prediction modeling is retrospective data.[31,34] The adoption of EMRs in most healthcare organizations has opened the door to the development of prediction models with hundreds of thousands of patients.[22] Secondary use of EMR data has many advantages and disadvantages. Advantages include its low cost, availability, granularity of the clinical data, and the fact that it reflects the "real data" captured routinely in patients during their interactions with the healthcare system. Having said this, a recent review found that researchers developing clinical prediction models using EMR data fail to take advantage of important features of the EMR, such as the capture of longitudinal data.[34] The major disadvantages of using EMR data are the missing or sporadic collection of some variables, the significant amount of unstructured free-text data in clinical notes, the fact that clinical problems might change over time and historic data sets may become irrelevant, and that new predictors cannot be evaluated if they were not collected and recorded.[31,35] Registry data, such as national cancer registries or multicenter quality benchmarking databases, are also often used to develop prediction models,[31] probably owing to the attractiveness of highly curated and complete data sets for tens of thousands or sometimes hundreds of thousands of patients.[36] However, a major disadvantage of registry data is that the level of granularity is usually low, with only a limited amount of variables recorded per patient.[8]

In the case of prediction factor research and biomarker discovery, prospective observational studies with biospecimen banking and analysis are the norm.[15,17] The major advantage of this study design is the ability to discover and evaluate new predictors, while the major disadvantages are the limited number of patients that will likely be recruited and the cost of such studies.

Regardless of the type of data collected, an important factor to consider is the availability of the data in real time in the clinical context in which the model will be used. While it might seem tempting to use all the data available for modeling, if any of the predictors in the data set were collected or reported at any time in the patient's clinical course subsequent to when the model would be used in a hypothetical implementation, it will be of little value. For example, a laboratory test that takes 24 hours to be resulted will be of no value in an emergency department triage model, neither would a discharge diagnosis when estimating the risk of clinical deterioration during the hospital stay. Furthermore, as novel predictors are discovered, it is important that researchers take into account the feasibility of measuring those predictors in a timely and cost-effective fashion in order to be clinically useful.[24]

10.3.3 Data Quality and Preprocessing

Biomedical databases are filled with erroneous data and missing values.[6,31,37] The sources for these errors can be found at any level of the data life cycle, from data collection all the way to archiving. Data quality is a key component of a reliable prediction model, so understanding the possible sources of error or missingness and mitigating these is a key aspect of the data preprocessing. A through exploration of the data and quantification of missing values and outliers should be an initial step of any prediction model development.[6] Data visualization techniques can be of help in this part of the project. Understanding the data or having domain expertise is also an important part of the data preprocessing. For example, simply eliminating outliers might introduce significant bias. While there are erroneous outliers that can be easily identified, such as a patient breathing >100% oxygen, there are also many outliers that are clinically meaningful, such as a serum glucose level >900 mg/dL.

Dealing with missing data is one of the main challenges of using clinical data for research.[6,31,37] Not all patients will have all the data points of interest and only analyzing patients who have all the data points (i.e., complete-case analysis) can be inefficient and introduce bias.[31] Data can be missing because they were collected but not recorded, recorded but lost, or never collected. The latter is common in medicine, where certain laboratory tests (e.g., arterial blood gas) or more invasive measurements (e.g., central venous pressure) are not obtained on patients who are not sufficiently sick to warrant those test or procedures. In these cases, one may assume that the unrecorded values are normal and a normal value or a population mean can be used to impute (i.e., fill in) the missing value. However, this approach ignores the fact that many missing values might be related to the recorded values.[37] An example would be a missing serum creatinine level, which can be related to the age, height, fluid status, and blood urea nitrogen level of the patient, among other things. In this case, an imputation method that models this multivariable relationship between the missing values and the recorded values, such as a regression or a nearest neighbor–based imputation method, might be more appropriate.[37] Careful handling of missing variables will improve model performance and decrease the risk of unwanted bias.

10.3.4 Feature Engineering and Predictor Selection

Feature engineering is the process of using domain knowledge to extract meaningful information from the data in order to develop good predictors.[38] For example, a clinical researcher might want to predict the likelihood of a life-threatening infection occurring in a pediatric inpatient ward and is interested in the features that can be derived from the heart rate recorded in the EMR. Things like the maximum heart rate in a given time frame, its variability, its trend, or the amount of change over time could all be features that the researcher may identify as potentially meaningful. Extracting features that represent these attributes without losing valuable information and without introducing noise is the basis of feature engineering. These features can then be further selected and used as predictors in a model.

Data transformation, which is closely linked with feature engineering, is the process of transforming data from raw values into predictors that can then be selected and used to train models. This process can range from codifying non-numerical data and generating composite variables to normalizing age-dependent variables.[31] A common data transformation process used in clinical prediction problems is to categorize continuous data into different discrete values in order to deal with the nonlinear relationship that the data might have with the outcome. While commonly used, this approach can eliminate important information about the relationship of the data and the outcome and should be avoided when possible.[6]

Finally, predictor selection is the process of reducing the number of predictors that are used to train the prediction model to reduce the complexity of the model and the likelihood of overfitting (discussed below). There are many approaches to predictor selection, and each one has advantages and disadvantages.[31] From backward selection using a generalized linear regression model to predictor selection using random forest, each approach has a risk of introducing bias and must be used with care.[31,39] Domain expertise can be helpful in this step by allowing the researcher to choose predictors that might have an advantage in a real-life clinical setting, such as greater generalizability or easier data capture.[40]

10.3.5 Preparing the Data Set

It is important to think of a data set for a prediction problem as a precious, limited resource. Every correlation or statistical test performed between a predictor and an outcome taps this resource and threatens the generalizability of the findings. With this in mind, it should be clear that a careful, structured approach to preparing the data set before performing analyses is preferred over a "shotgun" approach that performs countless tests and comparisons to look for anything that is significant.

One key consideration when developing a prediction model is what data will be used to develop the model and what data will be used to validate and estimate its accuracy. Some investigators use the entire data set at hand for both these tasks. However, accuracy measures derived from this internal validation procedure, called "apparent validation" in the statistical literature, are often unduly optimistic.[31] This is due to the fact that machine learning algorithms will unknowingly fit both the true signal in the data (i.e., the predictor-to-outcome relationships that will be generalizable across similar external data sets) and also random noise.[27] The drop in accuracy from one data set to the next as a result of an algorithm fitting too much random noise is called overfitting and should be avoided if at all possible. Separate model derivation and validation cohorts are therefore necessary to obtain a more realistic estimate regarding how well the model will perform in new settings.

Several methods can be used to create separate derivation and validation cohorts within a data set. The most common method used in the medical literature is a split-sample approach, where a randomly selected percentage of the data set is used for model derivation (often 50% or more) and the remainder of the data set is used for model validation. Although simple, this method has several disadvantages. These include the fact that omitting patients from the model derivation step by only using 50% of the sample can result in overfitting in smaller data sets. Similarly, only using 50% of the sample for validation may result in inadequate power to estimate model accuracy precisely.[41]

The limitations of the split sample approach have led researchers and guidelines to recommend other approaches to separating a data set into derivation and validation cohorts. One commonly used method is called cross-validation. This involves splitting the data set into several equal parts (often 5 or 10) and then deriving the model on all of the parts except for one and then testing model accuracy on the part that was left out. This is then repeated until every part has been used for both model derivation and model validation. Thus, in 10-fold cross-validation, 90% of the data will be used at each model derivation step, and all the data will be used for estimating model accuracy. Bootstrap resampling methods are also commonly used, where a random sample of the data set is selected for model derivation and accuracy is estimated on the remainder of the sample. These methods and other variations are recommended over the split-model approach when assessing model accuracy in a single data set.[31]

The goal of many clinical prediction models is to use them to care for future patients across multiple hospitals and geographic locations. If data from other centers are not available or if the model will be used only within hospitals sampled in the data set at hand, then splitting a sample based on time (temporal validation) is a useful way to estimate accuracy for future patients. If external data sets from other hospitals are available, developing the model in some centers and validating its accuracy in others (external geographic validation) may be preferred. This would provide more realistic results if the model will be disseminated across new hospitals not currently available in the data set used to derive the model.

Once the method for deriving and then testing model accuracy is determined, it is important to only use the validation cohort to test model accuracy. Thus, all data exploration, predictor selection, and tuning parameter selection (described below) that involve both predictor and outcome variables should only be performed using the derivation cohort.[41]

10.3.6 Selecting and Training Prediction Models

10.3.6.1 Overview of Machine Learning Algorithms

Machine learning algorithms are the engine of predictive analytics that transform data into predictions of outcomes in past, present, and future patients. These methods can also provide graphical displays of variable relationships and can be used to discover clusters of patients with similar characteristics. Input variables for these models may be nominal (e.g., race), ordinal (e.g., grade school, high school, or college education), or continuous (e.g., age). Outputs from the models may be probabilities of an outcome occurring for classification problems (e.g., dead vs. alive at hospital discharge) or a continuous output for regression problems (e.g., predicted length of hospital stay). Other outcomes can also be used in machine learning algorithms, including multinomial outcomes (e.g., predicting the likely infectious organism) and survival outcomes (e.g., predicting the time to cancer recurrence). Currently, there are hundreds of different machine learning algorithms and more are published and presented at conferences every year.[8] Below, we provide a broad overview of some of the more commonly used machine learning methods and focus on predicting binary classification and continuous regression outcomes.

10.3.6.2 Linear and Logistic Regression

Linear regression and logistic regression are linear statistical models used for continuous (linear regression) and binary classification (logistic regression) outcomes. The concept of correlation and regression originated from Sir Francis Galton, a cousin of Charles Darwin, more than 100 years ago while studying sweat pea seeds. The origins of logistic regression are also more than 100 years old, with Verhulst publishing three papers on the topic in the mid-1800s. These methods are the most commonly used models in medicine today, both for prediction problems and in exploratory epidemiological studies. They offer the advantage of simplicity, interpretable output formulas, and familiarity. Linear and logistic regression models can be as accurate or more accurate than other methods for prediction problems, especially when nonlinear effects of predictors are included during model fitting (e.g., by using splines)[27] (Figure 10.2a).

The simplest form of linear regression can be conceptualized by imagining a sample of data points with X and Y values on a two-dimensional plot. A simple linear regression model can create a "best-fit" line through these data points by taking the inputs (X values) and fitting them to the outputs (Y values). Adding more predictors to the model amounts to fitting a best-fit line through multidimensional space. Although many different methods are available to fit linear regression models, the most commonly used is least squares regression. This method finds the line that minimizes the sum of the squared distance between the actual data points and the line along the y axis.

Logistic regression transforms the binary outcome using the logit (log-odds) link to predict the probability of the outcome. This transformation restricts the outputted probability to a value between 0 and 1, such that the predicted likelihood of an event occurring will be between 0% and 100%. Logistic regression models are commonly fit using maximum likelihood estimation, which finds the predictor coefficient values that maximize the likelihood of the data used to fit the model.[42]

Penalized likelihood methods of model estimation, such as the lasso, ridge regression, and elastic net, can also be used for both linear and logistic regression. These methods can decrease the likelihood of model overfitting in small samples or when the outcome is rare. The lasso and elastic net have the additional advantage of automatically performing predictor selection.

10.3.6.3 Tree-Based Models

Tree-based models are based on decision trees that can be presented as a series of "if–then" statements in the form of a tree.[27,43] In order to determine the splits of the tree, the algorithm searches across all values of the predictors to find the predictors and cut-point that maximizes the difference in the outcome variable between the two groups that result from the split. Optimal cut-points are then found for each subgroup from the first split (leaves), and this process is continued until some

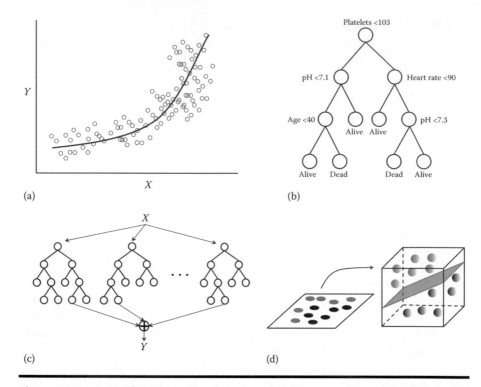

Figure 10.2 **Examples of machine learning algorithms used in prediction modeling. (a) A linear regression line (black) fitted using a spline to model the nonlinear relationship between the predictor X and the outcome Y. (b) A classification tree using several clinical predictors to model survival. (Note: the predictors and cutpoints used are for illustration purposes only.) (c) A random forest classification model using a voting scheme of the output of all the trees to predict outcome Y. (d) A linear support vector machine model based on the mapping of the two classes in the input data (left) into a high-dimensional space and the fitting of a hyperplane that maximally separates the two classes (right).**

stopping criterion is reached (Figure 10.2b). There are several methods to define an "optimal" split, including the Gini index and cross entropy. In practice, these methods typically yield similar results. A cost complexity parameter, which penalizes larger trees, can be used to find the size of the final tree that maximizes model accuracy using cross-validation.

To improve the accuracy and stability of the decision tree model, a procedure called bagging can be used. This involves taking random bootstrap samples of patient data and fitting a tree model to each sample.[43] The final output of the model is obtained by using the result of all the individual trees either by averaging the results (in regression problems) or through a voting scheme (in classification problems). Random forests modify the bagged tree procedure by only allowing a random number of the predictors to be considered at each split of each tree.[43,44] This results in trees that are less correlated with each other compared to bagged trees, and thus potentially increasing accuracy. The optimal number of trees and predictors to be considered at each split can be determined using cross-validation (Figure 10.2c).

Another popular tree-based model is the gradient boosted machine. This algorithm fits one tree at a time, first to all the outcomes in the training data and then to the residuals of the previous models, thus creating a combination of trees that increasingly weight the "difficult to predict" events to a greater degree.[43,45] The optimal number of splits for each individual tree, the total number of trees, and an additional shrinkage factor called the learning rate, which weights the contribution from each individual tree, can be determined using 10-fold cross-validation.

Single, small decision trees are easy to interpret. However, they are often less accurate than other machine learning methods. On the other hand, random forests and gradient boosted machines are among the most accurate machine learning methods available. Although less interpretable than single trees, graphical displays of predictor importance and other metrics are possible for these algorithms.

10.3.6.4 K-Nearest Neighbors

K-nearest neighbors (KNN) models use local geographic information in the predictor space to predict the outcome of a new sample.[27,43] For example, a KNN model utilizing five neighbors uses the outcome values of the five closest observations in multidimensional space, based on a distance measure, to predict the outcome of a new observation. The optimal number of neighbors can be determined using cross-validation. Of note, distance is scale dependent; hence, the predictors should be rescaled (e.g., to a mean of zero and a standard deviation of one) before model fitting.

10.3.6.5 Support Vector Machines

Support vector machines are a generalization of the maximal margin classifier and the support vector classifier, which fit a separating hyperplane in high-dimensional space to the data in order to separate the two classes[5] (Figure 10.2d). Specifically, support vector machines generalize the idea of creating a hyperplane that separates the two classes of interest (e.g., event vs. no event) with the farthest minimum distance to the training observations to the situation where the two classes are not completely separable and the hyperplane is allowed to be nonlinear. This class of methods is unique in that they ignore data points from each outcome class that are "easy" to predict when determining the structure of the boundary and instead focus on the points that are hardest to predict (i.e., closest to the boundary) and those points that are misclassified.[27,43] There are many options for the shape of the hyperplane boundary, including linear, polynomial, and kernel functions (e.g., radial basis function). The main tuning parameter for support vector machines is the cost penalty, with higher values penalizing misclassified observations to a greater degree. The optimal value can be determined using cross-validation. Similar to KNN, this method is scale dependent; thus, all predictors need to be rescaled. Support vector machines can also be used for continuous outcomes.

10.3.6.6 Neural Networks

Neural networks are nonlinear models inspired by the nervous system. They involve creating a set of linear combinations of the predictors and then using those as inputs into a hidden layer (or layers) of units, which then create new combinations of these inputs to output the predicted probability or value of the event of interest.[27,43] The weights for the different parameters in the neural network are typically estimated using back-propagation, with the sum of squared errors (for regression problems) or cross-entropy (for classification problems) used to measure model fit. Weight decay, which is a penalty term used to avoid overfitting, and the number of hidden units in the model can be determined using cross-validation. There are many other varieties of neural networks, and this method has seen a resurgence of popularity lately owing to the use of deep (multilayer) neural networks and their success in online data competitions and in computer vision problems.

10.3.6.7 Accuracy versus Interpretability

Given the large number of algorithms available, it is important to choose those that best fit the goals of the prediction problem. For example, methods such as logistic regression are familiar to clinicians and output interpretable coefficients. Although they can be less accurate than other methods, they work well for prediction problems where accuracy is not the primary goal and model interpretation is important. Conversely, support vector machines are flexible methods but are a "black-box" technique, which makes the model hard to explain to clinicians. Tree-based methods, such as random forests, are often very accurate and software packages that present model details are available, such as predictor importance and marginal effects for individual predictors (Figure 10.3). Therefore, these methods work well if accuracy is paramount and understanding the highest weighted variables of the model is also preferred. It is also important to note that different methods may be more accurate than others depending on the prediction problem at hand.[27] Thus, if multiple methods fit the goals of the prediction problem, then comparing different methods can often be a useful approach. Finally, combining multiple methods together into a single model through an averaging or voting scheme, an approach

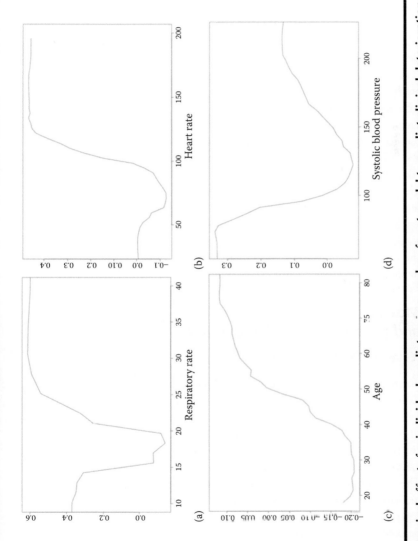

Figure 10.3 Marginal effects for individual predictors in a random forest model to predict clinical deterioration in hospitalized patients using: (a) respiratory rate, (b) heart rate, (c) age, and (d) systolic blood pressure. (From Churpek MM, Yuen TC, Winslow C, Meltzer DO, Kattan MW, Edelson DP. Multicenter comparison of machine learning methods and conventional regression for predicting clinical deterioration on the wards. *Crit Care Med.* 2016;44(2):368–374. Used with permission.)

called ensemble models, may improve accuracy over individual methods, although at the price of decreased interpretability.

10.3.6.8 Avoiding Overfitting

As noted above, machine learning algorithms, particularly those that are complex and flexible, can overfit the noise in the data, resulting in poor performance upon model validation. Avoiding this phenomenon is key to ensuring a more generalizable model that will work well with future subjects not used in model derivation.[27,31,41] One method to avoid overfitting is to ensure that the effective sample size to model predictors ratio is favorable. A common rule used for logistic regression is that 10 outcomes are needed for every predictor in the model to estimate a stable model and avoid overfitting.[31,41] This number has been challenged by some authors and more complex machine learning algorithms may need many more outcomes per predictor.[41] In smaller data sets, or those where the outcome is rare, omitting predictors based on prior published work can be an effective way to improve this ratio. Another way to avoid overfitting is to tune the model parameters that control complexity (e.g., the weight decay in neural networks, the lasso penalty value in penalized logistic regression, etc.) using cross-validation. Performance metrics from cross-validation typically track well with validation cohort accuracy; hence, choosing the model tuning parameters in this way can improve performance and decrease the likelihood of overfitting.

10.3.7 Measuring Performance and Comparing Prediction Models

10.3.7.1 Overall Performance

Model performance can be quantified in several ways, and these methods can then be used to compare different models to determine which to use in future implementation studies.[46] Overall model fit for models for continuous outcomes (e.g., length of stay) can be described by measures such as R^2, which states how much of the variability in the data is explained by the model. Versions of this metric and other measures are also available for classification outcomes and survival outcomes (time to event). The overall performance of a model can be further decomposed into discrimination, which describes how well a model separates subjects who experience an outcome from those who do not, and calibration, which describes the agreement between the predicted value or probability from a model and the observed value.[31] Although studies often focus on model discrimination, model calibration can be even more important in some cases. For example, if a clinical action is planned for patients with a greater than 10% probability of disease, then ensuring that the model probabilities are well calibrated is paramount.

10.3.7.2 Model Discrimination

Common metrics of model discrimination, which are used primarily for classification problems, include sensitivity, specificity, and the concordance (*c*) statistic.[31,41] Sensitivity is the proportion of patients with the disease of interest that are deemed positive by the model, whereas specificity is the proportion of patients without the disease deemed negative by the model. Two related metrics are positive predictive value, which is the proportion of patients deemed positive by the model that truly have the disease, and negative predictive value, which is the proportion of patients deemed negative by the model who truly do not have the disease. Because the predicted probability of a model can range from 0% to 100%, multiple thresholds can be used to separate those patients with and without the disease of interest. This leads naturally to the receiver operating characteristic (ROC) curve, which graphically displays model performance across a range of thresholds, with sensitivity (true-positive proportion) on the *y* axis and one minus specificity (false-positive proportion) on the *x* axis. The area under the ROC curve (AUC) can be calculated, with 1.0 denoting perfect discriminative ability and 0.5 denoting no discriminative ability. For binary outcomes, the AUC is equivalent to the *c* statistic and can also be interpreted as the probability that a randomly selected patient with the disease will have a higher model predicted probability than a randomly selected nondiseased patient. Versions of the *c* statistic are available for survival outcomes, and methods to compare the AUCs between models are in widespread use.

10.3.7.3 Model Calibration

There are also several methods to investigate model calibration. Simply creating a plot with the observed values on the *y* axis and predicted values on the *x* axis can be enlightening (a calibration plot), and areas of poor model calibration can be identified by visual inspection. For binary outcomes, this can be achieved using a smoothing method, such as loess, which plots a moving average of the mean proportion. The mean predictions can also be compared to the mean outcome value (calibration-in-the-large) and across deciles of predicted probability (the Hosmer–Lemeshow goodness-of-fit test).[31] The calibration slope is another important metric, which is calculated by regressing the observed outcome on the predicted probabilities from the model. Ideally, model calibration-in-the-large should be close to zero and the calibration slope should be close to 1. It is important to note that the assessment of model calibration should be done only in subjects not included in model derivation. This is due to the fact that model calibration in the subjects used to derive the model will typically be excellent as a result of how the models are fit by the algorithms. Poor calibration may be attributed to overfitting or changing patient case-mix from the derivation to the validation cohorts, and methods to improve model calibration have been developed.

10.3.7.4 Comparing Models

If multiple models are compared in a validation cohort, the user is sometimes left with several algorithms that differ in their discrimination, calibration, and complexity. Deciding which model to implement into practice is an individualized decision that has multiple considerations. As noted above, if the goal is to establish one threshold level to prompt a specific action, then model calibration and the positive and negative predictive values at that threshold of the different models will be more important than overall model AUC. The net reclassification index is a useful metric for classification problems that describes how patients are correctly or incorrectly classified across multiple decision thresholds.[46] This metric has been used to compare models with and without specific model features, such as biomarkers, to determine how useful these often expensive tests would be in practice. Other considerations when deciding on the optimal model for implementation include the complexity and speed at which the model output can be calculated, the generalizability of the features used in the models across different hospital sites, and the cost of collecting and implementing the different methods into practice.

10.3.8 Reporting Prediction Models

In order to include all the important information of the development process when reporting clinical prediction model, researchers are strongly encouraged to use a reporting guideline, in a similar way it is done for other study types like randomized controlled trials (e.g., CONSORT) and observational studies (e.g., STROBE).[5] One such guideline for reporting clinical prediction models is the *Transparent Reporting of a multivariable prediction model for Individual Prognosis Or Diagnosis* (TRIPOD) statement.[41] The TRIPOD statement contains a 22-item checklist that ensures the transparency of the model reporting in order to help assess its validity and usefulness.

10.3.9 Implementing and Evaluating Prediction Models

The ultimate goal of most clinical prediction models is to be used in a clinical setting and improve patient outcomes. There are many ways that a prediction model can be used in clinical settings, but perhaps the most effective way is through electronic clinical decision support systems.[3,47] Most of the design principles of clinical decisions support systems apply in the development of systems enabled by prediction models and should be followed whenever possible.[40,48,49] When designing an implementation, a common approach is to think of the output of the model as an alert for bedside clinicians once a certain risk threshold is achieved, but other outputs could be as effective, or even more effective, without contributing to the phenomenon of "alert fatigue." Implementations that stratify patients into different treatment regimens or care pathways, or that activate a different protocol at another point of the patient care process that is not directly at the bedside, such as at the pharmacy or blood bank, might have important impact in patient care without involving the bedside clinician.

Implementation is not complete without evaluation. Most prediction models would benefit from three different evaluation steps: a performance evaluation in the back end, interface testing with end users, and clinical impact and cost-effectiveness. Performance evaluation in the back end refers to running the prediction model on real-time data without reporting the output to end users.[8] This will allow the researcher to validate the performance of the model prospectively and also uncover any troubles that might arise from the algorithm running in a "real world" situation outside of the more controlled research setting. Evaluation of the interface with end users is another crucial aspect of a model implementation. If the timeliness, the message, or the actionable aspects of the prediction model do not align with the reality of clinical practice, the interface with end users will suffer. Best practices in the development and evaluation of other types of clinical decision support systems would be very helpful in this step.[48,49] Finally, the clinical impact of the model, both from a clinical outcome and a value standpoint, should also be measured after an implementation.[6] Pre- and postintervention comparisons or randomized trials can be used to measure clinical impact, whereas net benefit and decision analysis can be used to measure cost-effectiveness.

References

1. Kannel WB, McGee D, Gordon T. A general cardiovascular risk profile: The Framingham Study. *The American Journal of Cardiology*. 1976;38(1):46–51.
2. Wyatt JC, Altman DG. Commentary: Prognostic models: Clinically useful or quickly forgotten? *BMJ*. 1995;311(7019):1539–1541.
3. Bellazzi R, Zupan B. Predictive data mining in clinical medicine: Current issues and guidelines. *Int J Med Inform*. 2008;77(2):81–97.
4. Hemingway H, Croft P, Perel P et al. Prognosis research strategy (PROGRESS) 1: A framework for researching clinical outcomes. *BMJ*. 2013;346:e5595.
5. Tangri N, Kent DM. Toward a modern era in clinical prediction: The TRIPOD statement for reporting prediction models. *Am J Kidney Dis*. 2015;65(4):530–533.
6. Steyerberg EW, Moons KG, van der Windt DA et al. Prognosis Research Strategy (PROGRESS) 3: Prognostic model research. *PLoS Med*. 2013;10(2):e1001381.
7. Bates DW, Saria S, Ohno-Machado L, Shah A, Escobar G. Big data in health care: Using analytics to identify and manage high-risk and high-cost patients. *Health Aff (Millwood)* 2014;33(7):1123–1131.
8. Deo RC. Machine learning in medicine. *Circulation*. 2015;132(20):1920–1930.
9. Hastie T, Tibshirani R, Friedman J, Franklin J. The elements of statistical learning: Data mining, inference and prediction. *The Mathematical Intelligencer*. 2005;27(2):83–85.
10. Provost F, Fawcett T. Data science and its relationship to big data and data-driven decision making. *Big Data*. 2013;1(1):51–59.

11. Smith M, Saunders R, Stuckhardt L, McGinnis JM. *Best Care at Lower Cost: The Path to Continuously Learning Health Care in America.* National Academies Press; 2013.

12. Grossman C, McGinnis JM. *Digital Infrastructure for the Learning Health System: The Foundation for Continuous Improvement in Health and Health Care: Workshop Series Summary.* National Academies Press; 2011.

13. Anthony Celi L, Mark RG, Stone DJ, Montgomery RA. "Big data" in the intensive care unit. Closing the data loop. *American Journal of Respiratory and Critical Care Medicine.* 2013;187(11):1157–1160.

14. Iwashyna TJ, Liu V. What's so different about big data? A primer for clinicians trained to think epidemiologically. *Ann Am Thorac Soc.* 2014;11(7):1130–1135.

15. Riley RD, Hayden JA, Steyerberg EW et al. Prognosis Research Strategy (PROGRESS) 2: Prognostic factor research. *PLoS Med.* 2013;10(2):e1001380.

16. Huang E, Cheng SH, Dressman H et al. Gene expression predictors of breast cancer outcomes. *The Lancet.* 2003;361(9369):1590–1596.

17. Wong HR, Cvijanovich N, Allen GL et al. Genomic expression profiling across the pediatric systemic inflammatory response syndrome, sepsis, and septic shock spectrum. *Crit Care Med.* 2009;37(5):1558–1566.

18. Beck AH, Sangoi AR, Leung S et al. Systematic analysis of breast cancer morphology uncovers stromal features associated with survival. *Science Translational Medicine.* 2011;3(108):108ra113–108ra113.

19. Griffin MP, Lake DE, Bissonette EA, Harrell FE, Jr., O'Shea TM, Moorman JR. Heart rate characteristics: Novel physiomarkers to predict neonatal infection and death. *Pediatrics.* 2005;116(5):1070–1074.

20. Hood L, Flores M. A personal view on systems medicine and the emergence of proactive P4 medicine: Predictive, preventive, personalized and participatory. *N Biotechnol.* 2012;29(6):613–624.

21. Hingorani AD, Windt DA, Riley RD et al. Prognosis research strategy (PROGRESS) 4: Stratified medicine research. *BMJ.* 2013;346:e5793.

22. Churpek MM, Yuen TC, Winslow C, Meltzer DO, Kattan MW, Edelson DP. Multicenter comparison of machine learning methods and conventional regression for predicting clinical deterioration on the wards. *Crit Care Med.* 2016;44(2):368–374.

23. Kourou K, Exarchos TP, Exarchos KP, Karamouzis MV, Fotiadis DI. Machine learning applications in cancer prognosis and prediction. *Comput Struct Biotechnol J.* 2015;13:8–17.

24. Wong HR, Cvijanovich NZ, Anas N et al. Developing a clinically feasible personalized medicine approach to pediatric septic shock. *Am J Respir Crit Care Med.* 2015;191(3):309–315.

25. Moore WC, Meyers DA, Wenzel SE et al. Identification of asthma phenotypes using cluster analysis in the Severe Asthma Research Program. *Am J Respir Crit Care Med.* 2010;181(4):315–323.

26. Shah SJ, Katz DH, Selvaraj S et al. Phenomapping for novel classification of heart failure with preserved ejection fraction. *Circulation.* 2015;131(3):269–279.

27. Hastie T, Tibshirani R, Friedman JH. *The Elements of Statistical Learning: Data Mining, Inference, and Prediction.* 2nd ed. New York: Springer; 2009.

28. Hong J, Moon SM, Ahn HK et al. Comparison of characteristics of bacterial bloodstream infection between adult patients with allogeneic and autologous hematopoietic stem cell transplantation. *Biol Blood Marrow Transplant.* 2013;19(6):994–999.

29. Jenny MA, Hertwig R, Ackermann S et al. Are mortality and acute morbidity in patients presenting with nonspecific complaints predictable using routine variables? *Acad Emerg Med.* 2015;22(10):1155–1163.
30. Lee J, Maslove DM, Dubin JA. Personalized mortality prediction driven by electronic medical data and a patient similarity metric. *PLoS One.* 2015;10(5):e0127428.
31. Steyerberg E. *Clinical Prediction Models: A Practical Approach to Development, Validation, and Updating.* Springer Science & Business Media; 2008.
32. Kuhn M, Johnson K. *Applied Predictive Modeling.* Springer; 2013.
33. Breiman L. Random forests. *Machine Learning.* 2001;45(1):5–32.
34. Goldstein BA, Navar AM, Pencina MJ, Ioannidis JP. Opportunities and challenges in developing risk prediction models with electronic health records data: A systematic review. *J Am Med Inform Assoc.* 2016.
35. Cios KJ, Moore GW. Uniqueness of medical data mining. *Artificial Intelligence in Medicine.* 2002;26(1):1–24.
36. Delen D, Walker G, Kadam A. Predicting breast cancer survivability: A comparison of three data mining methods. *Artif Intell Med.* 2005;34(2):113–127.
37. Wells BJ, Chagin KM, Nowacki AS, Kattan MW. Strategies for handling missing data in electronic health record derived data. *EGEMS (Wash DC).* 2013;1(3):1035.
38. Feature Engineering. *Wikipedia: The Free Encyclopedia.* 2016; https://en.wikipedia .org/wiki/Feature_engineering. Accessed June 22, 2016.
39. Genuer R, Poggi J-M, Tuleau-Malot C. VSURF: An R package for variable selection using random forests. *The R Journal.* 2015;7(2):19–33.
40. Sanchez-Pinto LN, Khemani RG. Development of a prediction model of early acute kidney injury in critically ill children using electronic health record data. *Pediatric Critical Care Medicine.* 2016;17(6):508–515.
41. Moons KG, Altman DG, Reitsma JB et al. Transparent Reporting of a multivariable prediction model for Individual Prognosis or Diagnosis (TRIPOD): Explanation and elaboration. *Ann Intern Med.* 2015;162(1):W1–73.
42. Harrell FE. *Regression Modeling Strategies: With Applications to Linear Models, Logistic Regression, and Survival Analysis.* New York: Springer; 2001.
43. Kuhn M, Johnson K. *Applied Predictive Modeling.* New York: Springer, 2013: http:// dx.doi.org/10.1007/978-1-4614-6849-3.
44. Boulesteix AL, Janitza S, Kruppa J, Konig IR. Overview of random forest methodology and practical guidance with emphasis on computational biology and bioinformatics. *Wires Data Min Knowl.* 2012;2(6):493–507.
45. Friedman JH. Greedy function approximation: A gradient boosting machine. *Annals of Statistics.* 2001;29(5):1189–1232.
46. Steyerberg EW, Vickers AJ, Cook NR et al. Assessing the performance of prediction models: A framework for traditional and novel measures. *Epidemiology.* 2010;21(1):128–138.
47. Goldstein SL. Automated/integrated real-time clinical decision support in acute kidney injury. *Curr Opin Crit Care.* 2015;21(6):485–489.
48. Bates DW, Kuperman GJ, Wang S et al. Ten commandments for effective clinical decision support: Making the practice of evidence-based medicine a reality. *J Am Med Inform Assoc.* 2003;10(6):523–530.
49. Sittig DF, Wright A, Osheroff JA et al. Grand challenges in clinical decision support. *J Biomed Inform.* 2008;41(2):387–392.

Chapter 11

High-Dimensional Models and Analytics in Large Database Applications

Michael Brimacombe

Contents

11.1 Introduction: Detecting Patterns in Large Databases

Genetics, imaging, health outcomes, and large-scale clinical databases are all examples of settings where the amount of data is very large and complex, and the ability to analyze it is a challenge owing to the large number of subjects and variables. Simply organizing the data is often a serious endeavor, requiring major computational resources.

Genomic analysis, for example, may include gene expression patterns, networks of correlated gene expression, and the issue of how to relate expression levels to disease onset and possible treatment intervention [1]. There is also the fitting of specific models for such analyses and the assessment of latent variables and epigenetic factors. The analysis may also include the study of copy number variation [2] or more detailed RNA-based expression data [3]. Recent results in genetics have discovered more complex data types, including the presence of conserved DNA elements [4] and the importance of gene splicing [5].

Standard methods of statistical analysis are challenged in such settings. For example, when using the same model and data set to test several hypotheses regarding a common set of parameters, the family of signficance tests are conceptually linked and multiple comparison issues affect the interpretation of Type I errors, requiring careful interpretation [6]. Secondary individual tests require correction to control overall family Type I error, often rendering each test very conservative. Various methods have been suggested to make the individual hypothesis tests less conservative [7].

The growing field of data analytics, especially in the area of health analytics, reflects the need to deal with very large genetic- and health-oriented data sets that may not lend themselves to traditional statistical analysis. This often includes the refinement of data analytic and visualization methods, capturing basic patterns in the data. Indeed, often the focus in very large data sets is simply on the capturing, organization, and presentation of the data itself, with basic summary statistics and graphical presentations used to describe relevant patterns in the data [8]. From a statistical perspective, probability-based methods themselves may be of limited use in very large databases. If n is very large, standard errors have little meaning and p values may be of limited use as any effect size will be detected as significant.

On a practical level, health analytics focuses on organizing large amounts of data drawn from various sources into interpretable patterns. This implies a serious computational focus, the use of algorithms to structure and organize complex sets of measurements, variables, and other empirical structures that can help researchers identify and understand the data patterns they detect. Note that the standard approach of least squares can be interpreted as a one-step model-fitting search algorithm, heavily dependent on the assumption of a linear model and its geometric properties.

When there are more variables than subjects ($p > n$), the geometric intuition underlying the applications of linear models is altered [9]. Stagewise approaches are often used to cycle through the many possible restricted submodels with $p < n$, but these are subject to multiple comparison issues. Note further that application of linear models may not be appropriate if nonlinear functional relationships are present [10]. These are often relevant to growth processes and may be reflected in related genetic expressions. Newer statistical approaches for restricted or sparse situations ($p > n$), include least angle regression (LARS), usually extended via application of the least absolute shrinkage and selection operator (LASSO). A detailed review can be found in [11].

Outside of genetics, the areas of systems and network-related biology, imaging, clinical data repositories, Internet-based information, and other "large data" settings are all growing very quickly. Data Science or analytic-based approaches to identifying patterns in these large sets of collected data are quite varied, often reflecting a mix of methods drawn from engineering, computer science, and mathematics [12]. The statistically based approaches reviewed here apply also to these areas of investigation.

In this paper, we review aspects of analytic and statistical methods of high-dimensional data analysis. The challenges of interpreting observed data patterns in large databases is also briefly reviewed, noting that problems in the design of the database affect graphical and data-based results as well as statistical models. The effects of model misspecification are briefly discussed in relation to nonlinearity. We also briefly examine approaches drawn from mathematics and computer science that apply to the health analytic setting.

11.2 Database Structures and General Areas of Application

The raw material of large database analysis is often an integrated database composed of many variables, observed over various periods and collected on a set of subjects. This is typically observational data, and the goal is to look for patterns in the data on a variety of scales. Graphical methods and data summaries often motivate an initial study of the data and a linear model is initially used for predictive modeling if such modeling is of interest. If there is science to provide a narrower focus, then a smaller number of variables will be the setting, and nonlinear or other more detailed models applied.

The types of data that are to be found are wide ranging. In a primarily health analytics' study, the sets of variables given in Table 11.1 might be examined. This might also include patient demographics, medical history, billing information, clinical measurements, psychological assessments, genetics, family history, and other relevant variables. All such data collections require the careful selection of variable definitions (ontology) and assessment of any stochastic processes affecting the presence of missing data.

Table 11.1   Data Analytic Considerations

Computational Issues and Data Organization	Inferential Design Issues	Statistical and Probability Considerations
• Data architecture • Ontologies • Integration of multiple databases • Research databases • Initial data summaries • Graphical summaries • Privacy issues	• Bias • Comparability • Heterogeneity • Model assumptions, scaling of data • Scientific questions of interest • Missing data issues	• Law of large numbers • Central limit theorem • Standard errors • Multiple comparison issues • Correlation structures • Model selection • Model validation

The practical issues that arise in regard to the organization of such integrated databases are substantial. Computer architectural design issues are often an initial challenge when integrating different databases subject to privacy concerns and initial database structures. Ontologies may differ and may have altered over time. An administrative database is not a research database and the need to edit information to make it feasible to analyze is an issue. A list of related concerns is given in Table 11.2. For each database structural issue, there may be a related statistical

Table 11.2   Health-Related Applications

Large Data Type	Health-Related Issues	Medical Application
• Census tract • Population registry • Medicare data • Administrative and billing information • Clinical data repository • Imaging data • Genomics data • Internet-based data • Personal device related data	• Health outcomes • Health economics • Prevention • Resource utilization patterns • System efficiency • Smoking cessation • HIV and other infectious diseases: treatment and onset patterns	• Personal health-related behavioral patterns • Personal genomics • Rare disease onset and treatment • Pallative care and aging • Fetal and newborn care • Diabetes • Neurology • Cost patterns and prediction • Health quality assurance

design-related issue to consider. For example, data that are not missing at random may easily induce bias in a variable, set of variables, or cluster of subjects.

11.3 Database Issues: Observational Data and Simpson's Paradox

Much of the theory of statistical design and the design of experiments is developed with the goal of providing randomized, unbiased, and representative collections of data. This can then be aggregated into a database and summarized using graphical and statistical methods, estimating particular population characteristics or testing a hypothesis or set of hypotheses regarding those characteristics. If, however, the underlying database is a collection of data from many sources, there can be many challenges from a statistical and analytic modeling perspective.

A common challenge is Simpson's paradox [13], which states that overall patterns may differ from patterns within subgroups or substrata. If this cannot be ruled out, then each layer of information needs to be considered. If a stratification variable is left out, and in many settings we often do not know all relevant variables for the modeling of a given response, we are de facto aggregating over its levels and may obtain misleading results. Note that Simpson's paradox holds for all analyses, not just those that are probability based. Even simple graphical analyses or cross-tabulated tables can reflect this effect.

In the genetics setting, this "association reversal" phenomenon may arise owing to various triggers that seem to orchestrate genomic expression. Epigenetics, most simply in the form of DNA methylation suppression, affecting histone and chromatin levels, may stratify genetic expression [14]. With 20,000 individual genes expressing and acting as modifiers, promoters, and inhibitors of expression, these roles may alter in the presence of association reversal or favor a different set of triggers. When studying the onset of disease or cancers, these issues make analysis of genomics databases challenging and careful attention must be given to the stability of the findings obtained.

11.4 Large Sample Issues: Are All Empirical Patterns Scientifically Relevant?

A more subtle issue in large databases follows from being in the large sample context and thus subject to laws of large numbers and central limit theorems. This also includes other large sample phenomena such as power law patterns in data [15] and the Tracy–Widom distribution for the largest eigenvalue [16] and the implication of these when they are present (Table 11.3).

The question arises: Are we seeing actual empirical patterns in the response and other variables reflecting a biological or scientific reality, or are we seeing patterns

Table 11.3 Some Mathematical and Probability Laws Arising in the Analysis of Large Databases

Mathematical Law	Typical Formulation
Power law ($Y = aX^b$)	Relationship among variables. Some probability distributions have these patterns in regard to response (Pareto) or mean–variance relationship (Exponential Dispersion)
Law of large numbers	Convergence of average and other aggregate functions of random variables
Central limit theorem	Distribution of aggregated or averaged values
Benford law	Distribution of first digit in collection of observed data. Used to detect nonrandom patterns
Tracy–Widom distribution	Distribution of largest eigenvalue often reflecting properties of correlated networks of random variables or expressions defined across a threshold

attributed to the laws of large numbers? Should these be accepted as meaningful, or corrected for examining the residual elements for relevant scientific patterns? This is especially true if we do not process the data through a preexisting model structure or designed data collection procedure that can average out or parse out the various patterns in the data, relating them to the relevant variables or set of variables.

For example, in regard to power-law relationships between two measured variables Y and X, written $Y = aX^b$, where a and b are constants, these have been observed in regard to many biological and ecological relationships, for example, body size and metabolic rate across many sizes and strata of animal and organism type [17]. In relation to network data, the probability $P(k)$ that a vertex in the network interacts with k other vertices decays as a power law $P(k) \sim k^{-v}$ subject to two basic assumptions; networks exhibit preferential connectivity, and there is a higher probability that a new vertex will be linked to a vertex that already has a large number of connections. Networks are open and form by continuous addition of new vertices to the system, with the number of vertices N increasing during the lifetime of the network [18].

In relation to many naturally occuring growth patterns, power laws also arise in processes that can be viewed in terms of fractal and related chaotic behavior and multistage, nonlinear recursive growth systems, self-similar in nature [19]. Strong arguments can also be made that many power laws arise as a result of aggregation effects and large sample arguments, especially where we are counting the number of cases occuring over a set of distinct bins or types, irrespective of the underlying science [20].

11.5 High-Dimensionality and Linear Models

The standard linear model is typically expressed as

$$y = X\beta + \varepsilon,$$

where y is an $(n \times 1)$ vector of responses, $X = [x_1, \ldots, x_n]$ is an $(n \times p)$ matrix of p measured variables, and ε is an $(n \times 1)$ vector of error components. If all variables x_i are thought to be relevant, the fitted least squares model is given by $\hat{y} = Xb$, where $b = (X'X)^{-1}X'y$.

Often, many variables x_i have been collected and only a few are thought to be relevant to predicting the outcome y. Alternatively, many variables have been collected on relatively few subjects. Allowing only a few β_i values to differ from zero may help in finding a "best" underlying linear model using stepwise or stagewise methods. A sparseness restriction can be expressed:

$$\sum_{i=1}^{k} |\beta_i|^m < t,$$

for relatively small chosen values t and k. Sparseness restrictions typically assume $m = 1$ or 2. This is most useful in settings where only a few x_i are thought to be significantly correlated with the response y_i or when $p > n$ and the linear model suffers from less than full rank in the design matrix X and the least squares estimator $b = (X'X)^{-1}X'y$ does not exist in the overall model.

The LARS algorithm underlying the basic LASSO approach to fitting models in standard $n > p$ linear models [21] gives a fitted model of size m in m steps. This algorithm adds variables in a forward stagewise search approach using equiangular bisectors to find the most correlated variables in the data set, adding them sequentially. In the $p > n$ case, the LARS algorithm needs only to be slightly adjusted to accomodate a sparseness restriction. This approach has been extended to other settings [22].

11.6 Geometric Perspectives

To move from the standard $n > p$ geometry of least squares to the restricted $p > n$ setting, it is useful to begin with the standard setting. Letting $n > p$ and assuming all variables have been centered, the least squares estimator is given by $b = (X'X)^{-1}X'y$ and the related predictive value given by $\hat{y} = Xb = X(X'X)^{-1}X'y = Hy$, where H is the p-dimensional orthogonal projection matrix onto the linear span of the column vectors of X, $L(X)$. The residual vector $e = [I - H]y$ is the $(n - p)$-dimensional orthogonal projection of y onto the linear span orthogonal to $L(X)$. The orthogonality of these spaces implies $\text{Cov}(y,e) = 0$ as the cosine of the angle between them is 0.

In the $p > n$ setting, the loss of the usual residual space affects the geometry for analysis of the linear model as the dimension of the residual space $(n - p)$ is negative. Hall et al. [9] examined this setting without assuming a sparseness restriction or a linear model, studying geometric structures among a normally distributed set of variables as p increased with $p > n$. Subject to assuming the data followed a basic time-series structure, for large p, all data vectors cluster at vertices of an n-dimensional simplex. Further, these n directions lie approximately perpendicular to each other and form a simplex structure that can generally be written as

$$S = \sum_{j=1}^{n} \beta_j x_j : \beta_j \geq 0 : \sum_{j=1}^{n} \beta_j = 1$$

For large $p > n$, the observed randomness in the data is attributed to random rotations of the n vertices of this deterministic simplex structure. This has been shown to apply more generally [23]. Methods such as Singular Value Decomposition (SVD) [24] seem to work well when looking to cluster the large set of x_i variables in such settings as they already cluster at the vertices of the simplex.

11.7 Model Misspecification and Nonlinearity

As nonlinear relationships may underlie many genomic variables and related models, the immediate use of a linear model may lead to model misspecification issues. To fit linear models, algorithms often use correlation to motivate stagewise-fitting approaches. Correlation assumes linearity on some scale, and if there is a nonlinear pattern underlying the data, correlation-based algorithms may mislead.

Consider a linear model that we can express as a function of two sets of variables:

$$y = X\beta + \varepsilon = X_1\beta_1 + X_2\beta_2 + \varepsilon$$

where initially $n > p$. Assume the variables of interest are grouped in the X_1 $(n \times p_1)$ matrix with p_1 variables, with X_2 $(n \times p_2)$ matrix having p_2 additional variables, where $p_1 \ll p_2$ and $p_1 + p_2 = p$. The error term ε $(n \times 1)$ is assumed to have an $N(0,\sigma^2 I)$ distribution. If the true underlying model is nonlinear in the X_1 set of variables, linear model-fitting techniques may not accurately detect these variables. To see this, consider

$$y = F(X_1\beta_1) + X_2\beta_2 + \varepsilon$$

where $F(X_1\beta_1)$ is a nonlinear model for the X_1 subset of variables. Replacing $F(X_1\beta_1)$ with its Taylor expansion about β_{10} and using a model based on the local linear approximation gives

$$y = X_1\beta_{10} + X_2\beta_2 + \varepsilon^*$$

$$\varepsilon^* = \varepsilon + F'(X_1\beta_1)(\beta_1 - \beta_{10}).$$

This is a model with a biased error distribution $\varepsilon^* \sim N(F'(X_1\beta_1)\,(\beta_1 - \beta_{10}),\sigma^2 I)$, which affects the accuracy of estimators and model-based prediction. Stagewise methods that attempt to fit sparse models with $p > n$ are especially sensitive to such misspecification errors [25].

11.8 Graphical Methods

In the area of data analytics, graphical representation plays a large role. Often, in very large databases, they provide essential data-based summary tools for analysis, yet may be limited in their usefulness owing to the large numbers of variables and subjects. Graphics are, of course, limited by three dimensions, but can still be very useful if creatively developed.

A very useful approach is the method of principal components [24], which uses a linear transformation $Y = BX$ of the original data matrix X, whose columns are the variables of interest. The new variables, the columns of Y, are uncorrelated by design and the degree of total variation each demonstrates can be used to justify dimension reduction. A standard output is given in Figure 11.1a and b, where a simulated data set based on a set of 20 phenotypic measurements from an international collection of $n = 1000$ mummified skulls [26] is examined. The method of principal components finds that only eight principal components–defined variables are required to explain 80% of the total variation in the original data. The graphics plot the first two prinicipal components that show the correlation-based pattern of the original variables in this setting (loadings) (Figure 11.1a) and possible outliers at the subject level (Figure 11.1b).

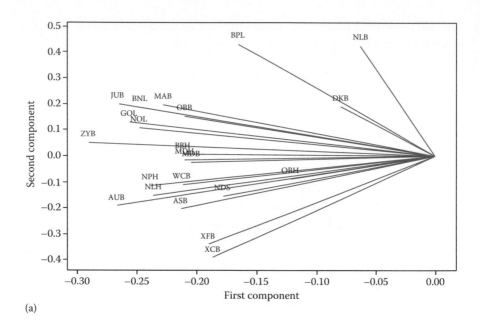

(a)

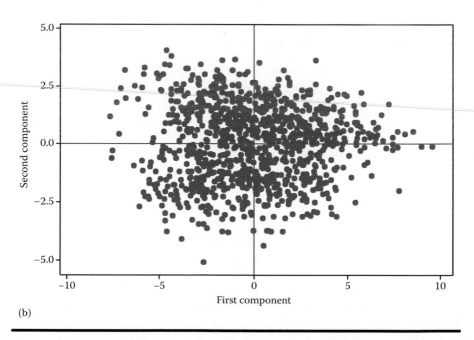

(b)

Figure 11.1 (a) Loading plot of variables on first and second principal components. (b) Scatterplot of first two principal components values for each subject.

Note, however, that just as correlation is not causation, patterns in a graphical representation are not necessarily representations of stable patterns and must be viewed with skepticism until replicated across multiple databases or randomly drawn subsets of the original database.

11.9 Replication

In general, replication allows us to better model the variation present in the response of interest. Several papers have discussed the surprising lack of replication of basic results in drug development [27]. Results that do not replicate are not stable results and there is obviously a serious need for data-based approaches and experimental designs to achieve stable and useful results in health analytics research. Variability in genomics studies, for example, may occur at the level of individual bioassay, shared platform, researcher, sample processing, and the individual response. These factors can affect the modeling of variation and data-based representations of patterns in the data in relation to both control and treatment subjects, confounding or biasing subsequent statistical or analytical study.

Other aspects of good study design in relation to data collection, such as controls to provide a useful baseline, are necessary, allowing for a relative interpretation of the data. For example, in genomic analysis, use of conserved genes can aid in the modeling of bioassay-related variation. Simple factor analysis can be employed to derive an overall "control gene variation" covariate [28] to help assess bioassay stability, though we do have to be careful to select conserved genes that are functionally related to the phenotype of interest.

In large databases, the requirement of replication does not alter. Many large databases are heterogeneous, reflecting the non–research-oriented basis for their development. Across the overall database or in specific subgroups, Simpson's paradox may also affect graphically based relationships just as those from fitted parametric models. It is important to note that, just like mathematically oriented models, unless replicated and vetted in regard to the underlying science or medicine, graphically based patterns may be misleading.

11.10 Likelihood and Bayesian Models

We note briefly that least squares–based methods can be extended to many types of underlying distributions and related statistical models. When fitting parametric probability models outside of the normal distribution to observed data, the likelihood function $L(\theta|\text{data})$ is often employed [29] and its mode, the maximum likelihood estimate, is used as an estimator of θ. With normal error, the likelihood approach yields least squares–based answers.

In large samples that may not assume normality, the central limit theorem for the maximum likelihood estimate converges to normality with the Cramer–Rao bound serving as a large sample estimate of variation. These results are standard and underlie the application of most generalized linear models, subject to regularity conditions. Note that in cases with $p > n$, the maximization of the likelihood function becomes a serious computing challenge, especially if subject to a sparsity restriction.

If the likelihood function can be modulated into a probability density on the parameter space via use of a prior density $p(\theta)$, this gives the Bayesian posterior density, which can be written $p(\theta|\text{data}) = cp(\theta)L(\theta|\text{data})$, where c is the constant of integration. For the purposes of inference, where θ is a p-dimensional vector of unknowns, the joint posterior density is averaged over the set of parameters not of interest, yielding marginal posterior densities for inferential purposes [30]. In many real-world settings, the likelihood or Bayesian parametric models may not be complex enough or may involve so many parameters that they are difficult to apply and interpret. This has led to a search for data-based approaches that are not so dependent on standard statistical formulations.

11.11 Complex Approaches to Pattern Recognition

The empirical data and computationally based sets of ideas viewed as analytics, or health analytics, are growing in application and complexity [31]. They tend not to be based on parametric model considerations, but rather observed data properties. While applied statistical techniques that are primarily empirical tend to be viewed as analytics, for example, cluster analysis, SVD, factor analysis, and object-oriented structure or dendograms [24], this is slowly becoming only a part of an overall set of approaches.

In the health analytic setting, the goals for the analysis of large data are often driven by the practicalities of health delivery and the need for standardized comparison and assessment of health treatments and outcomes. Much of the initial development of data analytics has focused on the development of platforms that can deal with very large amounts of data. Some common platforms and related tools include Cassandra, Hadoop (open source), and MapReduce [31], and these continue to be developed. Once the data are organized, the application of graphical methods, statistics, mathematical approaches, and computational search algorithms becomes practical.

11.12 Mathematical Approaches

Interesting mathematical ideas are finding application in the area of health analytics. The very large amount of data and variables in relation to complex medical applications have led to consideration of new approaches that can assess complex empirical patterns. These include statistical applications of topological functions and graphical summaries, and computer-based search algorithms.

11.13 Topology and Data Analysis

The need to find elegant geometric structures that summarize multivariable complex patterns in large databases has motivated work in the field of topology and topological structures. The complex interactions underlying the activity of the kidney, for example, in relation to the onset of diabetes, have been studied [32] from this perspective. Relating gene expression and other measurements taken over time to the onset of improvement from a specific treatment is very challenging when limited to linear measurments and related linear models. The attempt has been to find more complex nonlinear topological functions and shapes that can serve as interpretable means of summarizing treatment-related changes. These are often highly nonlinear and very flexible, and can be related by topological ideas of shape and metric invariance [32]. Invariance and transformations have a long history in statistical theory and data-based applications, but this is a more complex approach to their use.

The mapping of basic data properties, especially those data sets that can be represented as p-dimensional point clouds, onto topological surfaces and using these surfaces to summarize relationships or to look for differences over time are ongoing research [32]. Some standard topological shapes considered include the torus, sphere, and Klein bottle. A key concept is the idea of a persistent landscape, or persistent diagram, that has a topological invariance to it on some scale. Assessing whether such data-based summaries, often related to the identification of clusters, are statistically significant is a current area of research [33].

Rather than apply, for example, the simple linear transformation $Y = X\beta$ or $Y = AX$ underlying principal components and correlation or linear-based cluster methods, the topological approach attempts to develop idealized representations and mappings of data that may represent a wider variety of realistic shapes, while being invariant to distance norms or metrics [32].

It is interesting to note that design-related issues such as Simpson's paradox and the need for data replication would also be expected to affect topological data summaries. Whatever the approach to deriving statistically oriented summaries, if they do not follow the principles of good statistical and scientific design, the underlying data collection procedures need to be considered and will affect the relevance of the analytic summary obtained.

11.14 Computer-Based Approaches: Search Algorithms

Consider again the linear model $y = X\beta + \varepsilon$, where y and X are known data. Rather than apply least squares–based geometry to estimate β, what if we simply searched all possible values of the β vector in p dimensions and selected the one giving the smallest prediction error, where we can define error in terms of L_1 or L_2 measures of distance? In this setting, the least squares–based geometry or guidance is not necessary if we have a truly fast and complete search algorithm. Least squares itself can be seen as a one-step algorithm that uses the local geometry of the linear model.

The advances in computing technology and the ability to create search algorithms of tremendous speed lead to a rethinking of the place for statistical and mathematical models in the context of discovering patterns in a collection of data. While it is obvious that least squares provides a one-step optimal search algorithm, optimal in the sense of Gauss–Markov minimum variance, which itself requires the assumption of some mathematical and probabilistic structure on the problem, there may be no real need to assess search algorithms within this structure. Computational time and accuracy may be more relevant once computing speed is advanced [34].

For specific areas of application, for example, spatial patterns, the ability of algorithms focusing on pattern recognition to subdivide and localize pattern and graphical representation is very useful, providing researchers in epidemiology, health services, and other health analytic areas tools that provide insight into recent changes in disease onset.

The speed of computing algorithms has begun to allow for very simple definitions to drive the search for pattern, information, and best-fitting models. Algebraic information theory, complexity measures, and other related concepts are being used to define information theory at a primal level, often a coding level, to examine data for patterns [35]. Here, the function applied to the data often renders it a sequence of 0–1 elements for which optimal (minimal) coding length is the relevant function to minimize, rather than least squares–based departure.

Machine learning is a growing area of computational-based modeling [35]. Here, data-based classification trees can be derived and continually updated, and examined for robustness and predictive validity. Convex relaxation techniques have allowed for the development of greater computational speed in the maintenance of a large database and the processing and updating of fitted models summarizing patterns in the database [34].

11.15 Discussion

The analysis of large health-related databases is an interesting mix of statistics, large sample probability-based insights, data analysis, graphical summaries, and application to the health analytic issue or disease in question. The challenges implicit in the analysis of the large amount of data being collected have led to methodological development not only in health analytic–related areas but also in mathematical statistics, computer science, and mathematics. While most initial development has occurred in areas related to genetics, these approaches apply to a growing number of health-related fields.

Many standard statistical data analytic approaches and clustering methods involve assumptions of linearity. These are often not realistic in the complex health and medical science–based applications now being considered. This motivates the development of a broader set of methods for data analysis, and their integration into a data analytics field is an ongoing area of development. Note, however, that the need to interpret analytic results drawn from any of these sets of methods is a constant.

Poorly designed databases lead to poor results. The instabilities that may arise in any observational database, generally referred to as Simpson's paradox, can affect statistical, topological, and computational approaches. The need for replication is difficult to impose on large database collections in nonstandardized settings but is required for graphical or data analytic cluster-based methods to be viewed as validated.

As the databases to be analyzed grow in complexity and the related platforms and software improve, the opportunity to apply a variety of methods and approaches drawn from statistics, mathematics, and computer science to detect complex patterns will grow, with the goal being to develop tools and approaches that can obtain more realistic data-based methods that can better evaluate health-related disease onset, treatment, and outcome assessment.

References

1. Malone J.H. and Oliver B. (2011). Microarrays: Deep sequencing and the true measure of the transcriptome. *BMC Biology*, 9: 34. doi:10.1186/1741-7007-9-34.
2. Haraksingh R.R., Abyzov A., Gerstein M., Urban A.E., Snyder M. (2011). Genome-wide mapping of copy number variation in humans: Comparative analysis of high resolution array platforms. *PLoS ONE* 6, e27859.
3. Vollmers C., Schmitz R.J., Nathanson J., Yeo G., Ecker J.R., Panda S. (2012). Circadian oscillations of protein coding and regulatory RNAs in a highly dynamic mammalian liver epigenome. *Cell Metab.* Dec 5; 16(6): 833–845.
4. Lucas J., Carvalho C., Wang Q., Bild A., Nevins J., West M. (2006). Sparse statistical modelling in gene expression genomics. In: Do, K., Muller, P. and Vannucci, M. (editors), *Bayesian Inference for Gene Expression and Proteomics*. New York: Cambridge University Press, pp. 155–176.
5. Pan Q., Shai O., Lee L.J., Frey B.J., Blencowe B.J. (2008). Deep surveying of alternative splicing complexity in the human transcriptome by high-throughput sequencing. *Nature Genet.* 40: 1413–1415.
6. Draper N.R. and Smith H. (1981). *Applied Regression Analysis, Second Edition*. New York: John Wiley & Sons.

7. Storey J.D. and Tibshirani R. (2003). Statistical significance for genomewide studies. *PNAS* August 2003, 100(16): 9440–9445.
8. Berger B., Peng J., Singh M. (2013). Computational solutions for omics data. *Nature Reviews, Genetics*, 14: 333–346.
9. Hall P., Marron J.S., Neeman A. (2005). Geometric representation of high dimension, low sample size. *J.R. Statist. Soc. B* 67, Part 3: 427–444.
10. Brimacombe M. (2016). Local curvature and centering effects in nonlinear regression models. *Open Journal of Statistics* 6: 76–84. http://dx.doi.org/10.4236/ojs.2016.61010.
11. Johnstone I.M. and Titterington D.M. (2009). Statistical challenges of high dimensional data. *Philos. Trans. R. Soc. A* 367: 4237–4253.
12. Kambatla K., Kollias G., Kumar V., Grama A. (2014). Trends in big data analytics. *J. Parallel Distrib. Comput.* 74: 2561–2573.
13. Brimacombe M. (2014). Genomic aggregation effects and Simpson's paradox. *Open Access Medical Statistics* 4: 1–6.
14. Xu L., Jiang H., Chen H., Gu Z. (2011). Genetic architecture of growth traits revealed by global epistatic interactions. *Genome Biol. Evol.* 3: 909–914.
15. Sellis D. and Almirantis Y. (2009). Power-laws in the genomic distribution of coding segments in several organisms: An evolutionary trace of segmental duplications, possible paleopolyploidy and gene loss. Gene 447: 18–28.
16. Johnstone I.M. (2001). On the distribution of the largest eigenvalue in principal components analysis. *Ann. Statist.* 29: 295–327.
17. West G.B., Brown J.H., Enquist B.J. (1997). A general model for the origin of allometric scaling laws in biology. *Science* 276: 122–126.
18. Barabasi A.L. and Albert R. (1999). Emergence of scaling in random networks. *Science* 285: 509–512.
19. Bassingthwaite J.B., Liebovitch L.S., West B.J. (1994). *Fractal Physiology.* Oxford University Press, New York.
20. Jorgensen B. (1987). Exponential dispersion models. *Journal of the Royal Statistical Society, Ser. B (Methodological)* 49(2): 127–162.
21. Tibshirani R. (1996). Regression shrinkage and selection via the LASSO. *J. Royal Statist. Soc. B* 58(1): 267–288.
22. Tibshirani R. (1997). The LASSO method for variable selection in the Cox model. *Statistics in Medicine* 16: 385–395.
23. Ahn J., Marron J.S., Muller K.M., Chi Y.-Y. (2007). The high-dimension, low sample-size geometric representation holds under milder conditions. *Biometrika* 94(3): 760–766.
24. Johnson R.A. and Wichern D.W. (1992). *Applied Multivariate Statistical Analysis, 3rd ed.* New Jersey: Prentice Hall Inc.
25. White H. (1981). Consequences and detection of misspecified nonlinear regression models. *J. Am. Statist. Assoc.* 76(374): 419–433.
26. Howells. Skulls Data Set.
27. Begley C.J. and Ellis L.M. (2012). Drug development: Raise standards for preclinical cancer research. *Nature* 483: 531–533. doi:10.1038/483531a. Published online March 28, 2012. Clarification (May 2012).
28. Gagnon-Bartsch J.A. and Speed T.P. (2012). Using control genes to correct for unwanted variation in microarray data. *Biostatistics* 13(3): 539–552.
29. Cassela G. and Berger R.L. (2002). *Statistical Inference, 2nd ed.* Woodsworth Press.

30. Bernardo, J. and Smith A.F.M. (1994). *Bayesian Theory*. New York: John Wiley & Sons, Inc.
31. Raghupathi W. and Raghupathi V. (2014). Big data analytics in healthcare: Promise and potential. *Health Information Science and Systems* 2:3.
32. Carlsson G. (2009). Topology and data. *Bulletin (New Series) of the American Mathematical Society* 46(2): 255–308, S 0273-0979(09)01249-X.
33. Blumberg A.J., Gal I., Mandell M.A., Pancia M. (2014). Robust statistics, hypothesis testing, and confidence intervals for persistent homology on metric measure spaces. *Found. Comput. Math.* 14(4): 745–789. ISSN 1615-3375. doi:10.1007/s10208-014 -9201-4. http://dx.doi.org/10.1007/s10208-014-9201-4.
34. Chandrasekaran V. and Jordan M.I. (2012). Computational and statistical tradeoffs via convex relaxation. *PNAS*, Published online March 11, 2013 | E1181–E1190.
35. Kashyap H., Ahmed H.A., Hoque N., Roy S., Bhattacharyya D.K. (2014). Big data analytics in bioinformatics: A machine learning perspective. *Journal of LaTex Class Files* 13(9).

Chapter 12

Learning to Extract Actionable Evidence from Medical Insurance Claims Data

---

Jieshi Chen and Artur Dubrawski

Contents

12.1 Introduction

Medical insurance claims are a trove of data that have been collected and stored by various players in the healthcare industry for many years, primarily for recording purposes. These data have not been used much to support any other than billing, accounting, and actuarial needs. This voluminous and highly dimensional, but largely underutilized data contain, however, actionable information that can be leveraged to control the costs of care and to improve its quality. In this chapter,

219

we present a few case studies to demonstrate that medical insurance claims data can be effectively used to identify inefficiencies in the healthcare system that might unfairly drive up the cost of care and to spot opportunities for improved quality of care and better health outcomes for the individual patients as well as the general public.

The presented case studies rely on the machine learning methodology to implement data-driven analyses. Machine learning has shown the ability to create strategic value to all parties involved in healthcare industry by helping address a wide spectrum of problems ranging from mitigating escalation of costs of care to reducing variability of its quality [1]. For instance, insurance companies can use machine learning models to track outcomes to better align patient incentives with reimbursement strategies; monitor billing patterns to detect and eliminate fraud, waste, or abuse of the system; and enhance cost-effectiveness of care through improved membership management. Providers of care such as hospitals and physicians can achieve more accurate diagnoses and identify effective treatments based on patients' clinical data. Pharmaceutical companies could use clinical data and medical records to quantify and predict the effectiveness of drug therapies and identify physicians with suitable practices to facilitate clinical trials. Even individual patients could benefit from predictive analysis of possible diseases based on historical medical records and personal habits and take early action for improved health management and better outcomes. For government and public stakeholders, machine learning brings a great potential in detecting disease outbreaks, monitoring effectiveness of hospital usage of resources, guiding policy decisions on nationwide healthcare policies and medical surveillance programs, and monitoring and quantifying the outcomes of such decisions. All of that is motivated by the intention to help mitigate the soaring magnitudes of expenditures on healthcare and to elevate the quality and effectiveness of care to new levels. Machine learning methodology can provide creative solutions to alleviate challenges of scales and quality of data and, more importantly, produce strategic value for healthcare system players through approaches such as accurate predictive modeling including classification and regression, informative visualization and clustering, association analysis, and so on.

In this chapter, we demonstrate a few examples of applying this methodology to enable purposive analysis of medical insurance claim data. We chose these diverse examples hoping to motivate a wider adoption of advanced machine learning–based analytics to this and other similar types of readily available and currently underutilized data. The first case demonstrates how anomaly detection can be used to detect break points in billing patterns that may reflect systematic inefficiencies. The second case develops metrics to measure emergency room utilization by the chronically ill and exposes differences of efficiency of managing such patients between public and private insurers. The third case uses adaptive supervised classification to predict undocumented conditions from the history of a patient's medical claims. Finally, the last case illustrates how sequential rule learning algorithm can help identify patients suffering from rare and hard-to-diagnose diseases such as Gaucher disease by revealing characteristic patterns in their medical claims histories.

12.2 Detecting Break Points in Medical Billing Patterns

Healthcare expenditures in the United States reached $3.0 trillion in 2014 [2]. The costs are projected to reach $3.2 trillion, or $10,000 per person, in 2015 [3]. According to the National Health Care Anti-Fraud Association, the healthcare fraud is estimated to cause tens of billions of dollars of financial loss each year [4]. The healthcare fraud judgments, settlements, and additional administrative impositions in healthcare fraud cases added up to $2.4 billion in 2015 [5]. The most common types of fraud, such as false diagnoses and unnecessary treatment, identity theft, and fraud billing for more expensive than actually required services, carry a very high price tag for all stakeholders within the healthcare ecosystem. Thus, it is very important for institutional players, such as government agencies, healthcare service providers, and insurance companies, to closely monitor medical billing data for unexpected patterns, especially change points in billing behavior that may represent an illicit or inadvertently wasteful activity.

It is well known that coding and billing industry rules in the United States are subject to change from time to time owing to policy changes of Medicare and Medicaid systems or to disease coding system updates such as recent transition of International Classification of Diseases (ICD) coding standards from ICD-9 to ICD-10. Healthcare service providers such as hospitals demand more insights from the data for better management of their revenue cycles to optimize patient management and hospital resource allocation. Insurers or payers, both private and public, who are taking the greatest burden of financial risk of medical claim fraud and abuse, rely mostly on medical claims data to detect anomalous billing patterns and avoid or recover their financial losses. However, it is challenging to perform data analytics comprehensively against large-scale, complex, multidimensional data sets such as medical claims data. To address this challenge, machine learning techniques could be creatively applied to perform scalable, efficient, useful, and timely data analysis to detect unexpected patterns and changes within the records of medical claims so that they could be further investigated and subjected to audits.

Legitimate reasons notwithstanding, changes in billing patterns or code usage may be an indication of revenue optimization attempts by the providers or changing treatment patterns by the physicians who deliver care. To reveal such changes, a massive screening methodology can be deployed retrospectively or prospectively to detect billing pattern breaking points within the medical claim records across time and other dimensions of data, for example, to detect significant changes in frequency of claims involving a particular Diagnosis Related Group (DRG).

The example shown in Figure 12.1 presents such a significant change detected in retrospective analysis of data submitted by one of the hospitals in the state of

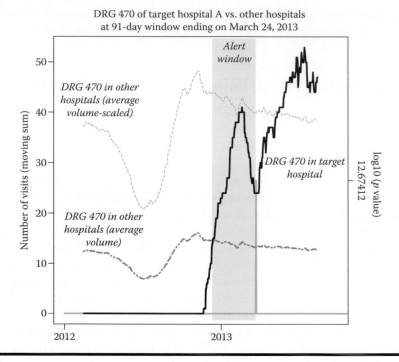

Figure 12.1 Detected unexpected shift of the volume of claims submitted with DRG 470 by one of the hospitals in California.

California. We observe a significant volume increase of medical claims submitted for the surgical DRG 470 (the code for a major joint replacement or reattachment of lower extremity without comorbidities or complications) by this hospital, compared to the number of claims for the same DRG in the other hospitals in California, during the highlighted 91-day time window ending on March 24, 2013. Based on prior billing activity of this healthcare provider, we expect to observe zero cases billed with DRG 470 during the current period of analysis, but we actually observe 37 such cases. Fisher's exact test of significance applied to a 2-by-2 matrix of counts of events is one of the methods that could be used to quantify the magnitude of the apparent anomaly. The upper left cell of the matrix typically represents the number of claims of particular characteristics recorded during the historical reference period of observation. In the example shown, these are the claims involving DRG 470 originating from the target hospital during 91 days immediately preceding the current window of observation, but the period of reference could be chosen differently (e.g., to account for potential seasonality, we could have chosen as a reference the same range of calendar days as the current window of analysis, but taken from data recorded in previous years). The upper right cell represents the same data observed in the current 91-day window at the same hospital. The lower two cells represent respectively the same frequency statistics computed cumulatively for all other hospitals in California. In this case, Fisher's test yields a p value lower than 10^{-12}, indicating that the probability of the observed change to be the result of random fluctuation of data is not greater than 10^{-12}, suggesting that we have a highly statistically significant finding that begs further investigation. The result would be insignificant if the proportion of current and past counts of the specific kinds of claims observed in the analyzed hospital more closely matched the proportion of the same DRG activity observed elsewhere. Note that Fisher's test is just one of the possible choices for the method of detecting anomalies in billing activity. We use it here as an example given its popularity and simplicity, but virtually any control chart approach can be used to complement the analyses, including computationally efficient chi-square approximation of Fisher's test, or the cumulative sum algorithm popular in public health applications. In any case, besides a potential fraudulent activity or inadvertent systematic mistake in coding by this provider, significant break points in billing patterns might also be explainable by benign reasons, as it is very likely the case in our current example, such as the target hospital opening a new specialization and hiring new surgeons to perform joint replacements at the end of year 2012, so that a number of new patients are introduced to the hospital for joint surgeries.

The result shown in Figure 12.1 is one of potentially very many statistically significant anomalies in billing patterns that can be found in medical claims transactional data by machine learning algorithms and data structures that facilitate massive scale searches through such data. It is worth noting that one can configure multiple alternative testing scenarios using various definitions of periods of analysis and reference, as well as various definitions of peer reference groups against which to compare the target. Truly comprehensive analyses will allow testing across a range of temporal resolution settings for both the current analysis and reference windows, and conduct tests against all dimensions of activity. Similar searches can and should be performed against other dimensions of medical claims data such as diagnosis codes, procedure codes, the Healthcare Common Procedure Coding System (HCPCS) codes, geographic locations (cities, counties), and other claim attributes, including patients' demographics. In addition, retrospective scans can be performed at arbitrary temporal resolutions, for example, by repeating those analyses at daily increments over the interval of time that needs to be reviewed. The multiplicity of choices and configurations at which the presented search for changes in patterns of billing activity often yields billions of hypotheses that need to be tested if the analyses were to be truly comprehensive. This justifies the popular nickname of this approach: massive screening. It also opens two practical challenges: high computational cost of performing these analyses, and statistical vulnerability of the results induced by testing multiple hypotheses.

The latter of these challenges can be addressed operationally by correcting for the escalated risk of Type I errors by applying one of the popular methods of significance threshold adjustment, for example, Bonferroni's correction or False Discovery

Rate method. To address computational scalability issues in the examples shown in this chapter, we relied on an efficient data structure called T-Cube [6,7]. It is a form of a data cube that caches statistics of data sufficient to very quickly compute, for example, Fisher's test results in response to arbitrary queries against highly dimensional databases of time-stamped or dated transactions whose fields are represented by categorical variables such as DRG codes or provider identifiers.

The ability to perform these analyses quickly and comprehensively eliminates the risk of missing important clues, and since the results found can be ordered by their statistical significance, the analysts can prioritize their attention to the most outstanding cases. An early and accurate detection of such anomalous patterns can help hospitals better allocate their clinical resources and correct inadvertent coding errors, as well as help insurance companies recognize the changes in the stream of claim reimbursements coming from specific providers, or across the industry, to optimize and negotiate corresponding reimbursement base rates and alternative treatment options in a timely fashion.

The T-Cube–based searches can include scanning through a range of time window sizes to enable identification of the time scales and persistence of the detected change patterns, as some of them may take longer to develop than others. The detection shown in Figure 12.1 highlighted the initial period of change but the increasing trend has extended beyond the span of the time window of the original detection of the anomaly, when the observed escalation of the unexpected activity was the most statistically significant. Figure 12.2 shows an example of a "spike" of activity. We observe a significant claim volume increase of DRG 392 (esophagitis, gastroenteritis, and miscellaneous digestive disorders without multiple complications and comorbidities) at a particular hospital compared to the same DRG in other hospitals of reference during the 364-day time window ending on October 30, 2011. At that date, the activity involving DRG 392 is actually already declining toward its historical levels. Clearly, this is an example of a sudden but temporary increase of activity, which did not remain at the elevated level for long. The possibility of this change to be random according to Fisher's test is approximately 10^{-16}, which is very highly statistically significant and still lower than the corresponding threshold of Bonferroni correction against risks of multiple hypotheses testing.

Increasing costs of operations and narrowing profit margins push healthcare providers to look for efficiencies. One of the conceivable approaches is to review one's own billing practices in an attempt to identify opportunities for increasing payoff from submitted claims while remaining within the boundaries of medical and ethical correctness of billed services and supplies. Occasionally, however, the optimization attempts may include upcoding. One type of an upcoding behavior is to capitalize on differences between negotiated reimbursement rates for treatments that carry varied costs depending on, for example, severity of the particular case and their comorbidities or complications.

Figure 12.3 shows an interesting example found via T-Cube–powered massive screening for swaps between claims involving pairs of medically relevant DRGs

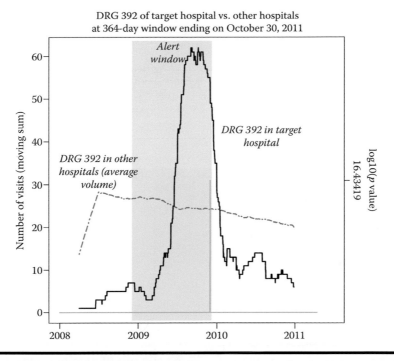

Figure 12.2 Detected unexpected spike in the number of claims submitted with DRG 392 by another hospital.

that differ in cost weighting. The algorithm flagged a particular hospital where, over a period of several months, one could observe a gradual but systematic pattern of interchange between the higher cost bearing DRG 765 (a code for cesarean section with multiple complications or comorbidities) and the lower cost bearing DRG 766 (cesarean section without complications and comorbidities). During the period of observation, the higher-cost DRG shows a systematically increasing trend while the lower-cost DRG shows a complementary pattern of decline. The cumulative volume of both DRGs remains almost constant throughout. The possibility of this change to be random is lesser than 1 in 10^{12}. Moreover, after the apparent change took place, the frequencies of claims involving both DRGs stabilize and remain at relatively constant levels moving forward.

That is an example finding of interest to the insurance companies who may want to check with this provider to confirm legitimacy of the apparent changes in billing patterns. Since the insurance reimbursement basis is much higher for the first of the DRG codes, this particular pattern of a suspicious code swap may be reflective of a financial optimization attempt by this hospital, or explainable by a shift of their specialization toward handling more difficult cases of late pregnancies. Conversely, the hospitals themselves may also benefit from monitoring their

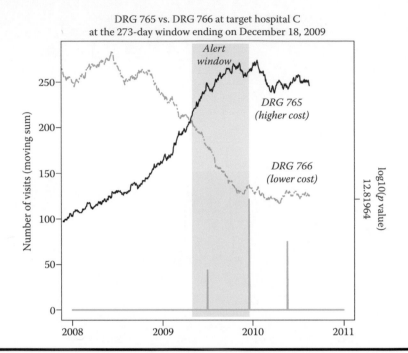

Figure 12.3 **A suspicious pattern of a systematic substitution of claims involving cesarean sections without complications and comorbidities with claims that include these factors and yield higher reimbursements.**

own outgoing streams of claims for possible inadvertent systematic down-coding episodes caused by, for example, overworked clinicians who prefer to avoid the hassle of fully documenting borderline cases merely for the cost recovery purposes. In either scenario, a large-scale machine learning–based anomaly detection can be effectively used to monitor streams of medical claims for statistically significant anomalous patterns that should be looked at by the analysts and adjudicators to verify their legitimacy and to potentially identify and eliminate previously unknown inefficiencies. The same approach can also be used to monitor outpatient, professional, and pharmacy claims.

To accomplish the analyses presented in this section, approximately 1.5 billion Fisher's tests of significance have been performed for the single DRG massive screening, spanning 470 unique DRGs and 8 different sizes of time windows of analysis. For the pairwise screening, the number of tests conducted equaled 65 million across selected pairs of DRGs, which shared similar distribution of the principal diagnosis codes present on their respective claims. This matching was done to encourage potential medical relevance of the paired DRGs. The computations performed on a single-core 3.4-GHz CPU took approximately 8 h. The relatively fast completion of these extensive computational tasks has been facilitated by using the T-Cube data structure to represent the underlying medical claims data.

12.3 Using Medical Claims to Analyze Resource Utilization

A 2010 report of the New England Healthcare Institute [8] estimated the overuse of US emergency departments (EDs) being responsible for the annual $38 billion in wasteful spending and increasing. One of the key drivers of ED overuse, despite recent efforts to strengthen primary care, is the limited access to timely primary care services, as stated in a more recent report by RAND Corporation [9]. This is especially evident in the case of chronically ill patients who, if properly managed at the primary level, should not require emergency services for primary complaints directly stemming from their chronic conditions.

A recent study [10] applied machine learning methodology similar to the approach described above, to analyze medical claims data to identify patterns of ED resource utilization by the chronically ill. It used institutional insurance claims collected from more than 400 hospitals in California between 2006 and 2010 and developed a metric called Relative Utilization Ratio (RUR) to quantify relative levels of utilization of ED by patients covered by different insurers, defined for a particular provider as follows:

$$p_{ij} = \frac{N_{ij}}{N_j}; \quad p_{-ij} = \frac{N_j - N_{ij}}{N - N_j}; \quad \mathrm{RUR}_{ij} = p_{ij}/p_{-ij}.$$

Here, N represents the total number of ED claims submitted by the provider during the period of analysis, N_j stands for the number of ED claims submitted to the particular insurer j, and N_{ij} represents the number of ED claims submitted to j with primary complaint corresponding to the particular chronic condition i. The RUR scores were computed and aggregated for a few types of chronic conditions over all institutional providers in the state of California over the 5-year period of analysis, stratifying for patient ages, and average scores and their binomial confidence limits have been estimated by aggregating across hospitals.

Figure 12.4 compares relative utilization of ED resources by diabetic patients covered by private versus public payers. The horizontal axis corresponds to the age group of patients (from young to old) and the vertical axis reflects the RUR scores estimated from data. For most patient ages, patients with diabetes who are covered by private payers put significantly less demand on ED services for episodes involving diabetes as their primary complaint, when compared to similar patients covered by public payers. Figure 12.5 splits these results into more detailed payer categories. We can see that self-paying category and patients covered by Medicaid show their

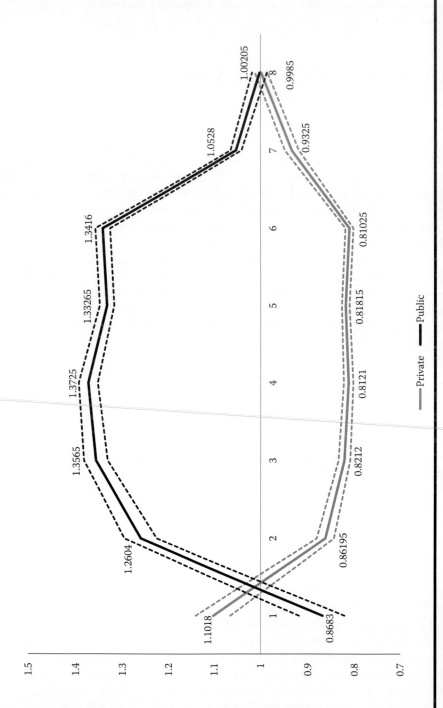

Figure 12.4 Comparison of RURs of privately versus publicly insured diabetics across patient age groups. The graph shows average RUR scores computed across hospitals in California over 5 years ending in 2010 and their 95th percentile confidence intervals.

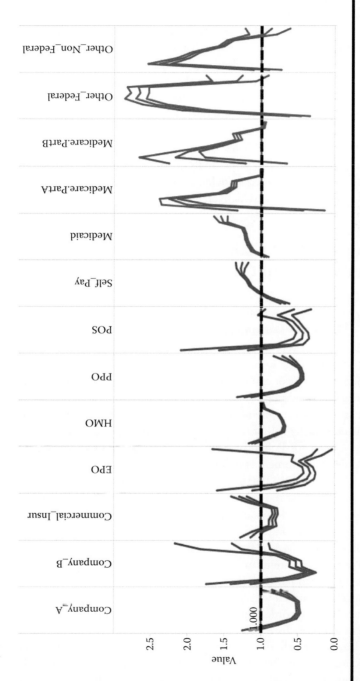

Figure 12.5   A closer view of the impact of insurance coverage type and relative utilization of ED resources by diabetic patients who report to ED with diabetes as their primary complaint.

demand for ED services for diabetes steadily increasing with age, while patients covered by other public sources show opposite trends to those covered by various private plans, controlling for age. Similar patterns have also been revealed for patients suffering from chronic asthma and arthritis. These results suggest that the privately insured are more effectively incentivized to manage their chronic conditions in primary care and avoid costly ED service than those carrying public insurance.

The study reveals an opportunity to indirectly quantify the effectiveness of managing chronic conditions, and consequently patient outcomes, by tracking ER resource utilization via medical claims as a proxy. It also brings the worthwhile awareness of the difference of efficacy between publicly funded plans and private health insurance providers. The same analytic approach can be applied to other diseases, or other hospital resources, including peer-to-peer comparisons of relative efficiency and effectiveness of care delivered by the individual healthcare providers.

12.4 Using Medical Claims to Predict Undocumented Conditions

In 2013, the US national health expenditures grew 3.6% to $2.9 trillion, or $9255 per person, and accounted for 17.4% of the Gross Domestic Product (GDP) [11]. For 2014–2024, the figure is expected to grow at an average rate of 5.8% per year, which means that nearly $1 in every $5 spent in the United States by 2024 will be spent on healthcare [12]. Among the components of the national health expenditure, Medicare spending accounts for 20% or approximately $585.7 billion in 2013. Inaccurate documentation of medical conditions or errors in medical claims data may result in incorrect risk score estimations for members of Medicare Advantage (MA) program. This exposes the insurers to the risk of financial losses, or it may cause the government to overspend. The Center for Public Integrity launched an extensive investigation into MA in 2014, publishing numerous reports that showed inflated risk scores and other errors between 2008 and 2013 that totaled a staggering $70 billion in overpayments to insurers. The report further shows that auditors were not able to confirm one-third of the 3950 medical conditions contained in patients' medical records, primarily because of insufficient documentation provided by physicians [13].

For patients in the MA plan or a plan purchased from Health Insurance Marketplace, insurers are reimbursed for healthcare services according to a risk score computed for each patient. This score is a function of the patient's diagnoses and condition codes claimed within a fiscal year. Latencies of billing processes and various inaccuracies in recorded data may obfuscate the visibility of the true condition of a patient and therefore affect their risk score.

Machine learning methodology can potentially be used to predict true latent annual risk scores and condition codes for the insured members that will be in effect by the end of the fiscal year before that date to hopefully mitigate revenue loss attributed to inadequate coding and to identify undocumented conditions to enable prompt medical follow-up with patients at risk of being undiagnosed for certain diseases. If a patient indeed has undocumented conditions, then their insurer will be underpaid for the risk they are taking. A similar scenario occurs when an insurance plan is taking new members. It is desirable to estimate their risk scores and unreported conditions even though the plan may have very limited visibility of each new patient's medical history at the time they are first enrolled.

The potential utility of such predictive model goes beyond reducing the business risk carried by the insurers. Health status of patients suffering from undocumented conditions may deteriorate until they are properly diagnosed and treated. Early detection of serious illness at its early stage and enabling its prompt management could make a significant difference for the patient and their outcome. If missing codes can be predicted well, then insurance companies have multiple options to correcting the patient's records. They may have a healthcare professional visit the patient's home, review the patient's charts, or incentivize their primary care physicians to have them in for an office visit. Accurate predictions of potentially missing conditions can be used to initiate the most cost-effective follow-ups for each patient.

We will now show an example of a successful framework for predicting undocumented Condition Codes (CCs) using machine learning methodology. The study builds and empirically validates computationally scalable predictive models to identify likely undocumented conditions and true latent annual risk scores from 28.6 million institutional claim records of approximately 330,000 MA members collected over three consecutive calendar years.

The base model takes the first three quarters of a year as input data to predict the presence of new and then undocumented CCs that were added to the patient's record in the fourth quarter of the year or during the four quarters of the following year. Each patient is represented with a binary vector, elements of which reflect the presence or absence of each of the 70 CCs under consideration within the first three quarters of their membership. The binary output variable indicates the presence or absence of a particular CC of interest during the next five calendar quarters. The study uses a Random Forest algorithm to independently train classification models, one for each CC to be predicted, and evaluates these models using 10-fold cross-validation. In this protocol, only the training subsets of data provide the machine learning model with the ground truth, that is, the appearance of new CCs during the following five quarters. However, the test data do not reveal this information to the model, they are instead used for evaluation of the model's ability to make accurate predictions. The results of the base 9-month model are compared to a more informed alternative that relies on 21 months (1 year and 3 quarters) of claims history for these patients for whom these much data are available. Therefore, the 9- and 21-month histories of claims are used as alternative inputs for making predictions, and the results are compared using cross-validated area under the receiver operating characteristic (ROC) score (AUC).

Figure 12.6 shows ROC curves and their 95th percentile confidence intervals obtained for predicting undocumented CC74 (seizure disorder and convulsions)

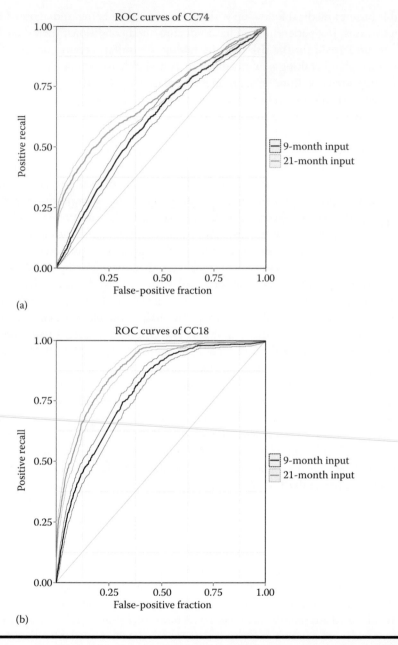

(a)

(b)

Figure 12.6 Receiver operating characteristic diagrams showing predictive ability of the models using 9-month and 21-month data to predict CC74 (a) and CC18 (b) to appear during the next five quarters.

and CC18 (diabetes with ophthalmologic or unspecified manifestation) during the next five quarters using claims observed during the past 9 (black lines) and 21 months (gray lines), respectively. As expected, the more data available (21 vs. 9 months of medical claims records), the more predictable the future conditions. Also, predictability of an undocumented condition varies between diseases.

More than 80% of the 70 considered CCs had AUC scores significantly above 0.5 (random chance level), and some of them were above 0.8, when using trailing 21 months' worth of claims data, as shown in Figure 12.7. Distribution of AUC scores of the models predicting the most prevalent 23 CCs (prevalence rates greater than 1% of member population) is plotted with a line relative to the right-hand-side scale. The results are sorted by the prevalence of individual CCs in data shown with bars with the scale shown in the left hand side of the diagram. The emergence of the previously undocumented CCs is readily predictable for these codes—none of the results shown in Figure 12.7 drops below an AUC of 0.65. Members who had recorded target CCs during the reference period have been excluded from evaluation so that only the newly documented occurrences count as true positives.

With the predicted presence of CCs, we are able to apply the published Centers for Medicare and Medicaid Services Hierarchical Condition Categories procedure to compute the predicted latent risk scores for each insured member. Figure 12.8 shows a ROC plot depicting the ability of the CC prediction model to prioritize recovery of missed revenue for the health insurance plan. The performance of a model that randomly samples patients for medical follow-up in order to identify any missing diagnoses follows the main diagonal of the diagram spanning the dimensions of the sample size (horizontal axis) and the recovered risk cumulative scores (vertical axis). We expect our machine learning model, trained to predict the missing CCs, to recover 50% of the unreimbursed revenue by reviewing up to 15% of the members at the highest predicted risk of missing some CCs, while improving accuracy of patient diagnoses and boosting quality of their health outcomes. The operationally optimal set point of this model may certainly differ from the one that corresponds to the showcased 50% cost recovery rate. It will depend on the ratio of unit costs of a false-positive detection (each of them leads to an unnecessary follow-up) and false negatives (unidentified undocumented condition), as well as the organizational capacity of the insurer and the providers to facilitate medical follow-ups with the prioritized members.

Undocumented condition categories can be predicted with a practically relevant accuracy. The presented approach can be useful in prioritizing follow-up actions to target the verification and documentation of missing conditions. It can enable better health management of patients and improved cost-effectiveness of healthcare delivery attributed to improved risk assessment.

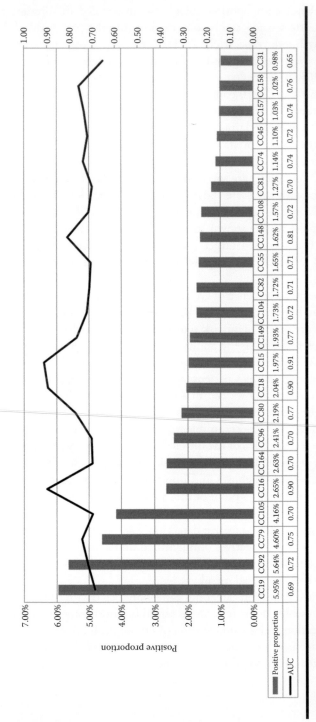

Figure 12.7   Area under receiver operating characteristic (AUC) scores and prevalence rates for the 23 most prevalent CCs.

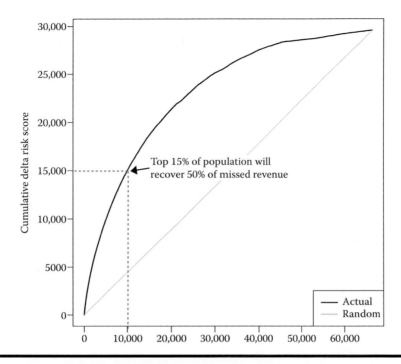

Figure 12.8 **Operating characteristic of the machine learning model ability to recover missed revenue by prioritizing members for medical follow-ups.**

12.5 Using Medical Claims to Identify Sufferers of Rare Diseases

It is not uncommon for patients suffering from rare diseases to be hard to diagnose. Their conditions may remain undetected for prolonged periods while their reported signs and symptoms as well as diagnostic test results can lead their care providers to erroneous hypotheses regarding the underlying health problems, prompting treatments for perhaps more common conditions these patients do not actually have, while not being treated for the real issue. This may obviously lead to an escalation of the untreated condition and expose the patients to the risks and side effects of treatments they undergo in error. If these patients could be identified accurately and early, the costs of unnecessary care could be avoided, their outcomes could improve, and they could be spared from the ordeal of potentially lengthy sequences of tentative treatments under wrong diagnoses.

While clinicians work hard to enhance the practice of diagnostics and improve detectability of rare diseases, machine learning models developed for analyzing sequential event data bring the capability to identify patterns in medical claim records that can make the rare disease sufferers stand out from the background of the rest of the patient population [14]. Patients flagged by a trained machine learning model as likely carriers of a particular rare disease can be prioritized for follow-ups, including genetic tests that are nowadays capable of adjudicating at least some such diseases with a very high precision.

Algorithms ideal for this purpose would scale well to large volumes and complexities of medical claims data and they would remain sensitive to target patterns despite a typically extremely low prevalence of the cases of interest in the available data. It would also be capable of taking into account sequences of claims in its predictions since we intuit that the rare disease cases would show distinctive sequential patterns in their claim histories.

We applied a sequential rule learning algorithm [15] to a data set of 1753 patients selected from a large database of members of one of the major health plans. The subjects were preselected to have medical histories that could be indicative of a Gaucher disease (GD), but only 25 of them have been confirmed as positive for GD so far. Corresponding records of more than 168,000 medical claims and 142,000 pharmaceutical prescription claims were featured separately for each patients into sequences of asynchronous events and regularly sampled time series based on their historical claim records as inputs for the algorithm. For example, an occurrence of a certain diagnosis code in a medical claim was counted as one event along the timeline of the patient's medical history. Thus, it was with other key attributes such as procedure codes, American Medical Association's Current Procedural Terminology—Healthcare Common Procedure Coding System (CPT/ HCPCS) codes, service provider codes, National Drug Codes (NDCs), DRGs, and so on. These types of events and their basic statistics, such as moving frequencies of particular event types, their standard deviations, peaks, change points, and so on, as well as generic statistics of claim activity, such as number of prescriptions filled in a period, formed the input feature space for the machine learning algorithm. The sequential rule learning algorithm was trained to adjudicate each test case and estimate the likelihood of them suffering from GD.

Figure 12.9 depicts the results predictive analytics obtained via cross-validation. Each case adjudication result includes the predicted probability of GD for the patient. These estimates can be used to rank all patients accordingly and prioritize follow-ups for genetic testing for those who rank high. The 10-fold cross-validation AUC score for the resulting sequential rule learning model is 0.8128, indicating a generally good predictability of the GD diagnosis. The left graph in Figure 12.9 shows ROC plotted in the familiar linearly scaled false-positive rate axis, while the right plot shows the same data using a decimal logarithm scale to emphasize the performance of the model in the very low false-positive rate range. Considering the practicality of costs of performing follow-ups such as genetic tests, we prefer a model achieving high recall (true positive rate) at low probabilities of generating false-positive detections. We can see that our model correctly identifies more than 25% of known positive cases while staying within 0.1% of the false detection rate.

The results also include rules explicitly used in adjudication, which are highly interpretable with sequential events. For example, Figure 12.10 illustrates one of

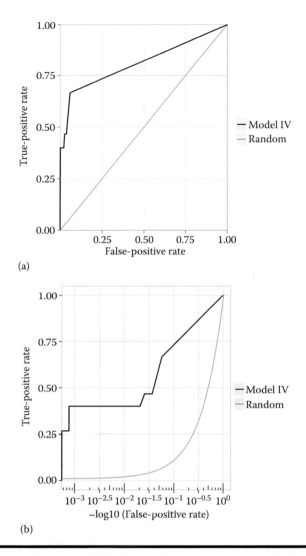

(a)

(b)

Figure 12.9 **Receiver operating characteristic curves for adjudicating Gaucher disease (GD) versus non-GD patients.**

these rules. The top box indicates the root node of the case adjudication tree, with "Event.7969" representing the ICD-9 diagnosis of "Other nonspecific abnormal findings." The text in the box indicates that among the 14 patients that have this particular ICD-9 code present in their claim history, 36% are confirmed GD sufferers. Compared to default prevalence measured on our preselected data set (note that this prevalence rate is much higher than that for the general population), this rule increases the probability of having GD for each patient who matches it 25 times.

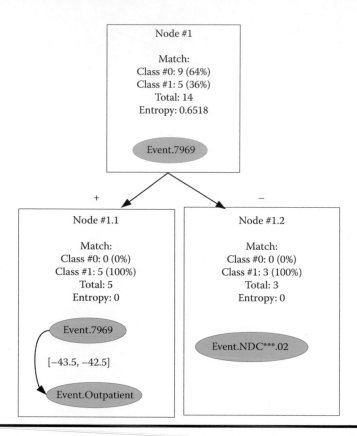

Figure 12.10 Example rule inferred from claims data and used in adjudication of possible Gausher disease cases.

Then, the rule develops to the next level of left and right branches. In the left branch Node #1.1 that combines the familiar Event.7969 (ICD-9 for other non-specific abnormal findings) with any outpatient claim observed within 43 claims from the occurrence of the Event.7969, we isolate five patients, 100% of whom are GD-positive. The right branch Node #1.2 reflects patients who do not have Event.7969 in their claim history, but who have been prescribed NDC 62756-0137-02 (gabapentin by Sun Pharmaceutical Industries Ltd.). There are three such patients in our reference data set and all of them are GD-positive. This is just one example of a quite simple and easy-to-implement business rule, automatically inferred from the routinely collected claims data that could be used to identify previously undiagnosed sufferers of rare diseases.

The key advantage of the presented approach to rare disease determination is that it can utilize information represented in the sequential relationships between events in claims history for each patient and reveal interpretable sequential patterns that indicate the cases of interest with a substantially higher than proportional probability. In addition, the underlying algorithm scales well to large volumes of diverse claims data and it can remain sensitive to target patterns despite a typically very low prevalence of the rare disease cases seen in such data. Machine learning methodology can therefore enable proactive monitoring of sequences of claims for patients with high probability of suffering from a rare and hard-to-diagnose disease in order to prioritize them for follow-ups with, for example, genetic tests for precise adjudication. These patients could be identified and diagnosed earlier than before and receive appropriate and timely treatment to reduce risk of complications and improve health outcomes.

12.6 Summary

Medical insurance claims are a rich source of actionable evidence that, if extracted, could substantially improve remediation of various challenges prevalent in healthcare industry ranging from ever-increasing costs to varied quality of care and its outcomes. These data historically have been, but also currently remain, largely underutilized. We have shown a few examples of how beneficial it could be when purposively analyzed using machine learning methodology. Our hope was to motivate more extensive use of medical claims records to utilize the intelligence embedded in them for attainable improvements of many facets of the healthcare industry.

Acknowledgments

The authors wish to thank Jeff Schneider, Ryan McDermitt, and Yue Wang for their numerous contributions to various aspects of research summarized here. This work has been partially supported by the National Science Foundation award 1320347 and by a project award from the Carnegie Mellon University Disruptive Health Technology Institute.

References

1. Michael R. Pinsky and Artur Dubrawski, Gleaning knowledge from data in the ICU. *J Respir Crit Care Med.* 2014 Jul 28; 190(6): 606–610. DOI: 10.1164/rccm.201404 -0716CP PMID: 25068389 PMCID: PMC4214111.
2. Centers for Medicare and Medicaid Services, National Health Expenditures 2014 Highlights, https://www.cms.gov/research-statistics-data-and-systems/statistics-trends -and-reports/nationalhealthexpenddata/downloads/highlights.pdf.
3. Centers for Medicare and Medicaid Services, National Health Expenditures Projections 2015–2025, https://www.cms.gov/Research-Statistics-Data-and-Systems/Sta tistics-Trends-and-Reports/NationalHealthExpendData/Downloads/Proj2015.pdf.

4. National Health Care Anti-Fraud Association, The Challenge of Health Care Fraud, https://www.nhcaa.org/resources/health-care-anti-fraud-resources/the-challenge-of-health-care-fraud.aspx.

5. Centers for Medicare and Medicaid Services, The Health Care Fraud and Abuse Control Program Protects Consumers and Taxpayers by Combating Health Care Fraud, https://www.cms.gov/Newsroom/MediaReleaseDatabase/Fact-sheets/2016-Fact-sheets-items/2016-02-26.html.

6. Artur Dubrawski, Extracting useful information from multivariate temporal data. In: Jay Liebovitz (Ed.): *Big Data and Business Analytics*, Taylor & Francis, 2013. ISBN: 9781466565784.

7. Artur Dubrawski, Maheshkumar Sabhnani, Saswati Ray, Josep Roure, and Michael Baysek, T-Cube as an enabling technology in surveillance applications. *Advances in Disease Surveillance*. 2007; 4:6.

8. New England Healthcare Institute, A Matter of Urgency: Reducing Emergency Department Overuse, A NEHI Research Brief, March 2010.

9. Kristy Gonzalez Morganti, Sebastian Bauhoff, Janice C. Blanchard, Mahshid Abir, Neema Iyer, Alexandria Smith, Joseph V. Vesely, Edward N. Okeke, and Arthur L. Kellermann, The Evolving Role of Emergency Departments in the United States, Research Report RR-280-ACEP, RAND Corporation, 2013.

10. Yue Wang, Artur Dubrawski, Lujie Chen, and Ryan McDermitt, Patterns of emergency care utilization by chronically III. *Online Journal of Public Health Informatics*. 2014; 6(1): e59. doi:10.5210/ojphi.v6i1.5146.

11. Centers for Medicare and Medicaid Services, NHE Fact Sheet, https://www.cms.gov/Research-Statistics-Data-and-Systems/Statistics-Trends-and-Reports/NationalHealthExpendData/NHE-Fact-Sheet.html (accessed August 12, 2016).

12. Dan Mangan, $1 of every $5 spent in US will be on health care, http://www.cnbc.com/2015/07/28/1-of-every-5-spent-in-us-will-be-on-health-care.html.

13. Fred Schulte, David Donald, and Erin Durkin, Why Medicare Advantage costs taxpayers billions more than it should, http://www.publicintegrity.org/2014/06/04/14840/why-medicare-advantage-costs-taxpayers-billions-more-it-should.

14. Jieshi Chen and Artur Dubrawski, Identification of sufferers of rare diseases using medical claims data. *Online Journal of Public Health Informatics*. 2017, http://www.syndromic.org/storage/documents/2016_Conference/abstracts/lightning_talks/isds16_lig_identification%20of%20sufferers_chen.pdf.

15. Mathieu Guillame-Bert and Artur Dubrawski, Classification of time sequences using graphs of temporal constraints. *Journal of Machine Learning Research*, 2016 (under review).

Chapter 13

The Role of Unstructured Data in Healthcare Analytics

Amanda Dawson and Sergei Ananyan

Contents

Advances in data science have solidified data as a key strategic asset and driver of company productivity.[1] Data's greatest potential for improving decision making rests in its ability to reveal undiscovered patterns across repeating situations. Yet, the ability to extract useful knowledge for data-enabled decision making has lagged behind technological advances in data capture, management, and structured reporting. In healthcare settings, the inability to use the vast quantities of clinical data already being collected to better inform clinical decision making has directly hindered our ability to achieve the Institute for Healthcare Improvement's Triple Aim of improving patient care, lowering the cost of care, and improving population health.[2,3]

This chapter focuses on one of the most challenging aspects of deriving actionable intelligence from healthcare data, namely, the continued proliferation and analytic burden of unstructured data. A recent analysis of data storage use estimated that 90% of all storage shipped in 2014 will store unstructured data.[4] Even with the rise of EHRs, it remains the case that most information about patients is being stored in an unstructured format, regardless of whether the data originated from the pharmacy, laboratory, radiology group, clinic, or hospital.[5]

Most commonly, unstructured data refer to textual or narrative data, such as clinical notes, but can also include numbers, dates, and even images. The primary criterion for data to be considered unstructured is that they are stored in an undefined format or ambiguous data model that prevents aggregation or further analysis. Unstructured data in their raw format are often unhelpful for answering tasks at hand, only deriving analytic value once they have been appropriately prepared and contextualized. However, the very failing of unstructured data is also their strength: by not forcing data into a predefined format, unforeseen responses and novel data patterns may emerge that enable organizations to not only answer the question WHAT is happening but also provide answers to the question WHY things are happening this way. Thus, the growing amount of unstructured data presents both an opportunity and a problem; additional data can facilitate making better decisions; however, finding and managing these facts are now more difficult.

The purpose of this chapter is to introduce data analysts to the challenges and techniques associated with the use of unstructured data in the healthcare domain, while also introducing healthcare providers and medical informaticists to analytic advancements that may better enable them to derive value from already existent data sources. After reviewing the techniques for processing unstructured text data, examples of applications to common healthcare questions will be provided, with a particular emphasis on how these different communities can work together to develop techniques that not only are analytically robust but also provide solutions relevant to the clinical goals for a given patient or population.

13.1 Underpinnings of Text Analytics

Natural language text is inherently a richer and more complicated media than structured data: textual documents have linguistic and semantic dimensions present in every word, phrase, and sentence. This makes text so powerful for expressing ideas and so convenient for facilitating complex communications between humans. Simultaneously, this makes the analysis of text documents much more complicated than the analysis of structured data. We need to determine the form and meaning of each word, its relation to other words, and its role in the considered sentence. The main objective of text analysis is to extract from documents features of potential interest and organize them in the form of structured data that can serve as an informative representation of the analyzed documents. Statistical techniques developed for the analysis of structured data are not suitable for the analysis of text; new techniques capable of understanding linguistic and semantic structure of text are needed.

Let us consider a typical example: a healthcare system desires to gain insights about patient experience in order to improve its operation. To achieve that goal, they ask patients to complete a survey which, in addition to structured questions, asks some open-ended questions allowing patients to elaborate on their reasoning behind low ranked questions. For example, the request to rank the customer perception of staff responsiveness is followed by the corresponding open-ended question soliciting details about the specific issues and experiences associated with their ranking. The responses to open-ended questions reveal concrete individual problems that should be handled by the company in order to improve patient experience. If the healthcare system collects responses from approximately 100,000 patients during a year, manual analysis of even this relatively modest amount of data in practice becomes a serious challenge. Thus, text analysis tools have been developed to process unstructured responses in order to extract potentially important features and relations between them. These newly structured attributes then become inputs for reporting and predictive modeling engines. Specifically, text mining systems automate the cleaning, regularization, HIPAA (Health Insurance Portability and Accountability Act) compliant anonymization, and categorization of the data in such a way that healthcare systems can monitor developments regardless of the original format of the data.

Text mining systems are composed of data storage systems; linguistic analysis toolkits; dictionaries and ontologies holding information about terms, their forms, and semantic relations (e.g., MeSH and SNOMED CT ontologies for healthcare); and a variety of rule-based and machine learning algorithms. Text mining systems are semi-automatic: they automatically run machine learning techniques and pre-configured linguistic parsing rules and dictionaries and enable the user to manually create multistep data analysis scenarios, evaluate the obtained results, and plan further analysis and reporting.

Text mining focuses on revealing the key structure and topics of the analyzed documents. To determine the meaning of documents, one needs to look beyond just a collection of sequentially organized words. When humans communicate with each other, they rely on their linguistic and semantic abilities to understand the form, meaning, and relationships of words with each other. The difficulty of incorporating this knowledge in machine analysis presents the main challenge for building accurate text analysis tools. Advanced text analysis systems combine three main types of analysis: linguistic, semantic, and statistical.

Linguistic analysis first aims at determining the borders of individual words and sentences and deducing the normal form of each word, as well as its part of speech. Going beyond individual words, linguistic analysis helps detect word phrases that represent single concepts, such as noun phrases and verb phrases, and determine the roles of individual words and phrases in the sentence and with respect to each other. In addition, linguistic analysis helps with detecting and interpreting negations, as well as sentences in imperative and subjunctive mood. An accurate understanding of the linguistic structure of documents enables the user to perform accurate feature extraction and classification of documents.

Semantic analysis is equally important for the correct interpretation of text documents. For example, when you hear someone saying that they see a car outside the window, you immediately know that the discussed object has wheels, can move, travels primarily by roads, and can carry passengers. You would not be surprised if another person refers to the same object as a "vehicle." However, none of these facts were present in the original statement, but rather they were invoked in the mind of the recipient of information based on the semantic model of the considered domain developed through that individual's past experience. By default, computers lack any semantic information about language that we as humans take for granted and use extensively when communicating with each other. Computers do not have similar experiences, nor do they have cognitive mechanisms for analyzing such experiences to develop semantic models of the outside world. To provide computers with knowledge of properties and relationships between different concepts in text documents, designers of text analysis systems must supply them with prebuilt dictionaries and ontologies that capture key terms and relationships that might be encountered in documents related to the considered domain.

Statistical analysis reveals the relative importance of individual words and phrases in the analyzed collection of text. For each concept, the system counts the number of documents containing this concept and the number of times it appeared in the documents. Additionally, the system captures the deviation in the use of each concept from the typical frequency of encountering this concept in a large collection of documents from the same domain or different domains. A significant excess in the frequency of a concept in the analyzed collection of documents compared to its background frequency signifies that the considered concept is an important feature of these documents.

Now, let us consider what text analysis techniques are incorporated in practical tools. Text processing typically begins with tokenization, where individual words are extracted and stored in a structured form for further analysis. Next, text mining tools augment information about the extracted words, such as the part of speech the word belongs to, the word's canonical form, or what group of words represents a single concept. With this information at hand, tools can focus on counting keywords or extracting standard entities such as the names of people, organizations, dates, and locations, as well as user-defined entities. Systems also identify phrases and their role in the sentence and in relation to other words or phrases. Together, these pieces of information represent key features of text that are used as input to classification systems assigning documents to predefined categories, clustering systems that group together similar documents, or reporting systems delivering easy-to-comprehend summaries of results to nontechnical users. The extracted information is stored so that it can be queried, used in a report, or integrated into the operation of external systems.

13.1.1 Language Detection

In order to correctly perform the sequence of steps involved in text analysis, one first needs to know what language the analyzed document is written in. A multinational organization frequently encounters collections of document written in multiple languages, without knowing upfront what language each document is in. For example, a pharmaceutical company can be receiving through a single channel questions from patients using their drugs in various countries of the world. The first step of text analysis is to automatically recognize the language each of the documents is written in and place documents in different languages in separate buckets that will invoke the corresponding language-dependent grammar modules. If you are certain that all your documents are in English, you can skip reading the rest of this section and move on to tokenization.

Text analysis tools use a combination of statistical and heuristic techniques to determine the language of each document. Of course, the first step is to check what set of characters is being used: documents in English, Russian, and Chinese would be easy to separate. Yet, documents in say English, Spanish, and French are all written in Latin characters and one needs more elaborate techniques for differentiating them from each other.

The idea behind the statistical analysis is that every language has its own signature. For each language, there is a certain probability to see the letter "a" in the first position of the document, another probability to see it in the second position, yet another probability to see it in the third position, and so on. Similarly, there are different probabilities to encounter the letter "b" in the first, second, and so on positions of the document. The same is known for all other letters of the alphabet. All these probabilities were determined a priori by scientists analyzing large collections of documents from each language. Armed with this knowledge, text analysis tools can determine the language of the document by looking at the sequence of first N characters of the document and checking which language signature it resembles the most. The longer the sequence of characters the system can analyze, the more accurate the results of language detection will be.

The obtained results can be further verified and modified if necessary by some heuristic-based algorithms. The system can look for frequently appearing words that are characteristic of a certain language, such as articles, prepositions, negation particles, and pronouns. For example, if the document contains articles "la" and "los," we can assume that the document is in Spanish, while articles "a" and "the" suggest that the document is in English.

13.1.2 Tokenization

Tokenization is the process of splitting documents into elementary structural elements: words, phrases, punctuation marks, and other symbols. The resulting elements, called *tokens*, serve as the basis for all further text analysis techniques. Systems collect information about each token, such as the length, the case, and the position, as shown in Table 13.1. Tokenization is the first tier of analysis in a text mining application, where the rubber meets the road.

Despite its apparent simplicity for English documents, the process of tokenization frequently presents challenges. These include the handling of punctuation: whether a dash symbol separates two words or whether the characters after an apostrophe character represent a separate token. For example, the tokenizer needs to be able to intelligently split fragments like "San Francisco-born" (where it makes more sense to make a split at the hyphen).

Also, idioms should be treated as single concepts. If you try to split idioms "bull's eye" or "jump the gun" into individual words, you are going to lose their meaning entirely. Other challenges of tokenization are the recognition of e-mail

Table 13.1 Tokenization of "Mister and Missis Smith"

Token	Position	Length	Case	Type
Mister	1	6	Proper	Alphabetical
and	2	3	Lower	Alphabetical
missis	3	6	Lower	Alphabetical
Smith	4	5	Proper	Alphabetical
.	5	1	N/A	End of sentence

addresses and website addresses (which include punctuation and some special characters in them), or the recognition of emoticons (when analyzing data from social media).

The process of tokenization becomes even less trivial for other languages that heavily use *clitics*, for example, Spanish, Italian, French, and Portuguese. *Clitics* are small words (typically pronouns) that stick to verbs. For example, in French, some words with a hyphen or apostrophe in them must be separated into several words: "*expliquez-moi*," "*qu'obtiennent-ils*," and "*a-t-il*." Yet other words with apparently similar structure, such as "*aujourd'hui*" and "*arc-en-ciel*," represent single words and must not be separated. In Portuguese, things become yet more complicated as *clitics* may appear inside the verb. For example, "Ele matar-se-ia" (translated as "He would kill himself") should be parsed as the following three separate words "Ele mataria se." Note that we had to dissect the second word and place the extracted part as a separate third word in order to perform proper tokenization here. Modern text analysis tools use sophisticated linguistic rules and machine learning algorithms to tokenize documents in different languages.

Tokenization becomes a real ordeal for the analysis of documents in Chinese where blank spaces are not used for separating words from each other. For example, a combination of two sequential symbols can represent a single word or two different words, depending on the context they are encountered in. Intelligent tokenization of Chinese documents becomes possible only through contextual analysis.

After separating a document into words, the document is typically split into sentences and paragraphs. A simple example of a sentence parsing algorithm iterates over the token list, looking for end-of-sentence markers like the period, exclamation point, and question mark, and assigns tokens to each sentence sequentially. An algorithm must consider whether a period is an end of a sentence or part of an abbreviation like Dr. or Prof., or part of an e-mail or website address.

Errors in the tokenization process can lead to errors in handling all subsequent text analysis tasks. This is similar to creating a foundation when building a house: without a solid foundation, the house will fall apart.

13.1.3 Morphological Analysis

In many languages, including English and other European languages, words can have different inflections producing different morphological forms of the same word: for example, "work," "working," and "worked." The canonical form of the word, in this example "work," which one would find to be representing this set in the dictionary, is called lemma. When indexing a document to produce a set of words, the occurrence of the word "work" in any of its inflected forms should be treated as a single entry because they support the same concept. This is a morphological abstraction of the document's contents.

The process of identifying correct lemmas for every word in the document is called lemmatization. To a large degree, this process can be completed through the use of a stemming algorithm. In short, a stemming algorithm repeatedly applies suffix and prefix stripping rules to a token to produce its root form. An example suffix stripping rule would be: if the token ends with the suffix "ly," discard the suffix. A stemming algorithm would ultimately convert the word "indefinitely" into "define" or "defin" or possibly "fin." Additional rules might restrict the length of the word and prohibit removing affixes if the result is too short.

In some cases, stemming algorithms cannot be used to produce the canonical form of the word. For example, stemming would fail to determine that "went" is a just a morphological modification of "go," or that "worse" is a morphological form of "bad." Such irregular words can be lemmatized only by looking in a dictionary.

While simple stemming makes for a good first attempt at automated morphological analysis, this approach can easily generate erroneous results. Consider applying the stemming algorithm to the word "filling" in the following two sentences:

"When filling a hole, apply pressure from both sides."
"Composite dental fillings are newer than amalgam."

As a result of simple-minded stemming, we lose the meaning of the second sentence. Why? Because we failed to notice that the word "filling" is its own noun rather than the present continuous form of the verb "fill." A robust lemmatization algorithm first considers syntactic relationships of the word in the sentence to determine its part of speech from the context and only then applies an appropriate version of the stemming algorithm. The more detailed representation of a word composed of its normal form and its part of speech is called lexeme. Modern lemmatizing algorithms perform context-based analysis and generate a list of lexemes on the output.

13.1.4 Indexing

To facilitate searching a collection of analyzed documents, one forms an index (also called a forward index), where every document is represented by the list of lexemes encountered in the document with their corresponding positions. The process of searching is performed against the index rather than in the original documents so that the system can locate all instances of the sought words, regardless of the morphological form they take in the considered documents. While this is a step forward from searching against full text documents, using the forward index for searching large collections of documents or executing large numbers of queries remains painfully slow.

To further speed up searching, text mining tools create an inverted index that alphabetically lists all words encountered in the complete set of documents together with the corresponding IDs of documents and relative positions of words within these documents. While it is a somewhat more complicated and time-consuming process to create an inverted index, the use of an inverted index dramatically decreases the processing time of search queries.

13.1.5 Spelling Correction

There may be many reasons why analyzed documents contain errors. For example, data representing call center transcripts and survey responses received from thousands of users of very different backgrounds are often ripe with misspellings, grammatical errors, and abbreviations. Also, systems that transform paper documents into digital text produce a significant number of errors owing to the nature of the optical character recognition process they are using. While humans can easily recognize and fix such errors, computers cannot do this automatically, and if errors are not fixed upfront, words with errors in them will never be included correctly in results of searches performed by the machine.

To better illustrate the nature of the problem, consider the following meme [12]:

> THE PHAOMNNEAL PWEOR OF THE HMUAN MNID
> Aoccdrnig to rscheearch at Cmabrigde
> Uinervtisy, it deosn't mttaer in waht oredr
> the ltteers in a wrod are, the olny iprmoatnt tihng
> is taht the first and lsat ltteer be in the rghit
> pclae. The rset can be a taotl mses and you can
> sitll raed it wouthit a porbelm. Tihs is bcuseae the
> huamn mnid deosnt raed ervey lteter by istlef,
> but the wrod as awlohe.

While humans are quite capable of processing this text using their amazing pattern recognition skills, computers fail miserably. Computers are symbolic processing systems with no tolerance for errors in recognizing symbols. Undetected (and thus not fixed) errors undermine the accuracy of statistical algorithms that use features like word frequency, length, and position as input. This leads to misclassified records and missing search results (low recall), which in turn leads to inadequate decision support. It is imperative for text mining systems to be equipped with robust algorithms for identifying and fixing errors in data.

Text mining tools incorporate string similarity algorithms measuring either edit or phonetic distances between words. Edit distance is a measure of the number of typographical operations required to transform one word into another. Typical operations are substitution, insertion, and omission. Substitution is the swapping of two characters, insertion is the addition of an extra character, and omission is a missing character. For example, "receive" and "recieve" are within one substitution operation from each other. This distance is incorporated into spell checking algorithms to suggest correct forms of a word by measuring the distance between the unknown word and the closest known words. Words with a smaller distance are more similar and are more likely to be the right correction for the misspelling.

Another technique for spelling correction, phonetic analysis, classifies tokens into phonetic categories. The original algorithm for phonetic classification is called soundex. The algorithm analyzes the characters of the input word and produces a phonetic class of words that sound similar to the human ear. For example, "heart" and "hard" share the same soundex class and therefore would be considered similar by the algorithm. Modern text analysis tools rely on an improved phonetic comparison algorithm called Metaphone.

13.1.6 Collocation Analysis

Collocation algorithms search for sequences of consecutive terms based on linguistic and statistical analysis. Recognizing a concept at the phrase level increases the result's semantic accuracy. For example, the term "post office" is not just a "post," nor is it just an "office." Idioms like "vicious circle" take on a completely new meaning as a phrase. Considering the constituent words individually does not capture the meaning conveyed by the complete phrase. By performing advanced linguistic analysis of multiword sequences and their relations with other words in the sentence, text mining applications can reveal a more accurate set of concepts adequately portraying key ideas that are not obvious from individual words.

Below is an example of how a text mining system parses the following text record:

"Having better response time to the call buttons (night time taking between 15–30 minutes)."

The same record parsed by the system is as follows:

[Having]/pver [better response time]/pnou [to]/ppre [the call buttons]/pnou ([night time]/pnou [taking]/pver [between]/ppre [15–30 minutes]/pnou)

13.1.7 Dependency Parsing

The ability to detect whether or not two concepts are present in the same linguistic context is of great benefit to text analysis. For example, when one is searching for records where patients are requesting to have a bigger hospital in their town, a record asking for "a bigger x-ray machine in the hospital" should be ignored. However, this record contains the same keywords ("bigger" and "hospital") and in close proximity of each other. Understanding linguistic dependencies between words in the sentence is the only way to resolve this ambiguity.

The most advanced text analysis systems today feature dependency parsing algorithms that can determine the roles of individual words and phrases in the sentence, as well as in relation to each other. A typical result of the dependency parsing engine looks like this:

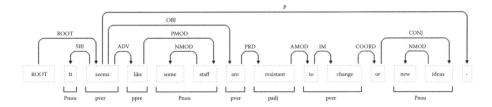

13.1.8 Semantic Dictionaries

Words can have different semantic relationships between them, for example, in relation to one another they can be synonyms ("destroy" can be equivalent to "break"), antonyms ("hot" is the opposite of "cold"), hyponyms ("a kind of" relation: "eagle" is a kind of a "bird"), or meronyms ("a part of" relation: "steering wheel" is a part of a "vehicle"). While humans can easily trace such relationships based on semantic models gained from previous experiences, computers are unaware of these relationships by default.

This problem is mended by equipping text mining systems with semantic dictionaries (sometimes referred to as ontologies) that capture various relations between terms. Generic semantic dictionaries aimed at capturing most standard semantic relations (e.g., WordNet) provide little help in practical applications because of the presence of scores of redundant relations necessarily stored in such systems. However, more domain-specific semantic dictionaries, as well as custom dictionaries, can significantly improve the recall provided by a text mining system (recall is a measure of how many documents potentially matching a search query were indeed fetched by the search system).

In the healthcare domain, the most important semantic dictionaries are the ones that are being developed and regularly maintained by large communities of industry professionals. The most prominent examples of such dictionaries are MeSH (Medical Subject Headings), SNOMED CT, and RxNorm maintained by the National Library of Medicine. Text mining systems that can incorporate such dictionaries in their analysis and capitalize on the structure of the corresponding semantic relations in their analysis deliver amazing results to users. For example, the user might be not even aware that "Pulmonary Valve Atresias," "Mitral Valve Disease," and "Eisenmenger's Syndrome" are specific instances of "cardiovascular disease." However, the search for "cardiovascular disease" associated with the use of hyponyms from the MeSH dictionary incorporated in the system diligently delivers all documents matching these specific conditions, as well as thousands of other issues associated with "cardiovascular disease" through MeSH.

Q ▼ Cardiovascular Infection

→ Hyponym (3) | → Hypernym (2) ↑ | → Meronym | ↑ Holonym | ← Antonym | ↕ Association | ◇ Others

Token

Cardiovascular Diagnostic Technique

Cardiovascular Diagnostic Techniques

Cardiovascular Disease

Cardiovascular Disease Specialty

Cardiovascular Diseases

Cardiovascular Diseases Specialty

Cardiovascular Drugs

Cardiovascular Infection

Cardiovascular Infections

Cardiovascular Model

Cardiovascular Models

Cardiovascular Physiologic Phenomena

Cardiovascular Physiologic Phenomenon

Cardiovascular Physiologic Processes

Cardiovascular Physiological Phenomena

Cardiovascular Physiological Phenomenon

Cardiovascular Physiological Process

Cardiovascular Physiological Processes

Cardiovascular Physiologies

Cardiovascular Infection

Noun

1. ⓘ **SCOPE NOTE Pathological conditions of the CARDIOVASCULAR SYSTEM caused by infections.;**

   ⓘ Cardiovascular Infection

   ⓘ Cardiovascular Infections

   ⓘ Infection Cardiovascular

   ⓘ Infections Cardiovascular

   ⊕ Add synonym

Hyponym

ⓘ *SCOPE NOTE Pathological conditions of the CARDIOVASCULAR SYSTEM caused by infection of MYCOBACTERIUM TUBERCULOSIS. Tuberculosis involvement may include the HEART; the BLOOD VESSELS; or the PERICARDIUM.;ANNOTATION coordinate IM with specific cardiovascular term (IM) or specific cardiovascular disease (IM).;* Cardiovascular Tuberculoses, Cardiovascular Tuberculosis, Tuberculoses Cardiovascular, Tuberculosis Cardiovascular

ⓘ *SCOPE NOTE Cardiovascular manifestations of SYPHILIS, an infection of TREPONEMA PALLIDUM. In the late stage of syphilis, sometimes 20-30 years after the initial infection, damages are often seen in the blood vessels including the AORTA and the AORTIC VALVE. Clinical signs include syphilitic aortitis, aortic insufficiency, or aortic ANEURYSM.;ANNOTATION coordinate IM with specific cardiovascular term (IM) or specific cardiovascular disease (IM); note entry term AORTITIS, SYPHILITIC;* Aortitides Syphilitic, Aortitis Syphilitic, Cardiovascular Syphilis, Syphilis Cardiovascular, Syphilitic Aortitides, Syphilitic Aortitis

ⓘ *ANNOTATION coord with specific bacterium /infections heading (IM) if pertinent; DF: ENDOCARDITIS BACT';* Bacterial Endocarditides, Bacterial Endocarditis, Endocarditides Bacterial, Endocarditis Bacterial

⊕ Add relation

13.2 Practical Tasks Handled by Text Analytics

A suitable solution for the analysis of large amounts of unstructured data appeared with the advent of techniques and tools for computer-based advanced text analysis. Let us consider the most frequently encountered text analysis tasks starting with unsupervised, or data driven, techniques and then moving to supervised, or analyst-driven techniques:

1. **Keyword extraction** is a data-driven technique focused on revealing the most important words and phrases that provide a simple representation of the analyzed collection of documents. This technique is used to gain a quick glimpse of key topics present in the analyzed documents, for example, survey responses. The results provided by keyword extraction are used as a starting point for further in-depth analysis.

2. **Summarization.** Document summarization is another data-driven technique that refers to the automated production of a concise representation of the contents of a document. This may be in the form of important keywords, phrases, or excerpts, a list of the most important sentences, or a paraphrased document. Most frequently, the result of summarization is a small collection of the most representative sentences extracted from the complete document.

3. **Clustering** identifies groups of documents that are similar between themselves in some aspects, and different from the rest of the data. Clustering helps one isolate collections of sufficiently similar documents and perform separate analysis of documents from each group.

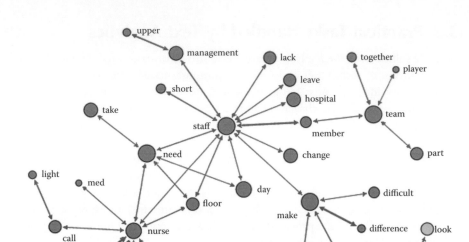

4. **Automated taxonomy generation**. This is a variation of clustering technique that attempts to automatically create a hierarchical structure of categories, each of which represents a separate cluster of documents. It uses the most important topics discussed in each of the clusters to name the corresponding category in the hierarchy.

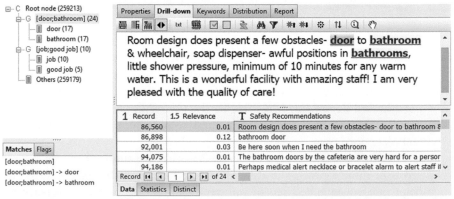

5. **Classification** assigns to every document a set of tags representing one or more predefined categories. Once the key concepts and relationships present in the text are revealed through data-driven analysis, the analyst can move to

supervised text analysis. This is where the analyst can capitalize on the results obtained by unsupervised analysis techniques that require no human input and realign the obtained results to better connect to key business objectives and produce actionable insights. The analyst typically builds a taxonomy representing a collection of hierarchically organized categories for extracting important features from the documents and performing document classification. The taxonomy categories are defined by queries expressed in Pattern Definition Language (PDL), supported by text mining software packages like PolyAnalyst, which can capture lexicographic, proximity, linguistic, and semantic patterns in text facilitating accurate extraction of the features of interest.

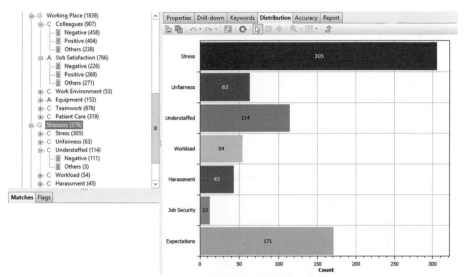

Alternatively, when one has a set of manually preclassified documents available, a text mining system can use machine learning techniques like Naïve Bayesian classification and Support Vector Machines to automatically build a model for document classification.

The taxonomy structure is used to score the original data in order to produce new attributes to be included in further analysis along with the associated structured attributes present in the original data. The construction of a useful and accurate taxonomy is one of the most important tasks of text mining because it allows the end user to perform many additional types of analysis on the data

6. **Sentiment analysis.** The techniques discussed so far were focused on revealing key topics discussed in the analysed documents. However, the objective of the analysis may sometimes differ: for example, we may want to know how customers responding to a survey feel about topics they are bringing up. What issues irritate them most and what issues make them happy? In other words, what is their sentiment toward various issues? To address this task, modern text mining tools offer Sentiment Analysis engines that use linguistic analysis rules to identify items that

please or aggravate survey respondents, extract the specific evaluation they are providing for each item, and rate the degree of their sentiment.

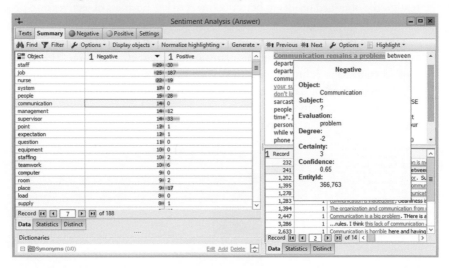

7. **Entity extraction:**

   a. *Named entity extraction.* This engine performs automated identification and extraction of standard named entities from documents. Such entities include names of people and organizations, dates, geographical locations, currency amounts, and personal information.

   b. *Data redaction.* Frequently, organizations encounter the need to disguise or remove certain elements of data. For example, when a medical system needs to send data to a vendor performing some service, they are required by HIPAA to strip data of any personal information, such as names of providers and patients, dates of birth, any type of ID, and so on (this process is referred to as data de-identification or redaction). Manual search for elements of personal information is extremely time consuming, tedious, and prone to error. A text mining system can automate this task, providing in many cases more accurate results and dramatic cost and time savings by eliminating the need for manual work.

   c. *Arbitrary entity and relationship extraction.* Modern text mining systems provide means for data analysts to build their own rules for automated extraction of arbitrary entities and relationships between them from textual documents. The development of such rules requires knowledge of more elaborate tools such as Extended Pattern Definition Language (XPDL) supported by text mining systems like PolyAnalyst. For example, you might need to extract from documents all prescribed medicines along with the corresponding dosage, frequency, duration, and method of application. One can write an XPDL rule automatically extracting results as displayed in the figure below.

medication	dosage	mode	frequency	duration	1.5 Con...	1 S...
Actonel	35 mg		q week		1.00	
Amitriptyline	10 mg	p.o. at	bedtime		1.00	
AMOXICILLIN						
Aspirin	81 mg		daily		1.00	
Feosol	325 mg	p.o.	every day		1.00	
Folic acid	1 mg	p.o.	every day		1.00	
glyburide	5 mg		bid cc		1.00	
Klonopin			PRN		1.00	
lantus	20 units		qhs		1.00	
Levothyroxine SODI	150 mcg	TABLET			1.00	
lisinopril					1.00	
metformin	1000 mg		bid		1.00	
Motrin						
Naprosyn	500 mg		b.i.d. p.r.n.		1.00	
Nexium	40 mg	Cap 1 capsule by mo	daily		1.00	
Norvasc	5 mg	orally	daily		1.00	
ondansetron			PRN		1.00	
Simvastatin	20 mg	Tab (Zocor) 1 tablet	every evening	ninety day	1.00	
Singulair	10 mg	Tab 1 tablet by mout	daily		1.00	
Tamoxifen	20 mg	Tab 1 tablet by mout	daily	thirty day	1.00	
Tylenol					1.00	
Tylenol #3			p.r.n.		1.00	
Zolpidem	5 mg	Tab (Ambien) 1 table	every evening at bet	five day	1.00	

- Nexium 40 mg Cap 1 capsule by mouth daily needed for diarrhea
- Zolpidem 5 mg Tab (Ambien) 1 tablet by mouth every evening at bedtime for five day(s)
- Simvastatin 20 mg Tab (Zocor) 1 tablet by mouth every evening for ninety day(s)
- Aspir...
- Tam... thirty day(s)
[Pleas... ed 6 refills.]
- Singu...
- Norva...
- lantu...
- metf...
- glybu...

Medications

medication:
   Simvastatin
dosage:
   20 mg
mode:
   Tab (Zocor) 1 tablet by mouth
frequency:
   every evening
duration:
   ninety day
Confidence:
   1.00
EntityId:
   15

1 Fre.   medication vastatin   20

13.3 Analytic Applications in Healthcare

13.3.1 Patient Diagnosis: Taxonomy Building for Predictive Modeling

One common text mining application to healthcare is to derive important patient symptomatology from clinical notes. While most EHRs enable clinicians to select from preformatted phrasing or from lists of standardized diagnosis codes (i.e., International Classification of Diseases diagnosis codes, or ICD-10-CM), rarely are clinicians relied upon to consistently and accurately provide all standardized data needed for healthcare management functions, such as obtaining reimbursement for care provided. Most healthcare systems have a second-level review of clinical notes by professionals in health information management who have been trained to read patient narratives in order to reliably and accurately apply one of 69,000 possible ICD-10 codes. Computer-assisted coding is a type of specialized text mining software that provides tools to assist, or potentially even replace, professional coders.

Once text mining processes are complete, that is, diagnosis-related dictionaries are prepared, classifiers are built, and phrases within the clinical notes are tagged, it is often commented that analyses can proceed as they would on any structured data set. However, unstructured data that have been syntactically or semantically parsed into a defined format often inherit characteristics that recommend certain statistical approaches over others. One predominant issue is that software that classifies text using primarily unsupervised, data-driven processes often produces a large number of data categories that may or may not be conceptually meaningful to the task at hand. Thus, it becomes incumbent on subsequent statistical analyses to employ methods that are appropriate for sparse and collinear data sets and which employ aggressive data reduction, often through the interleaving of supervised and unsupervised techniques.

For example, we looked to our narrative EHR data to help us investigate a common concern within the healthcare continuum, namely, that after discharge from the ICU, the right patient is being sent to the right venue for further care.[6] Hospital discharge summary narratives from the EHR were divided into separate 60% test and 40% validation data sets, and the test data set was then parsed and classified into a complete list of all possible diagnoses and comorbidities for each patient. We further paired these data with an additional predictor of the number of days spent in the ICU and the outcome measure of "successful" discharge destinations (discharges to venues that did *not* result in 30-day mortality or readmission).

The initial text mining classification resulted in 17,000 ICD-10-CM codes. We then applied a well-known hierarchical structure for ICDs, published annually by the Centers for Medicare and Medicaid Services, called the Hierarchical Condition Categories (CMS-HCC) model.[7] This step bundled the data-derived ICDs into 79 clinically related diagnosis code categories. Despite the combination of bottom-up and top-down approaches to identify relevant diagnoses, there were still too many predictors both from the perspective of developing a model and from the perspective of providing clinically distinguishable patient groups for use by practitioners. Thus, the CMS-HCC bundles of associated ICDs were subjected to a cluster analysis, and noninformative clusters and individual ICDs were discarded, for example, clusters were discarded for containing less than 3.5% of all patients, and ICDs were removed that occurred less than 1% of the time within a cluster. Clustering and automated taxonomy generation can be done as a separate step in a statistical package, but some text mining packages include these tools as part of their standard analytic output.

Individual ICDs from the remaining clusters were then sequentially entered into, first, a de-trended correspondence analysis (DCA) in order to exclude ICDs that were poorly discriminating of patient conditions and, second, a linear discriminant analysis (LDA) in order to determine which predictors (ICDs and the number of ICU days) were capable of discriminating between different "successful" discharge destinations. The cutoff for ICU days suggested by the LDA model was supported with an additional Chi-Square Automatic Interaction Detection decision tree model. The results from the DCA and LDA approaches provided ICD subclusters that were defined by proximity to one another, allowing us to describe patient similarity in terms of a customized distance metric for a specific clinical context.

Last, the ICD subclusters were reviewed by hospital physicians for clinical relevance by removing ICDs that fit within the subclusters but which were deemed not specific enough (i.e., more than 10% of eligible patients had that ICD). The final taxonomy was of 15 post-ICU condition categories (PICU-CCs) composed of just 361 ICDs, and a cutoff threshold for ICU days relevant to identifying a potentially "successful" discharge destination. This process was then repeated with the 40% validation data set in order to replicate the final solution set.

While the described analytic approach may seem complex, the issue that this example tackled—an unsupervised initial data structure that favors exemplars over coherent aggregations—is not uncommon in healthcare data. In statistical terms, unsupervised data analysis tends to generate lots of parameters with few data points, which leads to the dangers of overfitting the data and generating unstable estimates as a result of collinear predictors. However, the dangers of unsupervised analysis must be balanced with the recognition that model evaluation parameters, like area under the curve (AUC), tend to improve significantly when data-driven factors are added to existing knowledge-based factors.

13.3.2 Patient Prognosis: Sentiment Analysis in Risk-Adjusted Models

The previous example involved deriving clinical categories from EHR narratives by mapping synonyms from a medical dictionary to a set of well-specified diagnosis codes. However, there are subtler uses of unstructured EHR data for researchers looking to get past traditional analyses of diagnosis codes that may already be available in structured administrative and billing data sets. For example, we investigated whether the kind of language that attending physicians used in their admitting history and physical (H&P) summaries was indicative of later patient prognosis, and thus could be used as an additional risk factor in a predictive epidemiologic model. Unstructured physician H&Ps were classified according to affective tone (i.e., overall balance of positive and negative phrases, otherwise known as sentiment analysis) and specific language cues, for example, how often negation was used (e.g., "denies chest pain"), how the physician used temporality (e.g., "the patient had diverticulitis ten years ago" or "continues to experience headaches" or "still takes aspirin"), and who the experiencer was (e.g., "sister is being treated for breast cancer"). The classification results were entered into a hierarchical mixed linear model (nesting physicians within hospitals) together with covariates representing patient-related factors relevant to clinical severity and do-not-resuscitate status. The final results of the analysis provided us with a set of tools: an inverse prediction score to help us decide whether the data quality in a given H&P is sufficient for inclusion, sensitivity and false positive rates for our risk-adjusted model, and the ability to calculate class probability estimations of mortality prospectively on each patients for a given physician.

13.3.3 Patient Risk: Data- and Knowledge-Driven EHR Clinical Decision Support

We have similarly used narrative categorization in the development of new clinical algorithms to automatically flag patients in our EHR who are at high risk for falling and to provide clinical decision support by automatically recommending individualized fall prevention interventions. By text mining the narrative portions of incident reports of past patients that fell during their hospital stay, we have discovered risks previously unidentified by existing knowledge-based risk factor categories. Traditional knowledge-based risk categories are derived from reading incident report narratives but are difficult to process analytically because of complexity, volume, missing data, and the use of alternative words and expressions.[8] It has also been possible to use receiver operating characteristic curves to compare knowledge-based risk factors to knowledge-based plus text mining data-based risk factors, and to use boxplots of AUC values to show whether significant differences exist.[9]

13.3.4 Patient Imaging: Pattern Analysis to Identify Clinically Relevant Abnormalities

Last, one area of particular challenge and opportunity for unstructured data analysis in healthcare is in the evaluation of medical images. Image data are also a form of unstructured data, and on top of the usual challenges, we must also grapple with the fact that image data tend to be huge, high-dimensional, and complex.

Extraction of the most important features is daunting, in terms of both selecting what is relevant and using sophisticated sparse methods and dimensionality-reducing techniques. For example, one important goal in this area is to be able to assign clinical significance to abnormalities in medical images. In the case of brain research, new ways to treat, cure, and prevent brain disorders are dependent on understanding how behavior is represented in the brain. One important way in which brain–behavior relationships can be studied is by mapping specific patient symptoms to the location of brain lesions identified through magnetic radiographic imaging (MRI) or computerized axial tomography (CAT). In structural imaging–based lesion-symptom mapping in the brain, the structuring of imaging data is dependent on the ability to align radiographic images between different patients in a process called intersubject registration, or spatial normalization. Different brain images are fitted to a standard position template by aligning, pitching, or warping the brain and accompanying lesion using automatic mathematical algorithms, landmark-based manual transformations, or manual transcriptions of the lesion itself onto an overlay map. Despite the disparity in automated versus manual approaches, each method has been demonstrated to obtain satisfactory results in comparison to one another, or a gold standard, though some methods are more robust to a wide variation in the match between images (e.g., combining MRI with CAT scan images). A very active area of research in lesion-symptom mapping is the development of methods that would improve statistical power to draw conclusions. Because lesions vary in location distribution, and in a nonrandom fashion, the power to find differences varies regionally across the brain, reemphasizing the same challenges of data sparsity and collinearity seen in other forms of unstructured data (as well as a host of other concerns too wide too cover here).[10]

13.4 Conclusion

Many future advances in clinical care are dependent on the ability to analyze and act on unstructured data in the many forms in which they occur in the healthcare sector: high-dimension patient characteristics, electronic health records, medical device logs, patient satisfaction comments, staff notes, and medical imaging. For example, the greatest potential for EHR data to improve decisions about patient care rests in the use of machine learning and text analytics to identify patterns and trends, detect anomalies, and predict outcomes of future situations. Until greater capability is developed in these areas, the overwhelming majority of clinical staff will remain dissatisfied with the return on their time investment entering data into computer systems.[11] The recommended course of action for data analysts, healthcare providers, and medical informaticists is to establish a context for unstructured data, prepare text data to draw out the inherent clinical value of the data before using analytics, consider semantic disambiguation and syntactic analysis to find the most flexible format for text data, and focus on data quality, accuracy, and reliability.

References

1. McAfee A, Brynjolfsson E. Big data: The management revolution. *Harvard Bus Rev.* 2012; 90: 60–68.
2. Hillstead R, Bigelow J, Bower A et al. Can electronic medical record systems transform healthcare? Potential health benefits, savings and costs. *Health Affair.* 2005; 24(5): 1103–1117.
3. Berwick D, Nolan T, Whittington J. The Triple Aim: Care, health and cost. *Health Affair.* 2008; 27(3): 759–769.
4. Nadkarni A, Yezhkova N. *Structured versus Unstructured Data: The Balance of Power Continues to Shift.* International Data Corporation, March 2014. IDC Publication 247106. https://www.idc.com/research/viewtoc.jsp?containerId=247106
5. Jensen P, Lars J, and Søren B. Mining electronic health records: Towards better research applications and clinical care. *Nat Rev Genet.* 2012; 13(6): 395–405.
6. Unroe M, Kahn J, Carson S et al. One-year trajectories of care and resource utilization for recipients of prolonged mechanical ventilation: A cohort study. *Ann Intern Med.* 2010; 153(3): 167–175.
7. CMS-HCC Risk Adjustment Model. In: ICD-10-CM Mappings [database online]. Centers for Medicare and Medicaid Services. https://www.cms.gov/Medicare/Health-Plans/MedicareAdvtgSpecRateStats/Risk-Adjustors.html. Accessed March 1, 2016.
8. Sun J, Reddy C. Big data analytics for healthcare. Tutorial presented at: SIAM International Conference on Data Mining; May 2–4, 2013; Austin, TX. http://dmkd.cs.wayne.edu/TUTORIAL/Healthcare/
9. Shlipak M, Fried L, Cushman M et al. Cardiovascular mortality risk in chronic kidney disease: Comparison of traditional and novel risk factors. *JAMA.* 2005; 293(14): 1737–1745.
10. Kimberg D, Coslett H, Schwartz M. Power in voxel based lesion-symptom mapping. *J Cogn Neurosci.* 2007; 19(7): 1076–1080.
11. Meigs S, Solomon M. Electronic health record use a bitter pill for many physicians. *Perspect Health Inf Manag.* 2016; 13(Winter): 1d.
12. Rawlinson G. *The Significance of Letter Position in Word Recognition* [Dissertation]. Nottingham, UK: The University of Nottingham; 1976.

Index

Page numbers followed by f and t indicate figures and tables, respectively.